Mayo Williamson Hazeltine

Chats about Books

Poets and Novelists

Mayo Williamson Hazeltine

Chats about Books
Poets and Novelists

ISBN/EAN: 9783743328464

Manufactured in Europe, USA, Canada, Australia, Japa

Cover: Foto ©Thomas Meinert / pixelio.de

Manufactured and distributed by brebook publishing software (www.brebook.com)

Mayo Williamson Hazeltine

Chats about Books

CHATS ABOUT BOOKS

POETS AND NOVELISTS

BY

MAYO WILLIAMSON HAZELTINE

NEW YORK
CHARLES SCRIBNER'S SONS
1883

CONTENTS.

*The papers here collected, and in some measure
revised, originally appeared in the Sunday editions of the Sun.*

M. W. H.

New York, March 1, 1883.

CHATS ABOUT BOOKS.

GEORGE ELIOT.

THE achievements of two women, our contemporaries, have dispelled some venerable fallacies respecting the scope and faculty of the feminine intellect. The presumption, doubtless, remains in force that a less wide and rigorous training, whose defects are not corrected but accented by the subsequent exercise of functions relatively few and narrow, must tend to cripple, and in some directions paralyze, the constructive forces of the mind. It is likewise possible, if we may argue from analogy, that particular mental aptitudes, or incapacities, may be intensified by inheritance in a given sex. In this sense, therefore, it is still reasonable to speak of special laws which govern the intellectual work of woman. But these laws, which have sometimes been deemed inflexible, are now seen to be the affirmance of mere tendencies, which may be counteracted and largely overcome by the expansive pressure of remarkable dynamic qualities and an exceptional personal experience. This we know, because George Sand and, in a somewhat more decisive way, George Eliot, have done some of the very things which, it was supposed, women could not do.

If we accept the general verdict of men we shall admit that women had never until the present century attained high excellence on the higher levels of art. They had given us clever letters, like Madame de Sévigné, shrewd reflections on life and books, like Madame de Staël, character sketches, carefully drawn, but pale in color, and adjusted to a narrow canvas, like Miss Austen. But they had never produced a drama or an epic poem. Neither had they shown themselves competent to execute that elaborate and comprehensive work of art to which Fielding gave consummate form, and which, partially divested of the atmosphere of humor with which he clothed it, and informed with a more serious spirit, might fitly be called the modern epic. Some thirty years ago, however, appeared a woman who, within the horizon of an English vicarage, brought to bear an intuitive discernment and a power of dramatic synthesis which, transferred to a wider theatre, might have created a large picture of human life. Yet Charlotte Brontë was but the precursor of George Eliot, and can only be said to have demonstrated that a great female novelist was a possibility.

At the time when Mrs. Lewes published "Adam Bede," the conception of the novel popularly held in England had lost somewhat of the organic unity and symmetry which Fielding gave it. Conspicuously as Dickens and Thackeray outshone the elder novelist in specific lines of excellence, it would be not less idle to compare their narratives with "Tom Jones" in respect of coherence and cumulative evolution than to compare one of Shakespeare's plays with a Greek tragedy. These masters of irony and pathos were perfectly alive to their own shortcomings, and did not dispute the soundness of the principles to which they failed to conform. For what are the fundamental laws of the novel as laid down by the exemplar whom they never wearied of extolling? That this species of composition, like the drama, must be built upon a skeleton of strong and well-compacted plot, and that the outward texture must reproduce not a class, a coterie, or eccentric social types, but broad human nature in its multifarious aspects. Moreover, the novel, as Fielding conceived it, had one mark of decisive difference from the drama, that it contemplated the slow and graduated development of character under the shaping of circumstances and the growth and recoil of passions. On the other hand, what lessons and criticisms might be interjected by way of prologue and interlude, what spirit, whether of mirth or sadness, of superficial tolerance or contempt, or of earnest questioning and sympathy, would pervade the whole, would be determined by the taste and quality of the individual artist. It is doubtless true that one man's commentary may be more precious than another's text, and it is likewise probable that some creations of Thackeray and Dickens are niched more securely in the memory even than "Parson Adams;" nevertheless the fact remains that we commonly find ourselves dwelling less on what their actors do than on what the author says of them, and that a single chapter or page may be taken up at random without a painful sense of dislocation. That this is so may be accounted a signal tribute to the constant charm of the novelist's style, but it manifestly impugns the perfection of his narrative as a coherent artistic structure. The truth is, we cannot help thinking of Dickens or Thackeray as far brighter and more delightful than any one of their books, whereas Fielding lies buried beneath his greatest work, like an Egyptian king beneath his pyramid.

But those principles of dramatic narrative which the young writer who named herself George Eliot found partially obscured in England were still paramount in France. Indeed, the astonishing fruits which their application produced in the hands of Balzac fixed the laws of the novel so rigorously that even such spirited, vivacious histories as those of Erckmann-Chatrian are now assigned to a distinct category. Nor is it doubtful that George Sand had contributed not a little to enforce correct artistic form. She is almost always successful in weaving a consistent, progressive plot, which, like a Latin sentence, shall hold back its meaning till the end, and the action of her female characters under the play of motives and the pressure of events is often evolved with a sustained, deliberate touch which in a feminine writer was unprecedented. Her portraits of masculine nature, however, are less life-like, and she seems to have painted vividly only the many phases of her own experience, and those somewhat numerous types which came under her close personal observation. She had not Balzac's faculty of deciphering a whole biography from a word, a glance, a gesture ; and hence the middle and background of her canvas are peopled with shadows, and the long catalogue of her works cannot pretend to the title which Balzac not unreasonably gave his own, the *Comédie humaine.*

A comparison of George Eliot with Balzac might not occur to those who classify writers by their spiritual influence, yet it is pertinent, and the points of concord are not less suggestive than the points of contrast. Thus, in Balzac's ripest performances each incident serves not merely to project or unfold character, but is seen immediately, or subsequently, to be one of the pivots of the story. A like economy of materials is noticeable in " Scenes of Clerical Life," as well as in George Eliot's later books. Again, her actors, like those of the French novelist, are introduced in much the same way as they are made known to us in actual life, with cursory outward observations sufficient to frame a provisional judgment which further acquaintance will complete or modify. Neither are lay figures common on her stage, even subordinate persons as a rule being presented in clean, firm outline. The range of character which she thus interprets is too wide to have been gained by the study of living representatives, and implies the possession of that species of divining-rod which is one of the least common of human gifts. Finally we seem to discover in " Middlemarch " and " Daniel Deronda "—

dealing as they do with social grades and environments very different from those encountered in "Silas Marner" and "The Mill on the Floss," and yet different from each other—a distinct purpose to produce in the aggregate of her works an exhaustive picture of contemporary life. In all these respects, taken together, it will scarcely be disputed that no English novelist has approached so closely to the author of "*Scènes de la Vie Parisienne.*"

As an artist, then, George Eliot aims, not unsuccessfully, to continue the traditions of Fielding and Balzac. Some of the latter's faults, too, she not only shares, but may be said to emphasize. He was over-fond, for example, of parading recondite learning, which, it is known, had to be crammed for the occasion ; and, while Mrs. Lewes' acquisitions are unquestionably of a more solid kind, she is by no means free from pedantry. Balzac, however, for the most part, confines his display of erudition or of technical knowledge to the initial portion of his story, and sometimes may justify himself by the necessity of creating a specific framework and atmosphere ; but when the plot is fairly under way, and the characters on the stage, he rarely frustrates his central purpose of lucid, forceful exposition by resorting to metaphors or allusions not capable of instant and general comprehension. On the other hand, we have noted many instances in "Middlemarch" and "Daniel Deronda" where, at critical junctures of the narrative, the grasp of the author's thought is thwarted for the ordinary reader by somewhat fantastic references to mediæval or ancient literature. No one, of course, would attribute to George Eliot any of the foolish motives which are usually associated with pedantic writing, but we mean to say that she overrates the average culture of her audience; which is a mistake no less serious than for an actor to pitch the voice too low. Another familiar criticism of Balzac is levelled at his passion for analysis. Few men, certainly, have tracked the windings of motive with a more ruthless persistency and unerring scent, but to the conscious possessor of such powers the chase is apt to seem of more consequence than the game. But in .this form of self-indulgence Balzac preserved a certain timeliness and propriety, reserving his more dainty and patient manipulations for moments of suspense and preparation, for moods of doubt and vacillation, and contenting himself with swift, firm strokes at the critical stages of the action, or in the projection of strong feeling. George Eliot is not equally circumspect. More than once in "Daniel Deronda," for example, when our sympathies have been intensely wrought upon, we are suddenly called to take part in an operation which is as unwelcome as vivisection. Elsewhere, too, when analysis is in order, it is performed with an elaborate thoroughness which partially defeats its end, since in the multiplied flashings of the dissecting knife we lose sight of the slender filaments and nerve-centres we were asked to scrutinize. Many of her pages thus devoted to an exhaustive moral anatomy would have been compressed by Balzac into paragraphs, and doubtless much careful work would thus have been sacrificed. But the reader's mind would have retained a more distinct impression, and is not this a test of art?

If we pass from technical qualities of workmanship to the moral atmosphere of her books, and the spiritual nobility embodied in certain characters, we find George Eliot moving on a plain attained by few English novelists, and certainly not by Balzac. There is in the *Comédie humaine* no goodness in the sense of lofty principles consciously self-imposed and nobly fruitful. You encounter kindly, unselfish instincts, maternal yearning, filial affection, paternal devotion, and not seldom amorphous goody creatures moving sluggishly in the grooves of harmless habit, and who serve as foils to brilliant villains. But the clever people are always bad, and either Balzac's intuitive perceptions were sometimes dulled by rooted scepticism, or he never had the good fortune to meet such men as Deronda and Felix Holt, or such women as Romola or as Dorothea in "Middlemarch." On the other hand, in George Eliot's world all the robust, well-poised, regnant natures are sooner or later enlisted on the side of worth and purity and of truthful, helpful living; as if to her mind the tremendous leavening influence of right-wishing minorities were the one supreme sign of power in history, and as if she could not imagine a sound, strong intellect not yielding ultimate acceptance to those principles of sympathy and self-control which formulate the wisdom and aspiration of the race. In conformity with her view of the laws which govern the genesis and collision of moral forces, her vicious, egotistical persons are always weak, and invariably succumb in the end to the defeat or failure which awaits weakness. It is impossible to conceive of teaching more diametrically opposed to Balzac's, whose fifty volumes are so many sermons enforcing the gospel of self-seeking. We need not say that proofs and vouchers for the correctness of his doctrine were easily marshalled by one who considered a stalled ox and hatred therewith a more authentic measure of success than the scriptural alternative.

There are probably no depths like those of remorse in men sincerely wishful of better things, and therefore a writer whose path lies along the heights has yet ample occasion to fathom the profundities of human nature. It is certain that as we follow George Eliot's portrayal of life in its fundamental and interior relations, we are startled by a sense of comprehensiveness and penetration with which few writers in this century have impressed us. We may know life, indeed, intensively, through the exhaustive study of a few types, and yet want the knowledge of its outward and transient aspects, the evanescent moods, ideals, standards, the manners, habits, fashions, which make up the livery of a particular age, and which must needs be familiar to the novelist who aims to be in some sort the mirror of his time. How far George Eliot is conversant with this superficial lore we are only beginning to discover, since on a cursory glance

1*

her earlier works seemed to be bounded by one horizon —that of the humbler classes in the English community. Looked at more narrowly, they reveal important differences in this respect, one book, for example, dealing with the agricultural laborer, and another with the artisan of large manufacturing centres. Again, in "Middlemarch," we had a presentation of the middle class in a dull provincial town, while in "Daniel Deronda" the social environment assigned to the foremost persons is that of the aristocracy.

In this latest story the unfolding of character is managed with more than usual skill, and there are many evidences of intense sympathy on the part of the author with her work. The nucleus of the book is the fundamental antithesis in respect of conduct and destiny between two natures at bottom equally generous, but of which one has been warped and narrowed by habitual indulgence, the other braced and expanded by a sense of bereavement and isolation. The early planted conviction of illegitimate birth might have been expected to engender bitterness and resistance, but with Deronda it had an opposite effect. "As his mind ripened to the idea of tolerance toward error, he habitually linked the idea with his own silent grievances;" and again, "the sense of an entailed disadvantage, the deformed foot doubtfully hidden by the shoe, makes a restlessly active spiritual yeast, and easily turns a self-centred, unloving nature into an Ishmaelite. But in the rarer sort who presently see their own frustrated claim as one among a myriad, the inexorable sorrow takes the form of fellowship, and makes the imagination tender. Deronda's early wakened susceptibility, charged at first with ready indignation and resistant pride, had raised in him a premature reflection on certain questions of life ; it had given a bias to his conscience, and sympathy with certain ills and a tension of resolve in certain directions which marked him off from other youths much more than any talents he possessed." That, on the other hand, Gwendolen, the heroine, is not likely to be patient under crosses, and will probably marry for money the instant she is threatened with privations, is foreshadowed in the earlier pages. "The implicit confidence that her destiny must be one of luxurious ease, where any trouble that occurred would be well clad and provided for, had been stronger in her own mind than in her mamma's, being fed there by her youthful blood and that sense of superior claims which made a large part of her consciousness." Most readers will find it difficult to pity this young lady, who in her matrimonial venture had much ampler reason than most of her sex to know what she was doing, and in whose subsequent career stands forth the awkward fact that, being in love with another man, she allows her husband to drown. It is not surprising that Deronda should pity her, since he is rapidly falling in love with Gwendolen before the advent of Mirah, a Jewess and, superficially at least, a much more charming person. As might be inferred from the title, the main interest of the novel is centred in Daniel Deronda, who, under the shaping of personal disappointment and generous action on behalf of others, develops energies and qualities which would have been utterly thrown away in the *rôle* of an English country gentleman. Our sense of the fitness of things demands a larger field for him, and we therefore share his satisfaction when he turns out to be a Jew—that is, to belong to a race with whom and for whom an earnest, large-minded man may find something positive and urgent to do.

On the humor which relieves and lightens the dominant seriousness of the book we do not need to dwell. There are gleams and flashes of it from many subordinate characters, but the thread of comedy is chiefly sustained by Deronda's supposed uncle, Sir Hugo Mallinger, by Hans Meyrick, a painter, and by Parson Gascoigne. The motives of this mundane yet worthy ecclesiastic are set forth with the dry, incisive, and perfectly good-tempered irony of which George Eliot seems to have the secret. On the whole, more space is give in "Daniel Deronda" to the levities and gayeties of life than in the other novels of this writer.

As an artistic story, framed in strict accordance with the laws of form, neither of George Eliot's latest works need shrink from comparison with the great masters of narrative whom we have named above. As a reflex of contemporary manners, "Daniel Deronda" covers a broader canvas than "Middlemarch," but it is no less painstaking and true, and few men probably, whatever their creed or school, will rise from a perusal of the story without an impression strong upon them that this world is not Vanity Fair, as Balzac and Thackeray paint it, but a place of labor and endurance, where he is wisest and happiest who recognizes and fulfils his duty.

I. DRAMAS.

THE appearance of a new and revised edition of Victor Hugo's dramas directs attention to the scope and quality of the author's achievements in that direction. Although the prestige of the lyric poet and the novelist have in some degree obscured earlier triumphs in another field of art, yet it is certain that the plays which Hugo wrote some forty years ago did for a time illumine the French stage with gleams of its former glory. Moreover, they have been reproduced, in one form or another, in libretto, translation, or paraphrase, by the great theatres of the world, in London, St. Petersburg and New York.

Perhaps no young author has suffered more than Hugo from the difficulties and prejudices which beset the stage. Announcing himself as an innovator, he was, of course, proclaimed an outlaw. Splendid names, beloved traditions, revered canons of art, were invoked against him, until an outraged public opinion seconded a suspicious Government and inspired a truculent press. He began by a declaration of war and printed " Cromwell." Official bureaus, college lecture halls, drawing rooms and coffee houses were scandalized by the principles of dramatic art put forth in the preface and elaborated in the play. The Latin quarter, however, swarmed with partisans of the heresy, and the director of the Odéon was persuaded to offer his theatre to Hugo. "Amy Robsart" was acted and failed. Next the poet wrote "Marion de Lorme" and submitted it to the Théâtre Français. It ran the gauntlet of the committee, and thereupon was strangled by an interdict. But Hugo was indomitable, and soon had a fourth piece ready. Hitherto his opponents had contented themselves with skirmish and ambush, but the first representation of "Hernani" gave the signal of pitched battle. Provisioned with sausages and bread, the students faithful to Hugo mustered early in the field. Long hair and matted beards, wild eyes, catcalls and savage yells affrighted the proprieties of the place, while flaming waistcoats and ragged trousers, coats and hats of every epoch and shape confronted and astonished the suave elegance of Paris. Such contests have but one result. Enthusiasm infects the critic, the pit electrifies the boxes. "Hernani" secured for the moment all the triumph its author could desire, and the romantic drama gained a foothold on the stage of Racine.

In the next year, moreover, the Government of Charles Dix was overthrown, and the play ("Marion de Lorme") which had provoked its censure, was welcomed at the Porte Saint-Martin. These victories were encouraging but not conclusive, and the dramatic Luther had yet much work to do. It was still, in fact, an open question whether the novel heresy would end in schism or in smoke. Two years later "Le Roi s'Amuse" was in rehearsal at the Comédie Française, and again the literary reactionists massed their forces to repel the intruder. An intrigue, hatched at the side scenes, reached ministerial circles, and the piece was stopped after one night's performance; whereupon the author sued the theatre, and indirectly impeached the conduct of the Government. The courts rejected his claim. He hastened to complete "Lucrèce Borgia," and appeal to a different tribunal. The new play was produced at the Porte Saint-Martin, and tumultuous applause proclaimed the verdict of the people.

In the following year "Angelo" took possession of the Comédie Française; but the devotees of tradition, baited in their last stronghold, turned once more at bay. The Society of the Théâtre Français had bound itself to enact the works of Hugo so many times a year. It broke the contract. Obsolete rules were resuscitated to embarrass the author, and the claque was instructed to hiss him. Actresses whose robust vigor lent to other *rôles* a spurious vitality were ostensibly made ill by the recurrence of the detested novelties. The poet was at length compelled to sue for a mandamus and damages against the company. But meanwhile a silent revolution had been effected in public opinion. The Tribunal of Commerce sustained both his demands. The matter was carried to a higher court, but the decree was affirmed. The fight was over. Envy and prejudice might continue to sneer, but henceforth despaired of stifling Hugo. The conscientious artist now became a prosperous man. Like Corneille he had written for bread, but, unlike Corneille, he had never sacrificed convictions to necessities. We may fairly say that if the father of French tragedy had evinced the resolution and self-confidence of Hugo, the " Cid " would have had worthy companions, and such a direction would have been imparted to the Gallic stage as might have led Racine to consecrate his delicate genius to elegies and lyrics rather than dramas, and permitted Voltaire to profit by the hints he gleaned from Shakespeare.

The popular play of " Ruy Blas " was presented in 1837, and during the five ensuing years the dramatist was silent. At length to the Théâtre Français, which had so often slighted and betrayed him, he gave his masterpiece, " les Burgraves." This was his last drama. Since 1842 Victor Hugo has abandoned the theatre for the tribune of the novelist. He had persuaded a city to become his audience, and it is scarcely hyperbole to say that he now persuades a world.

To gauge the power and appreciate the innovations of Hugo, considered as a dramatic poet, we have to recall the creeds and opinions which governed Paris at his *début.* It was a period of reaction, the brief and bitter day of Charles Dix. They who had thought and legislated for one-half of Europe seemed to have retained neither laws nor convictions of their own. The city which had worshipped Mirabeau, struck with Robespierre, and summoned a Pope to crown Napoleon, now cowered before the voice of bigotry and prescriptive right. The Polignac Ministry did not hesitate to proclaim a cynical indifference for public opinion which even Choiseul would have disguised, the Church clamored for a censorship which would have strangled the Encyclopædists, while the courts of law betrayed precedent to policy with a supple compliance which Louis Quinze would have sought in vain from the old Parliament of Paris. Precisely as the political upheaval had resurrected the principle of caste, the social recoil determined a literary reaction. That self-dissection of Jean Jacques, which had once impressed a painful lesson, only alarmed and sickened the tender stomachs of the day. The wholesome reforms and bold method of Diderot's drama now became a butt and byword to charlatans who tricked by rule. The pulpit had quite forgotten the accents of Bossuet's courtly sincerity, while the tribune would have quaked beneath the temperate speech of the Gironde. And, finally, the press, reduced to choosing between a bribe and a gag, found all novelties dangerous, and merit in everything old. In a word, thought stagnated ; her arteries were choked ; only a thin and sluggish current crawled backward along shrunken veins. What hope was left to dramatic art, misled by unsound methods, perplexed by arbitrary distinctions, haunted by the memory of an echo, the shadow of a shade !

There were divers iron rules which cramped the energies of the French dramatist, but, above all, he was enjoined to respect the so-called unities. A glance at those dethroned despots may be permitted, for so long as men read Greek tragedies at school, and see French tragedies enacted, the ghost of the old quarrel is likely to revisit the stage.

In the history of letters there is no more impressive instance of the mental paralysis induced by a shallow and servile learning than the subjection of the French drama to the unities of time and place. Following Boileau with unequal steps, critics who read Seneca in French and Aristotle in a Latin translation presumed to interpret Athenian art and regulate their country's. They proclaimed Aristotle an oracle, forgetting that the keenest eyesight is confined by its horizon, and that he certainly was not infallible who submitted the effects of art to the microscope of utility. They seem to have overlooked or ignored the fact that the Greek tragedies themselves sometimes violate their pretended laws. In the "Eumenides," for instance, Orestes flies from Delphi to Athens, and the "Agamemnon" opens with the beacon fire which announces the downfall of Troy, while in the course of the piece the King has completed his voyage from the Hellespont to Argos. Altogether too timid to dream of correcting, or even verifying their master's dicta, the censors of the French stage were ready enough to pervert them. Aristotle had merely noted the historical fact that most dramas of his day happened to observe certain limits of time and place. To inquire, however, whether this peculiarity was essential or accidental seems not to have occurred to men who understood neither the functions of a chorus nor the mechanism of the Attic stage. But it is plain that under the conditions of the modern theatre the fervor of popular enthusiasm and the gush of genuine sympathy ignore the restrictions of their theory. We find it no tax upon him who has learned to love Desdemona in Venice to attend her to Cyprus, and easily as the Afrite in the Persian tale, "Hernani" transports the entranced mind from the palace of Ruy Gomez to the tomb of Charlemagne. So, too, in "Goetz von Berlichingen" we gallop from city to castle and from month to month with the reckless speed of his own troopers; yet our interest, still untired, sits rooted behind the saddle.

There is no doubt one sort of unity which any clear-sighted man who has witnessed a dozen plays recognizes quite as distinctly as the watchers on the critical Zion. The current phrases, æsthetic unity, unity of interest, of impression, of design, describe the same thing from different points of view. An effective drama undoubtedly must be coherent and determinate. It will neither perplex the judgment nor scatter the sympathies of an audience, but evolve a single catastrophe, decipher a central thought. No one would deny that to waft the imagination across long intervals, lulling meanwhile calculation and sustaining enthusiasm, may enhance the difficulty of the feat, but difficulty is a spur and not a wall to genius. It is clear, moreover, that a drama is not an episode; that a genuine unity of action implies, as Aristotle said, a beginning, a middle, and an end. In other words, great passions cannot be adequately conceived without a view of their development ; but how rarely is such perspective possible within the compass of a day or the limits of a single scene ! No doubt some frigid works may have owed compactness, but it is equally certain that noble plays have sacrificed vitality to the fictitious unities of place and time. Compare, for example, " Andromache " and " Le Roi s'Amuse." The action of Racine's tragedy takes place within thirty hours. We are shown at the outset four passions wrought already to the uttermost point of tension. The headlong appetite of Pyrrhus is ready to spurn the most sacred obligations and insult his affianced bride. On the other side, Orestes is swept by a flaming sympathy toward treachery and murder. In Hermione wounded pride has trampled upon modesty and pity, while Andromache's maternal tenderness is on the brink of self-immolation. Of course, the poet knew that his audience would call these passions to account, would instinctively demand their source and provocation. He was aware that the heart does not grow white hot in a single day, or without ample fuel, and accordingly a large part of the tragedy is purely historical. The persons of the piece recount their wrongs and justify their projects. The result is, we are moved, but by no means electrified ; attention is secured, but not *rapport*. It is otherwise in Hugo's drama. The action covers several weeks, and the scene is often shifted. We are made to see the budding heart of Blanche interpreting its secret, and slowly learning to comprehend her woe. The cruel levity of Francis has leisure to fancy, to pluck, and discard a flower. Again, the rage and despair of Triboulet do not merely daze and startle, like the play of transient lightning, but rivet the gaze like the blazing passage of some comet. In a word, throughout the piece we watch the growth and catch the fire of passion. Does it not appear from this instance that even illusion, which rigorous limitations were supposed to insure, may be lost in classic and favored in romantic plays?

It was a remark of Schlegel, which has been seized and expanded by later writers, that even the literature of the Greeks is rather plastic than pictorial, and his suggestion seems to throw some light on the whole method of their drama, as well as on the unquestionable tendency toward a unity of place and time. If we choose to admit that the Attic tragedy, yielding to a dominant instinct of Greek art, aimed rather at grouping than perspective, we shall at all events understand its exclusive recourse to the bold outline and austere simplicity of Hellenic myths. Whatever we may think of this view of the Greek drama, it is certain that the genius of romance languages obeys a different impulse, and prefers a broader argument. Her voice— if she would master us—must be freighted with our nearest hopes, and speak to our liveliest sympathies. It is probable, for instance, that an English audience would have crowned Phrynichus, and not fined him, for the effective stage treatment of a contemporary event.

Grant, however, that it is possible to find a modern theme whose scope consents to the limitations of classic rule, the second canon of French critics struck at the root of right method. Instead of applying gyves, like the pseudo unities, it communicated a taint ; or rather genius under their hands shared the fate of Atys, for a slavish devotion to the suave and fine mutilated virile art. To what should we attribute the artificial tone and dainty finish which distinguished the literature of the *ancien régime?* We cannot ascribe it to a secret bias of the language inherited from that most artful and involved medium of thought, the written Latin, for the Castilian literature, which is by no means finical, reproduces more faithfully the structure and idiom of the mother tongue. Neither does the influence of a court account for the persistent tendencies of two centuries. Undoubtedly that influence was profound. Art kissed the hand of patronage, and not seldom wore her livery, while to literature a modest station was allotted at the monarch's levees, provided she wore the costume and manners of the place. Pensions nourished and an academy crowned the lucky favorites of the hour. Versailles, indeed, flattered the tastes and foibles of Racine, until the author of "Esther" and "Berenice" consented to dignify in those figures the widow Scarron and Louise de la Vallière.

But although the printing press seems essential to the absolute independence of letters, the forcing house of patronage has sometimes failed to stunt their growth, or subdue their flavor. Calderon, for instance, was a courtier ; Chaucer was a *protégé* of princes. Clearly the peculiarities of personal character, the attitude and pressure of individual minds, which some sociologists would have us disregard, are factors indispensable for the solution of many problems. But for the weight of Shakespeare's authority, for example, the correct and scholarlike Johnson might have turned the scale against Marlowe and Fletcher, and, as it was, he held his own for almost a century. So, too, had Regnier lived to contest the supremacy of letters he would scarcely have suffered Malherbe and the pedants to chastise the graceful nonchalance of Ronsard, and affix that stamp of preciseness and propriety which has cramped the strings of the French lyre. Unquestionably the classic literature of France caught much of its elegance and polish from the court which fostered it, but it finally and utterly succumbed to the controlling charm of Boileau's pencil and the chisel of Racine. Of the drama at least this may be said, for it was long the creed of Frenchmen that Racine had given tragedy a perfect and immutable form—that she left his hands a flawless statue which his successors might multiply by casts, but were not to dream of tooling. A glance at the poet's life will best interpret the spirit of his work. As sympathetic as Goldsmith, and almost as shy as Hawthorne, his sensitive and pensive nature early sought a refuge from the fame which, in his brief career of courtier, had occasioned some hours of rapture and many tears. His home long withheld him from the theatre, and in the bosom of domestic joys peace healed and religion comforted a heart which seems to have been bruised and frightened by the shocks and clamors of the world. Now, bestow on such a man such a mentor as Boileau, place him for a season in the atmosphere of Versailles, and you may easily seize the posture of his mind, and forecast his method. Himself of a cautious temper, and tutored by the French Addison, Racine owed it to the stubborn fire of a creative genius that his plays were not as frigid as "Cato." But although Boileau could not clip his pupil's wings, he could, and did, direct his course. "Leave," you can hear him say, "to rude Shakespeare and Moorish Calderon their sublime flights and falls. Choose for thy safer realm the tableland of the beautiful, unvexed by the grotesque and trivial aspects of common life, unshadowed by the giddy summits, beset with so many dangers and so hard to scale." Such counsels Racine would embrace with ardor, since they countenanced his tastes. And, in fact, everything was disposed to favor his treatment of the drama. Corneille had disavowed the impulse which had once led him toward the Spanish theatre, and renounced the promise of the Cid, so that no rival theories disputed and no traditions embarrassed the stage. Even prejudice encouraged Racine, and he was destined to ennoble prejudice.

In his earliest piece Racine announced the principles of his art. Tragedy henceforward must look well to her gown, compose her features, and move with a measured step. The troubles and perplexities of domestic life, homely passions, vulgar griefs, are summarily banished to comedy and farce. The argument and characters must be drawn from remote times, modern history being discarded, as wanting in perspective and in the mist and halo which are conferred by age. Greek myths and Roman chronicles will afford the safest themes, but lest their rugged lines and sombre coloring offend a polished taste, let them be softened and mellowed, so that the eye which is overawed by grandeur may be won by delicacy. Some of the results of this method are amusing. Thus the savage fortitude of Porus, by a curious anachronism, is tempered to a Christian resignation, and a tinge of Gallic gallantry refines the Roman features of the son of Vespasian. The stern spirit of a Hebrew virgin might prove forbidding, but she will be sure, it seems, to awaken sympathy when she is made to breathe the gentle piety of Port Royal. In like manner the stalwart forms of Achilles and Alexander will gain in grace what they lose in majesty by kneeling to the tender passion.

Of course the studied refinement and chastened pathos of such compositions required a language of their own— a sustained and careful diction, tolerably elastic, no doubt, and sonorous, but modulated with nice precision, and confined to a limited range. And accordingly, if

Racine's style rarely startles or electrifies, if its dignity is sometimes inappropriate, we may be sure it will never shock, and will almost always please. Whatever we may think of his method, it is certain that Racine exhausted its capacity of charm. Great critics like Boileau proclaimed the beauty of his ideal, and appluaded the consummate realization. Minor critics, whose myoptic glance missed the plan and proportions of the edifice, could at least decipher the elaborate frieze and admire the mosaic pavement. Palace and boudoir loved him, and they love him still. It was shrewdly said of his tragedies, which have always been well received by the fashionable world, and by no other, that even in foreign countries they somehow find their birthplace.

This was the model and these were the principles of dramatic art which Victor Hugo found in possession of the French theatre. It was not in him to do them homage, for he was truly a son of the century, and his spirit owned no kinship with the laureates of the old *régime*. Passing part of his youth in Spain, and always an ardent admirer of England, he had studied the romantic drama in its birthplace and second home, and by comparison the classic tragedy of France appeared a false and frozen thing. Moreover, temperament conspired with training to shape the poet's course. A glowing fancy and an eager heart had made Hugo's youth lustrous and fruitful. He became a fervent and earnest man. While his nerves tingled with buoyant life and the blood ran lustily in his veins, he was not one to loiter and dream in a lotos land, or people with graceful shadows an artificial stage. Altogether too restless for reverie, realities alone had power to fire his sympathies. It is given to such men, through the crash and tumult of daily strife, to detect some flute-like notes of beauty, and while others seek a pathos distilled through ancient legend these have the skill to catch the fragrant balm as it oozes from the wounded bark. Those who, like Hugo, recognize a kind of priesthood in their function of poet hold truth always noble and elegance often false. All that which oppressed Racine—the rush and scramble of interests, the jostlings and tramplings of the street, smoke of market and din of forum—cannot tease or cloud a robust and sunny spirit, and while delicacy cannot seduce, so even the ridiculous cannot dismay him; hence all the levities, humors, and follies which had been exiled by the tragic muse are welcomed back by the apostle of romanticism to the French stage. In a word, Hugo's method sought to win from nature her effects of light and shade. Like her, he would compel the trivial to relieve or heighten the sublime. He will profit, too, by Regnier's hint that nonchalance is the refinement of artifice. And, finally, his canvas will disclose to us the Janus face and latent power of the grotesque, leagued on one side with terror and clinging on the other to the tendrils of pity.

Thus, to seek concrete examples, we are made to feel an awful irony in the contrast of Triboulet's cap and bells with his scheme of Satanic vengeance. And, again, throughout the play of "Ruy Blas" the friction of an elaborate etiquette serves to chafe an explosive passion. The trifling of Louis Treize accentuates the anguish of Marion de Lorme, while the despair of her sombre lover is sharply projected by a comrade's heedless levity. During the supper given in Ferrara, mirth and dalliance strew flowers in the path of treason, and a jovial drinking song preludes a chant of death. So, under the shadow of fatality which shrouds the fortress of the Burgraves, a knot of slaves amuse their misery with tales and lively jests.

Now, the sharp drawing and vivid tints which stamp Hugo's characters are mirrored in his diction. Abrupt transitions of style, a large diversity of tones, variety in rhythm and cæsura, help to discriminate personal traits and emphasize posture or feeling. To come to particulars, his old men in conversation are sometimes sententious, sometimes garrulous; his young men now fervid and now volatile. The prattle of girlish innocence sounds in his scenes arch and confiding, while the words of mature women are made impetuous and intense. To soldiers he lends the bluff speech of bivouac and foray; to lovers, melting accents of tenderness or thrilling bursts of passion. He allots pertness to ladies' maids, dignity to duchess and queen; is careful to confine elegance to courts, and leaves the cottage its simplicity. Faithful, in brief, to the laws of real life, the voice of every person is flexible, not monotonous, matches the sentiment of the moment, and soars or sinks through the gamut of emotion.

After all, this was Skakespeare's method, and needs no sponsor to English ears, but it was the mission of Victor IIugo to impart and endear it to France. The antique tragedy, which on Athenian soil was a genuine and noble growth, transplanted to a modern stage had become an anachronism and an absurdity; whereas that drama which, born and matured in romance languages, has been termed romantic, is native and alive. The wise scrutiny of Hugo has sought to probe the open wounds of humanity and listen to the throbbing heart, while the genius of Racine did little more than lay sweet garlands on a tomb. The romantic drama cherishes the naïve sincerity of truth, and reveals her naked loveliness; but it was the aim and boast of pseudo-classic tragedy to tutor her artless grace and imprison in sumptuous vestments the free lines of nature. Accordingly, docile to his teacher's behest, the patient style of Racine weeded out every blemish and planted in the crevice a flower. On the other hand, with characteristic contempt for finical elegance, IIugo gave to a prosaic date the initial line of " Cromwell."

Hugo was destined in his *rôle* of iconoclast to confound the traditional distinction of styles. The French theatre had branded their admixture as treason to the principles of art ; and our own stage has sometimes protested against the so-called irregular drama. Ben Jonson, for instance, would not countenance it. " Alexandre " and " Les

Plaideurs " are not more dissonant in tone and treatment than "Sejanus" and "The Alchemist." It is plain, too, that Dryden disapproved of Shakespeare's variable manner, and some professed partisans of the latter have failed to wholly understand it. That blending of the grave and gay, the *chiaroscuro* of romantic drama, proceeds not only from a conscious fidelity to nature's contrasts and vagaries, but perhaps also from a secret drift and bias peculiar to the spirit of modern life. Unclouded elevation, unclouded joy, were moods familiar enough to the Athenian; but is it possible to catch more than glimpses of them in modern skies? On the other hand, is it possible to translate into classic Greek without a paraphrase the complex ideas (involving a background and antithesis) suggested by "earnestness" or "sport"? And why not? Because the sensation of the moment was in a very literal sense mistress of the Attic breast, whereas the atmosphere of a Christian world is surcharged with hope and terror, and the senses are in theory and tend to become in fact only servants in the house of conscience. We may say that, like the oaks of their Dodona, the majesty of antique tragedies was rooted in repose, and that their sublimity had a background of serenity, like thunder from a clear sky. It is otherwise in Christian art. Faith and fatality checker the sober side of our drama with broken lights and shades. The poet's watchful attitude and serious mien betray the tension of a spirit stung by high aspirings and environed by gloomy fears, and we per-

ceive that, unrelieved by gayety, the heart might snap
beneath the strain. Therefore it is that Hamlet is
fain to seek in transient sallies a respite from stifling
thought or to lull with fitful raillery his agony, for
Ophelia's treason.

Even on the cheerful side of our literature there are
traces of a like recoil. There is sunshine truly, but the
wind is sighing in the trees, and a rainbow chronicles
the recent shower. In short, laughter which dimpled
the Grecian cheek reveals the wrinkles of our modern
care-worn faces. The mirth of Attic comedy exhaled
the heedless joy of purely sensuous existence, whereas
the humor of Jacques, of Don Quixote, and of Molière's
Ariste, is distilled from melancholy, and the pungent
liquor betrays the source. Thus it happens that to interpret the Athenian character you must supplement
Sophocles by Aristophanes, while you may almost say
that a single romantic drama (like "Hamlet" for instance) in itself reflects the scope and exhausts the pos-
tures of the modern mind. It seems probable that the
composite manner of Shakespeare reproduced by Victor
Hugo was not so much an invention or foible of the poet
as an instinct of the time.

Having indicated Hugo's method, we need dwell but
briefly on its fruits. An intuitive insight and a stern
(almost a grim) sincerity were guarantees that most of his
creations would be quickened with native fire. Should
he select, for instance, for his protagonist a sinful but
ardent soul, panting to redeem her shortcomings, he will

not fill her mouth with eloquent apology, but goad her into action and bid her live her misdeeds down. If it be a gentle, pensive shape which haunts his memory, he does not content himself with a kindly biography, but bids us dwell upon the winning features and mark the touching voice. Hugo has made some of the offspring of his brain our comrades and bosom friends. He may claim to have animated with men and women a stage which since Molière's death had been surrendered to dreams and shadows. Through the haze which had for many years shrouded the French theatre, his nervous and sinewy forms push their way toward the light and compel recognition. You will not refuse, for example, to greet Rodolpho cordially, for he is Romeo's cousin. Ruy Gomez had perhaps derived from Moorish ancestors his sombre, wakeful jealousy, and we, who know Othello, comprehend the pangs of a proud spirit perplexed in the extreme. There, again, is Don Salluste, in "Ruy Blas," who seems to stalk among the foremost of that cynical and ruthless crew which allows Richard Crookback and Iago the merit of a bad pre-eminence. To our English eyes Don Cæsar, in the same piece, seems more lifelike than Molière's wits, and should be not unwelcome to the merry board where Prince Hal and Biron clink glasses with Mercutio. And we doubt if any of Shakespeare's heroes might challenge with more sovereign justice than Hernani the devotion of a woman's heart. In loyalty and tenderness, in love and in war, he is a true son of the Cid. On the other hand,

2*

although Triboulet is a careful study in morbid anatomy,
Hugo's genius has for the most part shunned grappling
with profound and problematic natures like Faust, Hamlet and Wallenstein. He soars highest in his latest drama.
Prospero, Wolsey, and John of Gaunt had already portrayed for us the noble dignity conferred by suffering
and age, but we can hardly refuse to recognize their
peers in the venerable trio which controls the actions of
"The Burgraves." These august and massive figures
are made to type with bold distinctness the rugged hon-
esty, the ferocious independence, and the splendid aspiration of Germany under her great Suabian Emperor.
The same struggle between license and order, savage
virtues and wise restraints, which blazed forth for the
last time under Maximilian, inspired Goethe's famous
play, but we suppose that even a candid German would
acknowledge that "The Burgraves" is in every way
superior to "Goetz von Berlichingen."

Love governs with paramount authority the plot of
romantic drama. Indeed, even Racine and his followers
were constrained to obey what seems the master impulse
of modern life (at least as we see that life reflected in literature), and give Greek and Roman bosoms a form of
sentiment they rarely knew. But amid the classical scenes
and persons of Racine love is felt to be an intruder and an
impertinence, whereas in Spanish and English plays he
is priest and king. To explain the prominence and ideal
purity with which romance literature has invested the
sexual affection might possibly involve us in an analysis

of those tides and currents which form the undertow of life in a Christian world. Without essaying to define or trace the genesis of the complex modern passion, we may point out that Hugo is not content to photograph a single phase, but discriminates the shapes and hues which the sentiment of love takes from character and circumstance. He allots, for instance, a distinct treatment and different object to the rank *nisus* which has root in appetite and to the noble yearning which seems as pure as prayer. He makes the brimming heart of youth lavish of blind devotion, while the lonely steps and sobered hopes of later life are shown to be grateful for discriminative sympathy. Again, the women to whom Hugo presents us seem able to feel love and inspire it. Blanche in the " Roi s'Amuse " is a gentle being swayed by every emotion and alive to all kind impulses, resembling, in fact, Tennyson's Elaine. You are reminded of Burger's Lenore in the smothered fire and dreamy reverie of Spain's German Queen, and you feel that Ruy Blas had cause enough to love the gracious lady whose delicate sympathy and implicit faith go far to ennoble at once his person and his soul. Then, too, the betrothed of Hernani reproduces, warmed, however, and softened, the features of Corneille's masterpiece. Both are Castilians of blue blood, but Chiméne is the typical Spanish heroine of whom Calderon might have dreamed, Dona Sol the glowing woman whom the courtier-poet might have seen at the court of Philip III. But it is especially in the drama of " Angelo " that two winning, though opposite, feminine natures are contrasted with striking effect. Had Rodolpho, the hero of the piece, been younger in feeling and experience, we are made to infer that La Tisbe's sumptuous beauty and magnetic vitality would have compelled his worship ; but the spring-tide of his youth is past, and her charms are powerless to dim the mild image of her rival. Caterina's tenderness is veiled by a sweet timidity, and she has the fervor of Murillo's virgins, chastened by their perfect modesty. But La Tisbe adds lustre to a type which the drama has often studied, being one of those erring, but generous, women whose faults accuse an ardent temperament rather than a perverted heart, misguided certainly and evil-starred, but not ignoble—like Adrienne Lecouvreur. One does not know whether to envy more the poet or the audience who saw such artistes as Mlle. Mars and Mme. Dorval interpret the heroines of "Angelo."

We cannot dismiss historical plays without a glance at the degree of fidelity with which they reflect the tints and texture of their supposed times. We know it is a nice question how far a dramatist should even try to re-produce the letter of history. But waiving that, nobody will concede to Hugo all the accuracy he claims. In "Cromwell," particularly, there are numerous an-achronisms and some errors more material. For in-stance, a *rôle* in the plot is assigned to one Syndercomb, who, as it happened, had previously died in prison. Again, Hugo makes Carr (Kerr), whom he calls an "old sectary," a bigoted partisan of the Long Parliament, and reiterates with some minuteness in the notes a statement of the text that in the rebellion of 1650, " Carr, seconded by Strachan, withdrew his forces from the Parliamentary camp." He could scarcely separate from that to which he was never attached. It is well enough established that this cross-grained fellow, Kerr, had raised some regiments in the West of Scotland for the Commission of Estates, and refused to join—not, of course, the English, whom he was in arms to oppose, but — his brother Scots under David Lesly. Neither can we like the contrivance by which, in Hugo's drama, Cromwell aims to convert his installation into a coronation, and filch, as it were, a crown which he had already solemnly declined. Such underground procedure would have galled the man's haughty temper, and, irremediably affronted the English people.

The laborious research which has commonly preceded the construction of Hugo's plays demonstrates, however, a literary integrity which dramatists rarely display, and we have touched some errors of detail only because the author asserts in prefaces and notes a punctilious exactitude to which few historians even can pretend. It appears to be the privilege of genius, as of royalty, to lavish large gifts with a careless hand, while it is rather the humble acquisitions derived not from nature or fortune, but from severe toil, to which they point with satisfaction. Thus, Milton dwelt with peculiar complacency on the learning which adorns the " Paradise Regained," and the author of " Childe Harold " recalled with especial fondness his dull paraphrase of the "Ars Poetica." So much is certain, that in Hugo's dramas we breath the atmosphere and glow with the passions of their times. He has approached, for example, the great Protector in the precise temper of Cromwell's Ironsides, a wholesome mixture of naïve sagacity and sober admiration, of candor and respect, equidistant from the resentment of Ludlow, the prejudice of Clarendon, and the hero-worship of Carlyle. Drawn from such a point of view, the portrait is instinct with spirit, and delivers the lineaments of life. Talma, we are told, complained to Hugo that he had played warriors and heroes, but never a man. Had he lived, he was to have acted Cromwell.

It will scarcely be disputed, doubtless, that the central aim of the drama is purely æsthetic. Nevertheless, the beauty which a dramatist aims to incarnate may be at times a spiritual beauty, a beauty which supposes an ideal and implies inward adaptation—in short, a reflex of moral perfection. Accordingly the creative power and ethical worth of a dramatist will often be found in nice proportion. If only his art be sufficiently incisive and veracious he has (perhaps against his will) pronounced a sermon. We can discern the intimate relation of art to ethics within a certain field by contrasting Racine's "Phèdre" with Victor Hugo's "Lucrèce Borgia." Both are fair women and syren-tongued; both are capable of murder and of darker sins; both invoke sympathy—let us see which commands it! Phèdre robes a brutish appetite in soft and graceful fancies, and pushes a vile design behind a mask of sentiment. She proposes to atone for a ruthless deed by a tardy compunction and to shift the responsibility of guilt by cursing the accomplice who has anticipated her secret wish. In the treatment of her illicit passion there was manifestly much to soothe, and nothing to chafe the conscience of Mme. de Montespan. Consequently, the critics of Versailles protested that Racine had, so to speak, purified Phèdre. The truth is, the poet had washed her in strong acids—the cleansing kills. The wicked woman of Greek tragedy has shrunk to a guilty ghost. Racine, no doubt, was a good man as well as a great artist, but throughout this piece his method seems to truckle to a perverted morality, and unquestionably engenders an abortive art. You feel that Phèdre's languors and raptures are the trappings of a filthy purpose, the weapons of cunning desire. And so, in spite of her smooth rhetoric and vehement tears, she is revolting rather than pitiable, meretricious and not beautiful.

At the outset of Hugo's drama, on the other hand, we are informed of the Borgia's atrocities, yet from her entrance upon the stage she enlists a measure of sympathy —and why ? Not because her beauty captivates some engaging person of the piece, and so involves an audience through a vicarious predilection in the meshes of her wiles. On the contrary, from *début* to climax she is the target of hate and scorn. Neither does the poet seek to mask a cancer which he means to burn away.

He suffers no contagious gayety to relieve, no persuasive plea to extenuate, the sins of her past career. But the monster is a mother. Her business in a licentious city is to visit an only son, the same wistful solicitude which had tracked his steps from youth having led her now to Venice to gaze upon his features. The contact with the young man's upright and sunny nature seems to electrify her torpid conscience and to strike like a knife at the ulcers of her soul. Remorse sets in, and her penitence goes far to cleanse, if it cannot respite. Accordingly, when the Duchess meets the retribution whose shadow is descried from the outset of the piece, we do not find ourselves cajoled or tricked into a mawkish sympathy, but won to an honest pity. We are made to feel in one and the same pang that the wretched woman does indeed merit chastisement, but not from a filial hand. This would seem to be wholesome art—art tending to those summits where poetry and religion walk hand in hand.

It is strange, considering how often rude and distorted versions are presented, that no attempt has hitherto been made to produce on the English stage some of Hugo's dramas in translations not unworthy of the poet's text. Such an undertaking would be fraught, we think, with large enjoyment and profit to the playgoer. Moreover, it may almost be pronounced a duty to one who, in our own day, has commended to France the aims and methods of Shakespeare's art, not as Voltaire commended it—by arid critical analysis—but by the fervent and fruitful homage of imitation.

II. LATER LYRICS.

ONE of the most charming contributions to recent literature is the volume of poems by Victor Hugo which bears the title of " L'Art d'être Grand-Père."   There is something profoundly touching in the spectacle of this old man eloquent bending wistfully over a cradle and sinking the voice which rang out so sternly in " L'Année Terrible" to the accents of a lullaby.

Although Victor Hugo is the least impersonal of artists, and in his " Contemplations " offered us a sort of autobiography, yet the present book was needed to show us the man.   The generation of readers which welcomed his first lyrics has, for the most part, passed away, and to their successors these verses, in which a poet grandsire prattles to or dreams over his grandchildren, will reveal the fountain of loving kindness in a nature which has often seemed surcharged with bitterness. Some there are, however, who will be reminded by this volume of earlier lines printed some thirty years ago, and in which the hopes and griefs of the parental relation are portrayed with the same tender grace and poignancy.   Indeed, we have found nothing in the " Art of Being Grandfather," stored with exquisite household idyls as it is, more daintily sweet than two poems beginning, " *Elle était pâle, et pourtant rose,*" and " *Elle avait pris ce pli dans son age enfantin,*" which appeared in the second volume of the " Contemplations."   But when these were penned the author was in the prime of manhood ; the horizon of the artist and the patriot was at the widest ; most of his work was yet to do, and thus it is not surprising the domestic affections should have claimed less space upon his page than we can now see they held in his heart.

Since the grandfather who here speaks to us is Victor Hugo, we should expect the volume to sum up all the impressions, memories, and experiences, all the phantoms, smiling or sombre, all the hope and disenchantment which may abide in the mind of one who has seen and accomplished much. Accordingly, in whatever key his verse is pitched, however blithe or trivial the text may seem, we are presently brought back to the solemn drama of human existence—to the problem which, as he has said, emerges from the enigma of the cradle to culminate in the enigma of the shroud ; which begins with a smile, and is continued in a sob. The meditations, fancies, visions into which we enter, are all intensely fraught with Hugo's characteristic spirit, yet, because the author is a great poet, the reader finds in them not a little of his own individuality, and sees reflected the very thoughts with which, surveying the dawn of a younger life, he has looked back over his own.

The first part of the present volume seems to have been produced at Guernsey during the poet's exile. At this time his grandson, George, was not three years, and the little girl Jeanne, but fifteen months old. One day in summer the children go out to walk with grandpapa

—Jeanne, however, being in the immediate charge of George, who, we are assured, is a perfect little man. Such young girls as Jeanne already occupy his mind, and he never tires of admiring her diminutive rosy fingers, and contrasting them with his own stout fists, which have battled some three winters with the world. Nevertheless, Master George is not unconscious of his masculine advantages ; he will point out, now and then, to the passers-by the curious fact that Miss Jeanne can only creep, while he himself moves with a firm stride, and he is likely to shake his head with an air of ˙critical disapproval when the young lady thrusts a finger in her mouth.   George is the guardian of this little sovereign, but her subject and slave is grandpapa.   On another occasion, when she is shut up in a dark closet for some grave dereliction, the old man goes stealthily to the chamber of penance, and slips a pot of sweetmeats through the door—a proceeding which naturally provokes remonstrance from those domestic powers who uphold the public order and security.

Jeanne often goes to sleep with her little hand tightly clutching one of grandpapa's fingers.   This is the moment the latter chooses for reading conservative newspapers, which, as a rule, are not accustomed to treat Victor Hugo with much deference.   One insinuates, perhaps, that the author would be an unpleasant man to meet at night in a dark place ; another recites the atrocious circumstances under which the poet demolished the Louvre, and put the hostages to death.   A third suggests that this alleged incendiary, poisoner, and assassin might have turned out a less sinister personage if the Emperor, Napoleon III., had deigned to make him a Minister. While the Bonapartist jackals are thus snarling at the majestic exile, his grandchild sleeps ; but, as if the dreamer besought him to bear and to forbear, he feels the soft pressure of her hand.

When times have changed and a new France rises on the ruins of the Empire, grandpapa takes his babies to Paris and makes known to them that place of wonders, the Jardin des Plantes. We are not surprised that the sweetest idyls in this volume should have been fashioned in this same garden. We can see the aged poet leaning on his cane, and watching the fearless motions of his innocents, while between the bars, behind which crouch the types of cruel instincts, they toss posies and sweetmeats, and while the joyous tinkle of their laughter blends strangely with a sullen roar, big with wrath and with rebellion. Nor are we surprised that, penetrated by the poignant contrast thus presented, and longing to readjust the seeming inequity of nature, he should have been led to reproduce in a passage of singular beauty the old theory of the transmigration of souls.

What, he says, if the antique conjecture, the wild dream of Chaldean magians, of Hermes and Pythagoras, had, after all, some groundwork of fact ! What if the myth of Tantalus did but figure an awful reality—the anguish of the brute condemned to live in the presence of humanity ! And were it true that these cramped skulls, flattened foreheads, distorted and vacant features are but the sombre masks of a dethroned intelligence—if these beings pent within the tomb of the bestial appetites, and straining with groans inarticulate to interpret their torment to our ear, are, indeed, the spirits of the damned, expiating on an earth which is to them a hell, the crimes of an earlier existence—then with what ineffable surprise, with what a shiver of awakened hope must these outcasts of creation, forsaken of God and abhorred of man, hear all at once beside their prison bars a peal of children's voices !

When a grandfather calls himself Victor Hugo—is, in other words, not only a poet, but a patriot—he will not forget amid his raptures and visions to add a word of sober monition. He would not have the young recruits of the future begin as he began, with the worship of false gods ; and, therefore, in the last section of this volume, under the heading, " For the little ones to read when they are big," he tells his grandchildren their duty, toward France first, and next toward humanity. In the outburst of fervor and unshaken constancy entitled " Patrie," he bids them know that their grandfather was not of those who, seeing ruffians lord it for a day, lose heart and confidence in the right. Neither was his faith in the fatherland at all disturbed because in the reflux of events fate had dealt it another and a more fatal Rosbach. In the record of the last hundred years you come oftener upon an Austerlitz than a Waterloo. But the benignant spirit of the grandsire poet cares not to flourish in these strophes names which are so many firebrands of international hate, but seeks to instil wider sympathies and a larger purpose than patriotism can kindle.

The hundred lines thrown together under the caption "Fraternité" contain the whole social philosophy and religion of Victor Hugo. His dream, he says, is a people enlightened rather than disciplined ; therefore, he is laureate of the love which wills, the hope which fires, the faith which builds—of equity, kindness, pity, long-suffering, and a vast forgiveness. "Oh, brothers," he cries, "wind-tossed, wave-tossed, battling for an hour in the night and the storm, succor each other, pardon each other." In a world whose to-day is the inexorable outgrowth of yesterday, where the human will dashes in vain against the walls of heredity and environment, it may be that the name of Justice is too often on the lips of men. Or rather her ministers can never have seen her real lineaments, for this is the portrait of the goddess whom we are taught to think stern and blind. On a certain day, the poet tells us, he beheld an unknown woman who seemed to float out of a cloud. Winged she was, and it seemed that honey was on her lips and heaven in her eyes. Now, this woman did naught but point out the right road to foot-sore and heart-sore wayfarers, and it seemed that her voice said only, "Lo ! ye have missed the way." And when he drew near, he saw that this woman's eye had blessed whatsoever it looked on, so piercing yet mild it was, and that this gush and overflow of unstinted, unmeted kindness made some to think her crazed. Then he fell on his knees and worshipped, for he deemed he knew her features. But she, reading his thought, said, sadly, " Dost thou, too, know me not ? My son, thou deemest me Mercy ; not so, my name is Justice."

By these gentle words of a poet grandfather, as by the solemn tones of " Les Châtiments" and " L'Année Terrible," and by his dramas and narratives, no less than by his lyric verse, one curious, we might almost say anomalous, fact is pressed upon the reader. In all the works of Victor Hugo the figure of the author fills the foreground, yet, strange to say, the artist is scarcely thwarted, but rather aggrandized by the man. We can affirm so much of but four names in the history of artistic achievement, and the coincidence may well be marked that the foremost of living artists is as indissolubly associated with the republican aspirations of France, as were his great predecessors with the civic liberties of Athens and Florence and with the English Commonwealth. The place of Victor Hugo is with those patriot poets who challenge the homage, not of wonder only, but of a loving reverence by the rare accord of a consummate art and an exhaustless sympathy with mankind.

III. " LE PAPE."

VICTOR HUGO's book named " Le Pape" seems to challenge attention not merely as a poem, but as a manifesto.   Indeed, when we note the remarkable attitude here taken by the foremost of living Radicals toward the Papacy, we are constrained to overlook for a moment the man of letters in the patriot. These shreds of verse, half lyric, half dramatic, fragmentary enough and sometimes incoherent, yet fraught for the most part with the author's intense and infectious eloquence, embody an extraordinary suggestion. An invitation is extended to the Catholic Church to discard at once and forever its profitless league with the monarchical and oligarchical principles, to repudiate King and Kaiser, who have plundered and betrayed it, to revert to the democratic, not to say communistic, spirit of its infancy, and to preach, frankly and exclusively, in organization and in work, those doctrines of equality and fraternity which it once proclaimed, and has at no time utterly overlooked. Whether or no this projected alliance between the Papacy and the new democracy is purely a poet's dream, we may be assisted presently to determine by the concordant hints of a shrewd Catholic thinker. At all events, these words of Victor Hugo deserve a thoughtful hearing, even through the medium of a prose translation, as the respectful, conciliatory utterance of a great republican poet, who has been swift enough in the past to mark the shortcomings of the Roman hierarchy.

In the poem itself, such a reversion on the part of Rome to the unselfish teachings which filled the Catacombs, and the strange, scarce thinkable alliance with the extreme popular tendencies of the day, are seemingly relegated to dreamland. It is night. The Holy Father is asleep in his bedroom within the Vatican. He dreams ; and, after following his night wanderings, we are brought back to the same apartment where the poet, as if admitting that his picture had more of longing than of faith in it, makes the Bishop of Rome mutter, on awakening, "I have dreamt a frightful dream." But a moment's reflection suggests that a poet-patriot does not give so much pains to the portrayal of an impossible vision, and that his perception of the function which events may press upon the Papacy is not unbrightened with a hope of its acceptance.

In an early scene of this cloud-drama, the Pope, who has been striving to spell the lessons of the Creative One written in the starry heavens, scans with pitying looks the file of monarchs which sweeps past him in august similitude of the most Christian and most Catholic defenders of the faith. We next see him on the threshold of the Vatican, about to abandon that stronghold and symbol of the old compact between priest and king, and go forth like the first Bishops of Rome, those lowly, often unlettered, expounders of the gospel of humanity. He whom the suffrages of the conclave have placed on the throne of St. Peter is represented as speaking in the spirit of the primitive propaganda to the city of Rome and to the universe. "Listen," he says, "all ye living, shrouded in shadow, led astray by the long imposture of the slavish centuries : know that thrones are black, the sceptre vain, the purple vile. Beneath the vast sky yonder, impenetrable and mild, love is the only purple, innocence the only throne. The night and the dawn, two combatants, front each other in the breast of man. The priest is a pilot ; he must accustom his eyes to the sunlight, if he would whiten his soul. As it is, I am blind, like all the rest of you, my friends ; I know not man, or God, or any part of the created world ; the triple crown about my brow is but a threefold emblem of ignorance. I know not why I dwell here in this palace, why I wear a diadem, why they call me Lord of Lords, Sovereign Pontiff, Heaven-chosen King. This thing I know—I am a poor creature. Therefore, I get me gone. I quit this palace, trusting that all these treasures and this luxury will not curse me for usurping them—I, whose roof should be of thatch. Man's conscience is my sister, and I go to talk with her. I will know no law but to hate evil, without hating the evil-doer. Henceforth I will be only a monk, like Basil, and like Anthony. I go. I set forth on foot over the earth, as chance leads me, into the dawn, into the night ; having the wind and the rain for clothing, if it please Heaven ; owning nothing but the passing moment ; and mindful that the moments are short. I know that man suffers. I go to succor the flagging spirit, the drowning heart ; I fare amid deserts, amid hovels, among brambles and rocks, vagrant even as Jesus, the divine, barefooted wayfarer. For him who owns nothing, 'tis to gain the world, thus to march through the profundities of humanity, to heal aching hearts, to prop sinking faith, to quicken souls about his path. From kings, then, I seize the earth ; to the Romans I give back Rome ; I go home to God's house, which is no other than the lowly house of man. Give me way, people ! Rome, farewell ! "

Now, we cannot shut our eyes to the astonishing vitality of Latin Christianity, or deny that the Roman Church, shorn of all its temporal possessions, remains on the whole the mightiest organization upon the earth. To measure the profound and massive foundations of its authority we need but to compare the influence of the present Pontiff with that of any of the disinherited princes whose ancestors have at times seemed to control or compromise the Papacy. The truth is, that in the great reaction which followed the German Reformation, the Church of Rome did, in fact, appeal to the masses of the people, and since that epoch she has probably lost much more than she has gained by her alliance with the monarchical principle. At all events, she must be held to have proved her power of self-protection ; she can stand alone. She can thrive in a republic, and who will say, in view of her origin, and of the successive reversions to the spirit of self-abnegation exhibited by the Franciscan, Dominican, and Jesuit fathers, that she might not adapt herself even to the Utopian commonwealths which Proudhon, Louis Blanc, and Karl Marx have contemplated ? But, while we concede to Latin Christianity the suppleness and elasticity which belong to living tissues, we cannot but recognize the blight of decay and

a rigidity which resembles that of death in the Church
of Eastern Christendom, which counts among its nom-
inal votaries some 80,000,000 of souls. It is beyond dispute that both wings of the so-called Orthodox body—
the Russian and the Fanariote clergy—are smitten
through and through with king-worship and the greed
of carnal things, cursed at once with spiritual apathy
and intellectual sterility. Accordingly, the reformer
of Moscow or St. Petersburg is invariably a Nihilist ; he
can find no place for the Church in a regenerated State ;
and it would never enter his brain to intrust the Greek
Patriarch or the Russian Metropolitan with the *rôle*
which Victor Hugo has assigned in "Le Pape" to the
Bishop of Rome. The difference in the ductility and
energy of the Byzantine and Roman organizations seems
to foreshadow a very different fate under the pressure of new social conditions. This wide divergence of
character and destiny is emphasized in a striking scene
of the present poem, where the Catholic Church, identified in the person of the Supreme Pontiff with the obscurity, the hardship, and the aspiration of humble
folk, is brought into sharp contrast with the garish accessories and essential nullity of the Eastern hierarchy.

The Synod of the Orient is in session ; in the place of
primacy the Patriarch of the East in pontifical robes
and a tiara on his brow ; around him a throng of Bishops, their copes and mitres heavy with gold. The superb prelate has deigned to expound to the awe-struck
congregation the scope of his apostolate, and has con-

cluded with pronouncing a gracious benediction upon them. To him enters, pushing his way through the crowd of Bishops to the altar, a man clothed in black drugget, holding in his hand a wooden cross. "To bless Heaven," cries the new-comer, "is well; to bless hell would be better. Yes, priest," he explains to the astounded prelate, "bless the pains and woes that make man's hell. Bless tears; bless the cankered but repentant heart where good with evil grapples. Bless hunger, rags, the prison where the convict drags his chain; bless the humble soul darkened by perpetual hardship and the heart worn out with hope deferred. Bless the reprobate, the pariah, all those for whom never yet thou didst lift voice in prayer. Bless hell!" Who is this man? exclaims the Patriarch, and the reply is: "Bishop of the Orient, the Bishop of the West salutes thee; I am thy brother." Then follows a remarkable dialogue, from which we can cite only the concluding lines. The exponent of Latin Christianity, in its imagined mission of fervent co-operation with the laboring masses, tells the prelates of the East that he has emerged in fear and horror from their night of callous indifference and blind self-seeking. "What!" he cries, "it might have been said of me, this man had in charge a great idea, the highest and noblest that ever dawned on our terrestrial twilight; he was the organ of the homage which the soul owes to Heaven, the one cable of safety between a foundering vessel and its port, the one flash of light between stumbling man and the abyss of annihilation and despair. What ! because these phantoms whom men call lords, princes, sovereigns, Kaisers— because false gods made up of accidents, the chance of conquest or the chance of birth, chose to come to me, the watcher who hath no function here on earth but to shout Hosanna, and point with upward finger to the soul eternal; me, whose duty is to ever ponder, amid sobs over wrong chastised, how to change God's light into God's pity—because these Kings, these shadows, these dealers in dust and ashes, come to my door, stern and haughty, and bid me do their will, must I therefore take their side ? Should it be said that the appointed almoner of Heaven had become the broker of these slave-merchants, cheapening at their bidding truth, honor, justice, law; filching its rights from a starving people to enrich a king; praying for the hand that smites, and cursing the head that falls ? Shall it be said that I degraded Jesus into Attila's lacquey ? Shall humanity look me in the face and say, " He had our soul in trust and lost it; the day was dawning and this man sold it; he has prostituted the morning star ? " The Patriarch breaks in with, " You blaspheme, Pope !" The Pope rejoins, " Proud priest, be humble ! Gilded altar, quit thy gilding ! August mouth, part thy long muzzled lips and speak the truth ! Enter once more into thy patrimony, disinherited man ! Women, children, possess rights at last ! People, be conscious of a soul ! Come, priests, preach the truths that I proclaim. Be lowly of heart ; draw nearer to little children that ye may draw nearer unto God. Believe that the meeker the Pontiff, his temple is the more sublime." But these verities, like those uttered by St. Paul, are to the Greeks but foolishness ; they vanish and leave silence around the Roman, who continues : "What, the priests fly, the altar falls ; even so Babel crumbled in the fore time. I am alone. Nothing left but shadow." Then from the far heart of the Infinite a voice whispers, "I am there !"

Before passing to those pages in which the Pope of Hugo's dream pronounces before a crowd of paupers and outcasts and malefactors such an harangue as may have been heard from Savonarola in Florence streets, let us quote some lines in which the poet suggests a form of propaganda with which Catholic priests are by no means unfamiliar, and which accounts in a large measure for the hold of village curates in France on the affections of the rural population. The scene is a garret. It is winter. A poor man and his family are huddled together, cold and famished, on a straw bed. The poor fellow mutters hoarsely : "I do not believe in God." The Pope enters, and with, "You must be hungry, eat," divides his slender store of bread, and gives half to the father. "And my boy ?" returns the other sullenly. "Take the whole," then says the visitor, and puts the remnant in the child's hand. "How good it tastes !" the boy cries, munching eagerly. "Children are angels," says the Pope to the father ; "suffer me to bless him." "Do as you will," replies the latter, not very graciously. Then the Pope, emptying his thinly garnished wallet on the straw—"Look, here is money to buy blankets." "And wood, too," says the poor man, softly. "Yes, and to clothe the little boy, his mother, and you as well, my brother; alas!" the priest continues, "'tis a harsh life. I will find you work to do. These winter nights are hard to bear. And now let us talk of God, my brother." The poor man answers, "I believe in Him."

And this is how the Supreme Pontiff of a younger and brighter day may commune with his brethren of the streets : "From the depths of night, the depths of woe, the depths of tears, come to me, all ye that tremble, that suffer, all ye that bleed and ye that sob, the convict, the beggar, the incurable, all that know want and wretchedness, all that are beaten in life's battle; I am your yoke-fellow, one of yourselves, my bones ache with the same fever, I am racked with the same agony. Come, ye ragged ones, ye dishonored, ye chastised ones, I am the servant of your servitude, the fellow-captive of your gaol. I whom they name first among the Kings will be the least among you. I love you, and have no other excuse for living. I am only a poor creature owing service to all. Do ye help me, O ye sufferers! I claim my share in the griefs of earth. O ye poor, give me all you have—your hungry days, your unwarmed lofts, your footsore walks, your cares, pains, murmurs, angers, your sighs, your prayers, your tears."

After all, the poet who would carry to such heights

the gospel of fraternity scarcely goes beyond the teachings and the acts of St. Francis d'Assisi. This is one of the coincidences with historical fact which make it impossible to regard this poem as in any sense a satire. But before examining in the light of some Catholic writings the practicability of the new alliance which seems to be commended with so much eloquence to the Papacy, we would direct attention to one or two other extracts of peculiar interest. In the following passage Victor Hugo rebukes distinctly and sternly the excesses into which French Radicals have sometimes been betrayed. In view of these lines it is impossible to calumniate the poet by conceiving him as an apologist for the bloodshed and devastation which dishonored the last days of the Paris Commune. "As to ye," he says, "working men, on whom your burden weighs, ye that own the strength of lions, yet whom they treat as ants, I bid ye lose not patience, but learn to wait, my friends. Shall you come to blows—a trial of main strength? Not so. Certainly it is your supreme right to live, to obtain bread to eat, to ask larger wages for less toil —so much I concede. The immense universe owes you a share of its vast blessings—life, harmony, love, joy, hope's aureole. The future is not dark—already morn tinges with rose the tiny fingers of the newly-born laughing in his crib. Thou shalt claim, O workman, the guerdon of robust toil, defend thy hearth-stone, yea, confront the laws whose false wisdom violates thy simple rights. Yet while thou feedest thy child, thou shalt

3*

not slay thy brother, thou shalt not bruise thy fatherland, or stab thy city. No Saint Bartholomew must
mar the clear record of your fraternal creed. There is
no place in the promised land for death. Hope was
not born to drown in hot, salt tears. Remorse and
infamy are not for us ; the people's cause needs no
butchers. I abhor a red-handed victory, and God's
paradise would be hateful if we had to enter it across a
murder. Liberty shall not accept an assassin for her
instrument. Progress has nothing providential in it if
it must sound hell in order to scale heaven."

And now we recall a part of the final scene, in which
the Holy Father, having striven to fulfil the poet's
conception of his mission, returns in his last days, not
to Rome, but to Jerusalem. A sad old man, the time-
worn comrade of hardship and heartache, the Pope
draws near to him who revealed here below so much of
God as may be embraced in man. He surrenders Rome,
and takes for his abiding place Jerusalem, which, he
tells us, is the veritable shrine of holiness. The shadow
of the Christian's faith lies on the Capitol—its soul on
Calvary. To the throne of Leo and Gregory the Pontiff
prefers Christ's sepulchre. For Jesus he forsakes Cæsar.

Those who are disposed to see in the central idea of
"Le Pape" only a poet's dream, and to regard the co-
operation, or even the coexistence of the Catholic
Church with the modern Socialist party as impracticable,
may do well to compare the suggestions of St. George
Mivart in the essay entitled " Contemporary Evolution."

Mivart points out that the elevation of the artisan class, once effected, would put an end to their hostility to the Church, since that hostility has mainly arisen from a belief that the action of the Church was prejudicial to their elevation. He reminds us too that, although the abolition of existing religious orders might be temporarily enforced, it would be almost impossible to interfere with the practice of the evangelical counsels—voluntary poverty, chastity and obedience. Each successive epoch of crisis has been fruitful of fresh modes of their manifestation, some new embodiment of the ascetic spirit appearing on the crest of the advancing wave of Christian aggression on the world. Hard work and charity, under one form or another, were universally obligatory upon the old religious orders; and to this day the Trappist works like a day laborer. It may well be, then, that manual toil in other forms, and a new modification of fraternal charity, will cause religious congregations to be as heartily welcomed and beloved by a Socialist community as ever they were in the ninth, thirteenth, or sixteenth centuries. Indeed, a body of workmen who should be only distinguished from their fellows by a larger spirit of fraternity and a disposition to take a greater share of labor from others, while at the same time they appropriated a less portion of its fruit, would speedily be popular; and a love for God might soon be appreciated when it was seen to be attested by a self-sacrificing love for man.

Neither St. George Mivart, nor, we imagine, Victor

Hugo, looks forward to any incongruous alliance between the Papacy and the Paris Reds. To the extreme revolutionary party in France politics are a religion whose cardinal articles are probably held with as much intensity of feeling as can be commanded by the Roman Catholic Church itself. Perhaps, if the Church should take the line indicated in Hugo's poem, it ought rather be regarded as a rival power bidding against the Reds for the friendship of the poorer classes of society. It would be quite as little hampered by any stereotyped reverence for economical laws. For different reasons capital is scarcely less hateful to the genuine ecclesiastic than to the Socialist, and we are not sure whether the doctrine that property is a trust held for the benefit of the needy might not prove quite as attractive to the beneficiary as the rival theory that property is only legitimate when it has been distributed among the poor. At all events, this is the attitude which "Le Pape" supposes the Catholic Church to have assumed, not so much striving to win over its vehement antagonists as offering to the great mass of the people, who are as yet neither Reds nor Catholics in any definite sense, a creed full of sympathy for their sufferings, yet untrammelled with promises which it might prove difficult to perform.

IV. "LA PITIÉ SUPRÊME."

IN a notice of "Le Pape" we dwelt on the dual interest attaching to the utterances of one who is at the same time the foremost of contemporary poets and the most conspicuous advocate of republican ideas. We find the same fusion of aims, the same striking coalescence of artist and statesman, in Victor Hugo's later work, "La Pitié Suprême. While parts of it undoubtedly vibrate with piercing strains of lyrical eloquence, this remarkable poem will be naturally regarded in some quarters as a political manifesto. From this point of view, the singular mildness and benevolence of its tone, its exhibition and inculcation of a placable and moderate spirit, is a fact of large significance. It means that a man of the ripest experience and the keenest insight, placed at the focus of affairs, and commanding the widest horizon, esteems republican institutions impregnably grounded in France ; that, in other words, the hour of partisan conflict has passed, and the hour of sage and sober counsel has arrived. It is the lesson of this poem that class hatreds are anachronisms, and that the injuries which rankle in the memories of many French Republicans should henceforth be rather studied as historical phenomena than avenged as crimes. That such a doctrine should be preached by the author of "L'Année terrible" is of itself a kind of revolution. Perhaps nothing that has been said or written in France since the collapse of the empire is more calculated to dispel the apprehensions and fortify the confidence of friends of order than such a change of front on the part of the patriot-poet, who has long been ranked with Milton among the most rancorous opponents of priest and king.

There are, indeed, some curious points of likeness in these two men, whether we consider their relation to the literary or the political movement of their times. Both evinced in youth some instinctive leanings toward the interesting and romantic associations which, to a sensitive fancy, invest conservative institutions with a species of glamour. Both promptly shook off such illusions as the power of insight was quickened and the habit of judgment asserted its regnant function. Once become republicans by conviction, they were impelled by the intensity of the poetic temperament toward sweeping reform and headlong revolution. The Long Parliament was not progressive enough for Milton ; the Assembly of '48 was too slow and circumspect for Victor Hugo. Each saw his dream of a commonwealth broken by the incubus of Cæsarism, and the diverse action of the two men in a somewhat similar juncture was dictated by the obvious difference of circumstances. However shocked and disenchanted by the usurpation of Cromwell, the Puritan enthusiast could afford to serve one who was himself the outcome of the republican upheaval, who upheld, upon the whole, the principles of civil liberty at home, and who stood forth the champion of religious freedom throughout Europe. The French patriot, on the other hand, could not stoop to compromise with a sham Cæsar, who was to Cromwell what a chicken thief is to a pirate, and whose dynastic, religious, political and literary credentials were all equally counterfeit. The fourteen years which Milton passed in blindness and seclusion after his hopes were shipwrecked by the restoration of Charles II. may be compared with the two decades spent by Victor Hugo in Guernsey, when he was, as Swinburne called him, the greatest exile, and, therefore, the greatest man of France. It was in these analogous periods, when the field of political energy was no longer open, that each poet gave himself with undivided mind to letters, and produced the works by which their names will be longest known. It was not given, however, to the creator of "Paradise Lost" to witness the pacific revolution by which a part of the gains won by his republican coadjutors were recovered and forever assured to England. More happy than his Puritan counterpart, the author of "Les Misérables" and "Les Châtiments" lived to see France emerge from the slough of political and social corruption, and rear once more—and this time on broad and firm foundations —the fabric of a free State. If we may trust his own estimate of the future implied in the book before us he has lived to see those reactionary forces which Milton eyed with well-grounded dread and vigilant animosity shrink into objects of philosophic review and thoughtful pity.

Kings, nobles, the rich, the lucky, all those who are born or drift into splendid opportunities, deserve, we are told, compassion rather than envy, and the keenness of our sympathy should be exactly proportioned to the extent of the temptation. This view of man's surroundings, and of the compensations inherent in social inequality, is trite enough to us, and no doubt it is familiar on the lips of village curates in the rural districts of France. But we may be sure that it is a strange, paradoxical, and repugnant statement to the operatives of Paris, Lyons, and the other great cities, who constitute the vital nucleus of the Republican party. As a rule, the French artisan has ceased to read the Bible, and as yet he has only learned the rudiments of the evolutionary philosophy. He has acquired the catch-words "heredity" and "environment," and he finds them useful to explain, as they unquestionably do, the intellectual shortcomings and the vices of his class. He has heard that inherited tendencies to pauperism, drunkenness, insanity, and crime can be checked and gradually eliminated in an improved social medium, and he holds that every community owes such facilities of melioration to all its members. But it seldom occurs to him—certainly he is never reminded of it by his spokesmen in the Legislature, or by the writers for radical newspapers —that the objectionable and odious traits of the once privileged classes, of the aristocrat and the capitalist, may be easily accounted for by the same simple formula. If, given heredity and environment, you have an exhaustive statement of all the factors that evolve character and conduct in the case of the neediest workingman portrayed in "L'Assommoir," it can be no otherwise with the most opulent and insolent of nabobs, or with the most oppressive of autocrats. The naked fact that wealth is so seldom employed with the disinterested philanthropy of a Howard, or power with the wise beneficence of a Marcus Aurelius, might seem to carry with it the proof of specific and irresistible temptations incident to such exceptional conditions. But it may safely be affirmed that Victor Hugo is the first Republican leader who has ventured to press home this obvious truth to the French Proletariat, and to enforce upon them the expediency, the duty, the moral dignity and beauty of applying to the excesses and deficiencies of their political opponents the same principles of interpretation and apology to which they appeal on their own behalf.

Victor Hugo does not forget how often he has figured in less auspicious times as the passionate denouncer of those who sit in the high places, and as the prophet of a chastisement to come. In some fervid strophes he gives utterance to the inveterate rancor and hunger after revenge of those who have suffered too acutely from the abuses of power to scan them with the eye of a philosopher. "The bitter student of the world," he says, "finds himself beset by implacable facts, and crushed beneath the stupendous ugliness of history. Grief-smitten by the doleful spectacle of the wave of humanity incessantly shivered on the same reef—wrought to indignation and savage rigor by the eternal divorce of right and law, by the inexorable triumph of sword and axe—he forgets the circumspection and sobriety of the analyst, and sees positive turpitude where the patient Darwinian would discern nothing but ill-fortune. To such a one

the crown is a crime, the right divine of kings a hor-
rible miasma.　For four thousand years, the claim of
privilege and of authority has racked and strangled mankind.　In all those centuries humanity has sobbed and
ground its teeth, and now that breath is found to curse
with we must not ask it to pick its words.　In the night
of its infinite anguish we must not expect it to descry a
ray of extenuation, and, after all, every monarch, whatever history may style him, is but a fold of the vast
winding sheet in which the gropings and strivings of
man have been stifled and interred.　The best of them
wring groans, draw blood.　Trajan proscribes, Titus
assassinates ; they are all akin, wolves and lions.　While
the people, in its death agony, swings from the gibbet,
no strand of the rope can be deemed innocent.　While
the world lies in irons, each link has its share in the
crime of the chain.　Can there be indeed such a thing
as a good, an estimable king ?　'No,' said Epictetus
and Plato ; 'No,' said John at Patmos ; and Zeno said,
'Why, yes ; good kings as there are good axes.'　Even on
the whitest of the Bourbons, on Henry IV., the verdict
will run, 'He was not a bad man, no, but he was a
king.'　Yea, no kings are good or kind ; the statement
involves a flagrant contradiction in terms ; all are contained in each, each is implied in all.　Let them expiate,
then, in the detestation of the race the wrong-doing of
forty centuries.　All are branded on the forehead with
history's bloody hand—imprecations on them all !"　It
is just here, after thus setting forth the sombre indict-

ment, that Victor Hugo strikes the key-note of his poem. It is precisely this corporate atrocity, he tells us, this frightful iteration and universality in the abuse of power, which suggested a species of fatality, and shook his vengeful purpose by infusing a doubt of responsibility. "Yes," he goes on, "I find myself smitten with a strange inscrutable pity, groaning over the untoward fate of kings, doubting whether the austere judgment of posterity is right, whether history has arrested the real culprit, whether these men after all whom we dub kings were at bottom worse than others. Is it not the fatal air of Rome which engenders the Cæsars? Must not Memphis and Thebes continue to spawn Pharaohs so long as the veil of Isis is hung before man's reason? Is it not the tainted atmosphere of the throne which begets the Tudor in London, and Belus in Babylon? No human being is born a fiend, begotten half flesh, half marble. He who fashioned humanity did not plant the tiger, the snake, the rat, in the child whose dimpled fingers clutched sweetly its mother's gown. No; if the heart is frozen, 'tis because you yourself have quenched the fire; if the soul's wing is broken you yourself have bruised and crushed it within a cage; if this or that man is hideous, 'tis because his plastic nature has been flung into a mould of deformity and crime."

"After all, whose fault is it," he continues, "that a child is born upon a throne? What has he done, this poor innocent, that he must needs be transformed by the iron force of circumstances into the curse of his kind, into the chimera of history, environed by all spectres' shapes and appliances of horror ? Must he alone then, ye thinkers, be condemned for succumbing to his environment while you absolve the man-eating Maori, the Papuan, the Ashanti, and the Kaffir that washes his assegai in blood ? You can pity the gypsy, who knows no country, the landless moujik of Muscovy, the ryot of Coromandel ; you can find pleas for their shortcomings—the wolf, the dog, the ass, you say, obeys his instinct. You can even follow the gaol-bird to his cell, measure his skull, spell out his story, and sue for mercy to the homicide, the ravisher, and the thief. And can you not perceive that the despot is more fatally immeshed in the trammels of his surroundings than is the beggar ; that his purple robe and the ragged coat are all one in the night ; that in the dense shadow wherein man is plunged by his brutal instincts, where lies tempt him and truth eludes him, he who shares the pauper's ignorance ought to share likewise his excuse ? "

These are general considerations, whose effect, in the author's luminous and vigorous imagery, is, of course, very rudely outlined in a prose paraphrase ; but they are enforced by the portrayal in detail of the apposite example furnished by the career of Louis XV. The remembrance of the old monarchy still rankles in the French people, because its restoration is still the object of machinations. And as the one name that commends the white flag to France is that of Henry IV., so the name of Louis XV. is identified with all that is most loathsome and detestable and formidable in the *ancien régime.* Yet of the whole dynasty, this member owed the least part of his execrable offences to heredity, and most to his environment. Next to the first Bourbon sovereign, he was the most happily gifted of his line that lived to fill the throne. It may be doubted whether even his kinsman, the Regent Orleans, had quicker natural parts, or had received a more adequate training of the intellect. Compared to his great-grandfather, Louis XIV., he might be fairly accounted an accomplished and even a learned man. So far, too, as his parents were concerned, he could have inherited only the worthiest propensities. His father, the Duc de Bourgogne, even after we have made allowances for probable exaggeration in the report ·transmitted by obsequious biographers, must apparently be accounted one of the purest, kindliest, most intelligent, and high-minded beings that ever breathed the sultry atmosphere that enfolds a throne, and his mother was a chaste, gentle, and winsome woman. So strong, indeed, was the congenital impulse toward a correct and honorable manhood, that the domestic life of Louis XV., up to the age of twenty-seven, was a model of continence and rectitude. But a monarch who, as a child, had been held up in the arms of the old Marshal Villeroy in the face of a jubilant metropolis and told *" tout ce peuple est à vous, Sire,"* was not likely to forget the noxious lesson when superlative seductions assailed his self-control. That the absolute master of twenty millions of Frenchmen should have remained so long an irreproachable prince is, indeed, a signal tribute to the sterling fibre of his inherited qualities. That he succumbed in the end, and having once asserted his right to self-indulgence, deteriorated with a frightful rapidity, was, as Victor Hugo says, well nigh inevitable in the appalling conditions of his existence. Nor, remembering the caprices and excesses of his busy career, can we doubt that the most robust and self-contained of all the Bourbons, that Henry IV. himself, would have undergone the same moral eclipse had he come earlier to the throne without the wholesome discipline of prolonged danger and privation. As it was, the secret correspondence lately published by the Duc de Broglie shows how stubbornly native sagacity struggled to exert itself even on the part of the most debauched and infamous of French rulers. In the brief intervals which satiety imposed on self-indulgence, this unhappy Prince bethought himself of his majestic opportunities, and in a fitful, feverish fashion sought to vindicate his capacity for higher spheres of kingcraft than the mysterious diversions of the Parc aux Cerfs. It is in short from this man's tragical experience that Victor Hugo deduces his most pertinent and conclusive arguments for tolerance and condonation.

To comprehend and pity the moral gangrene which, engendered near the throne, gradually infected the whole nation—to excuse the file of titled concubines which, beginning with the daughters of Crusaders, sank with a Du Barry to a woman of the town—to forgive the Parc aux Cerfs, whose wretched inmates were denied even the poor solace of protracted and published infamy —to overlook the moral debasement, the military humiliation, the social disintegration, and the financial bankruptcy of France—in a word, to fathom, and therefore to pardon, Louis Quinze,—certainly for French republicans the demands of philosophy, the austere requirements of equity, could no further go. And that Victor Hugo has been able to adopt such an attitude toward the most detestable representative of the extinguished monarchy is, as we have said, an impressive voucher for the safety of the re-established commonwealth. To his mind, at all events, the time has come for partisan invective to give way to deliberate, dispassionate inquiry. Nor will any student of events fail to deem it a note of happy promise that we should hear the laureate of the republic, whose verse throughout the term of liberty's eclipse breathed only wrath and retribution, now grown more sober and more mild,

> Retreated in a silent valley sing
> With notes angelical.

THERE are signs that the American novel will get itself written after all. Against the ingenious theories which explain its essential impossibility we are now able to set an encouraging fact. Notwithstanding the hard practical spirit ascribed to our society, the investiture of genuine native types with artistic form of a high order has of late been twice attempted with creditable success. We refer to the treatment of our disparaged raw material exhibited in "The American," by Henry James, Jr., and in Julian Hawthorne's "Garth." These experiments lead us to suspect that what other writers lacked was not the inspiration of a romantic environment and the stimulus of a highly cultivated audience, so much as insight and an adequate command of the creative faculty.

It may be thought that the capabilities of American fiction had been already revealed by Mr. Bret Harte. But his earlier etchings, remarkable as they were, might with some show of reason be pronounced rather hints and promises than demonstrations. The short tale is to the comprehensive picture of human life what the ode is to the epic, or a carved cup to a temple frieze. It is not certain that the nimble hand which executes the one can compass the other. In the "Sketches by

Boz " we discern the workmanship, but not the power of large, organic achievement displayed in " Dombey and Son." Small assurance of " Vanity Fair " lay in a " Shabby Genteel Story." It would be folly to set arbitrary limits to the possible accomplishment of the author of "The Luck of Roaring Camp," yet it is not the less patent that he has not yet written a novel of extended scope. He began one in " Thankful Blossom," but just as the stage had begun to fill with characters potential, and the plot to acquire breadth and complexity, the author seemed to lose heart or will, his hand relaxed, and the nascent drama came abruptly to a close.

It was by short stories, likewise, that Henry James, Jr., at first commended himself to American readers. During some ten or twelve years he portrayed a large variety of scenes, outlined a good many types of character, and it was observed that his canvas, although narrow, evinced a ripening discernment and a growing technical efficiency. These small pictures attested several things which rank among the prime qualifications of the novelist. Taken together, they betokened a wide, patient, and incisive study of men and things which seems to have been furthered by a singular lucidity of judgment, by sympathies quick and delicate though by no means impassioned, and by an agreeable immunity from most kinds of prejudice. They discovered a clear perception of the right methods of composition, and, what is more to the purpose, an increasing power of evolving conceptions through the action and self-utterance of his characters. We wish we could have also recognized an equally successful effort to relegate description and analysis to functions thoroughly and constantly subordinate. As regards the instrument of the novelist's art, Mr. James seems to have applied himself with deliberate and vigilant pertinacity to the forging of an effective style, which, although it bore for some time the marks of hammering and tooling, is now flexible, elastic, bright. Indeed, his diction, if it wants the affluence of Lowell's and the delightful grace of Howell's, is not inferior to either in aptness and *finesse*. A characteristic token of his prose is its aroma of good company, and this leads us to note that no American writer has depicted with such adequacy and exactitude what is known as "society" proper, the social plane which, in an æsthetic sense, may be fairly enough called the highest, and which, at all events, is the most coveted. With the coarser, but seemingly stronger texture, and the rough, angular, yet more picturesque surface which belong to American life between the Sierras and the Alleghanies this writer has given no evidence of personal contact. But the proficient in the science of human nature, like the adept in biology, can undertake the work of reconstruction with very fragmentary materials, and it is safe to assume that Mr. James would make the most of such types and samples as strayed within his ken. Finally, we should say that certain qualities which the English masters have taught us to exact of the first-rate novelist were but faintly represented in his minor works, and we shall probably deem their absence the conspicuous short-coming in the present performance. But while in some respects—in humor, and the piercing, heart-shaking pathos which is seldom found divorced from humor—neither he nor any other contemporary American can be named beside Mr. Harte, yet as regards the average technical excellence of his work, and those merits most easily communicable by translation, he is perhaps superior to the latter.

In spite of its name, Mr. James's book appears on a cursory review not to be an American novel, for the scene is laid in Paris, and all the persons of the story, with the exception of two clean-cut but merely ancillary figures, are French. Some persons may incline to see in the book only a careful study of Gallic manners, and we are bound to say that, regarded solely from this point of view, it is a creditable *tour de force.* Not that it pretends to compass the range of incident and character presented in Bulwer's "Parisians," but it offers an exhaustive, realistic, and luminous revelation of the Faubourg St. Germain, whose counterpart does not exist in English, and which we might find it difficult to parallel in any living writer of French fiction. Not many of the *feuilletonistes* of the gay capital are supposed to have the *entrée* of the noble Faubourg, neither have they Balzac's power of evolving from his inner consciousness the ideas, habits, tastes, traditions of an impenetrable sphere. It is indeed a surprising anomaly which our countrymen are perhaps less likely to appreciate than are the readers of the *Revue des Deux Mondes* (to whom by the way Mr. James is not a stranger), to find portrayed in an American narrative that sequestered Legitimist world which every Frenchman in his heart esteems the finest and grandest, and of which his native novelists are pronounced ludicrously ignorant.

This book, however, is something more than a *tour de force*, something more than a vivid reproduction of the most artificial, polished, and fastidious of human societies. If there is anything in the law of contrasts—and is there not everything in it—what medium so apt as this, of such peculiar and consummate fitness, to project the central figure of the novel, to emphasize the frank defiance of formula and convention, the uncouth, resolute self-assertion, the rugged individuality of the typical American? We shall acknowledge, no doubt, that the hero of the story is in sooth the typical American, for although some persons may not account him the highest type, yet, if they will turn their eyes away from a few seaboard cities and take a candid view of the whole country, they will recognize in him the national representative type. Happily, too, for the dramatic intensity of this narrative he is precisely the person whom well-bred Europeans, not having confined their observation of our travelling fellow-citizens to the members of the New York clubs, persist in thinking the typical American, and whom in that capacity they cordially detest. The truth is that the author is so determined to sink his hero down to the normal and undiscriminated level of our population that he has positively made him an ex-Brigadier-General of volunteers.

To introduce this incongruous personage into the core of the exclusive Faubourg, to deal with him in such sort that he must needs provoke the ineffable disdain and the instinctive, unconquerable aversion of its conventional refinement, and yet elicit a sympathetic recognition from its deeper insight and a loyal esteem from its substantial worth; this, the author's pivotal conception, was bold and strong, but the embodiment was plainly beset with uncommon difficulties. It would be relatively easy to portray, as this writer has elsewhere done, a perfectly-bred American whose appearance in a Legitimist salon could by no possibility offend, although it might surprise; and on the other hand it is quite possible, as Mr. Bret Harte has demonstrated, to commend the coarsest outlaw of our frontier to the liking of his own countrymen. But by what continual, yet cautious, shifting of standards and measurements, by what subtle interchange of atmospheres, by what deft suggestions and shrewd silences shall a reader be made to comprehend how one and the same man could justify the love of a daughter of the crusaders, and the inveterate repugnance and instinctive loathing of her kindred? In a word, to formulate the dilemma from a European point of view, the problem was to make a hero of a cad.

That Mr. James should have found the solution, that he should have brought upon the stage a man of manifest charm and honor and an indubitable cad in the same person, and that neither of the two should have effaced the other, constitutes an achievement of no mean order. And the merit of the artist is enhanced for us when we consider that this juxtaposition of seemingly incongruous elements is contrived, not in a farce or comedy, but in a piece which is essentially a melodrama, over which from the outset of the action broods a fatal certainty of disappointment. Obviously, the more arduous part of such a task was to indicate and yet hold back in shadow the superficial traits which rendered the American stranger obnoxious to certain members of the house of Bellegarde. We cannot stay to mark the adroit touches by which the purpose is carried out. It is seldom effected by plain statement or by hints too trenchantly pictorial; but we are allowed to guess by arch innuendoes and glimpses between the lines that the hero has most of the tricks, perversities, and rawnesses of manner which would particularly chafe a highly refined community. We can perceive that his favorite posture is to sit with his nether limbs outstretched at full length, or with his feet propped against a railing and his chair tipped back on its hind legs. That he is in the habit of showering tips on the lackeys of a noble mansion, at which he has leave to call. That he is quite as ready to laugh *at* people as smile *with* them, and is not unlikely to break into a loud guffaw in presence of the most august personages, as, for instance, of that grandest dame of France, the Duchess D'Outreville; that he is hopelessly obtuse to those æsthetic delights and discriminations which grow out of familiarity with art; and, finally that his nerves, although unshaken by annoyance or danger, are by no means proof against complacency, which, to the unspeakable disgust of his entertainers on the occasion of a *fête* given in his honor oozes from him at every pore. In short, "Mr. Newman of San Francisco," is a man who, if he used tobacco in any form, would indisputably chew ; and for that reason his creator will not suffer him even to smoke. We may add that this Crœsus of the West seems to avow with brutal candor his conviction that wealth is an all-sufficient passport to society. On the other hand, inasmuch as he never names his grandparents to any of his fine acquaintances, the latter are perhaps justified in inferring that he never had any.

These are the impressions produced upon the Marquis de Bellegarde by the Western savage, and which the hypersensitive reader might be disposed to share if he had leisure to ponder hints and make deductions—a proceeding from which the author is careful to divert him. Surface crudities and asperities are not allowed for a moment to obscure the essential virility, sweetness, and nobility of "the American's" nature, lest we might fail to understand the quick appreciation, blossoming at last into profound and even passionate regard, which he wins from Madame de Cintré, who is certainly a most dainty and ethereal creation. We are constantly made to see that this imperfectly cultivated stranger is a good fellow and a strong man, because all the good people in the book are instinctively drawn toward him, whereas all the weak and vicious instinctively avoid him.   Neither is this unconventional person at all wanting in delicacy amid circumstances where experience has taught him that another's feelings may be wounded, or where the fervor of affection illumines his intellect and informs his tact.   We should like to quote the characteristic words in which this plain, honest man asks the daughter of an ancient house to marry him.   But we could not give them all, and they would be spoiled by mutilation, since Mr. Newman was not the sort of person to discourse in epigrams.   We prefer to cite as indicative of the hero's character and attitude toward the lady of his affections, and at the same time illustrative of the author's style, the following passage :

Madame de Cintré seemed to him so felicitous a product of nature and circumstance that his invention musing on future combinations was constantly catching its breath with the fear of stumbling into some brutal compression or mutilation of her beautiful personal harmony.   This is what I mean by Newman's tenderness : Madame de Cintré pleased him so exactly as she was that his desire to interpose between her and the troubles of life had the quality of a young mother's eagerness to protect the sleep of her first-born child.   Newman was simply charmed, and he handled his charm as if it were a music box which would stop if one shook it.   Certain of Madame de Cintré's personal qualities—the luminous sweetness of her eyes, the delicate mobility of her face, the deep liquidity of her voice—filled all his consciousness.   A rose-crowned Greek of old, gazing at a marble goddess with his whole bright intellect resting satisfied in the act, could not have been a more complete embodiment of the wisdom that loses itself in the enjoyment of quiet harmonies.

There seem to be one or two trivial slips and one somewhat more important defect in the management of this story. It is not, for instance, made sufficiently clear to most readers why the dowager Marchioness of Bellegarde should give a great ball by way of announcing her daughter's engagement to Mr. Newman, when the intention of discarding the latter and replacing him with her own kinsman, Lord Deepmere, had already taken root in the old schemer's mind. Another objection is of more moment. How is it possible that Newman, being the man he was, should undertake to coerce the relatives of Mme. de Cintré by a threat of publishing their odious crime ? Waiving altogether the moral quality of the act, how could a man possessing the mental perspicacity ascribed to this American, fail to see that, even granted the temporary success of his venture, Mme. de Cintré, who intuitively "feared her mother," must guess the source of his strange authority, and that the knowledge of the secret and of her lover's use of it would crush a proud and sensitive heart ? We do not say that any avenue of escape from disappointment lay open to Newman. We are disposed to think that, given the character of the dowager Marchioness, there was none. But of sundry futile expedients, one, at all events, might have been chosen which should not gravely belittle the character of the hero, besides going far to rehabilitate, by contrast, his personal enemies.

4*

Mr. James has at no time discovered a lively sense of humor, or, at all events, the power of interpreting humor to his readers. We are less disposed, however, to regret the absence of this quality in the present volume, because, as we have said, the action turns on more than one incident of a tragic or melodramatic nature. But we cannot so easily condone a certain constraint and frigidity discernible in passages which might be fraught with intense pathos. It is probably a consciousness of certain shortcomings in this direction which is chargeable with one of Mr. James's very few technical faults. He is sometimes led to mar a climax, going back to the picture and retouching it again and again, as if he suspected that another might have infused more fervor and poignancy. This is true, for instance, of two specially impressive scenes—the death bed of Valentin de Bellegarde and the final interview of Newman with Madame de Cintré. And, generally, it may be said that, in grave and moving crises, Mr. James drops too frequently into a tone of gentle cynicism, almost of persiflage, as if he felt the strain on his sensibilities excessive and intolerable. So much for qualifying suggestions. It is not the less true that this novel, "The American," is a meritorious work of art, and, if we compare it with the writer's earlier essays in fiction, an augury of still riper and more highly vitalized achievements.

It is creditable to American readers that Mr. James's story should have won hearty recognition. Yet we are constrained to add that another novel has been published during the present year which deserves an equal, and perhaps a larger measure of approval, although it seems to have received less. In the first place the narrative is longer, and obviously, provided other conditions are equally well satisfied, this circumstance of itself betokens a more remarkable performance. Before indicating, however, some of the merits which distinguish "Garth," it may be well to ask what is attested by the pecuniary success of novels. Of course, on the threshold of criticism lies the inquiry, does the book please ; for a novel is interesting or it is nothing. But interesting to whom ? It is known to booksellers that there has never been any great demand for the tales of Poe and the elder Hawthorne. Again, the works of Howells, of James, even of George Eliot, cannot pretend to vie in interest, if circulation be a criterion, with the precious piece of inanity current in the United States during one brief summer under the name of "That Husband of Mine." The essential quality of charm, no less than the ancillary proprieties belonging to a work of art—whether novel, picture or statue—can only be authoritatively affirmed by people of taste, and the question for the mass of men must needs be, not whether they like a book, but whether they ought to like it. But it must be owned that while they are fain to query, what is beauty, they will not always stay for an answer. Fielding and Balzac find few readers in this country, and it is probable that the authors of "The American" and "Garth" must content themselves with an esoteric audience. We can see, nevertheless, that the former story would appeal to a somewhat larger class, since there is a more widespread curiosity touching the doings of a fellow countryman in Paris than about his experiences at home. It is a fact, too, which we are not called upon to stigmatize or justify, that a majority even of those cultivated Americans who are qualified to enjoy imaginative works of a high order, are vastly more interested in a portrayal of the Faubourg St. Germain than of a New England village. They think they know all about the latter, but this is a great mistake. While it is plain, therefore, that Mr. James has hit upon a luckier theme, we are by no means to infer too hastily that he has made the better novel.

After all, however, it is inexplicable to us that the mass of homely folk who follow with hungry eye the dramas of life unfolded in the daily press, should not scan such a book as "Garth" with eager interest, just as we have heretofore been confounded by a bookseller's assurance that the "Gold Bug" and the "Murder in the Rue Morgue" are in no considerable request. For this story of "Garth" has what so many famous novels have wanted, a strong, inscrutable, yet compact and organic plot. The plot is intricate, but the intricacy is that of a watch, where every spring and wheel, each tiny cog and wire, has its nice functions, so that when the appointed sum of revolutions is complete the hour strikes and the tale is told. Regarded merely as a piece of mechanism, the plan of Mr. Hawthorne's narrative is scarcely less worthy of dissection than the skeleton of "Tom Jones." And when we reflect how many readers a dexterous construction of plot, almost his only merit, has rallied to Wilkie Collins, we marvel that all seekers of sensation have not been tempted to track the windings of the strange history set forth in the pages of "Garth."

The truth probably is that many persons have glanced over the first chapter of this story, and, finding it filled with a description of an old New Hampshire homestead, have put down the book convinced that nothing lay before them but a tame, homely record of rural existence, where the labors of the plough and the scythe are supposed to be enlivened by such mild diversions as sleigh rides, corn huskings, and maple bees. And yet, if they look a little narrowly at this rough-hewn Yankee dwelling, they would feel that the antique mansion to which Balzac gave so many pages of his *Recherche de l'Absolu* was not more steeped in mystery. So, too, for a careful eye the conditions of life amid the New England hills, where the same family may have tilled the same farm for two hundred years—the immobility, monotony, sobriety—seem not unapt to foster those robust, massive, gnarled, and angular natures which, once caught in the gripe and flame of passion, become the fittest tools of tragedy. Poor in incident and rich in individualities, such sequestered phases of existence are peculiarly adapted to the study of those grave problems which deal with the scope and potency of inherited tendencies. You notice that it is not in new but in old countries that the simpler sort of folk talk of curses and blessings as overshadowing and moulding a particular race. Thus, in a remote tranquil scene like that which Mr. Hawthorne has chosen for his novel, it may well be that the pressure of hereditary taint, uncontrolled by any change in the environment, would gather momentum till it seemed inexorable.

It is a problem in the difficult equation of heredity and environment to which Mr. Hawthorne has addressed himself in the present work. He has discovered that a family is a man of larger growth and more complex character, yet of individuality not less distinct.   " It is young ; it grows up prosperous and dies ; its years are generations, each one inevitably moulding the next.   At last comes a year when all its evil is arrayed against all its good." As regards the particular family whose record is here taken up at the crisis of its history, the author makes one of its members say that "the Urmsons have generally been worsted by their old Adam ; yet no one of them was ever utterly wicked ; " and it is inferred that the decisive battle has not yet come off, and that there is still a chance to vindicate the inborn angel. But " he, in whom the struggle culminates, must be thoroughly Urmson—a compendium of the race—no diluted alien, for the more stubborn the devil in him the better worth the victory."

While, however, there runs through the core of this book a *motif* large and serious—for is not the *vis major* of inherited impulse the scientific equivalent of destiny?

—the most frivolous person need not fear that the author has indited a philosophical treatise or evinces the slightest pretension to teach anybody anything. His business is to please, and if we learn something from him it is because no transcript of human life prepared, not with the camera's mechanical fidelity, but with the artist's finer insight, can want significance. It is certain that while this writer has infused into certain scenes the weird uncanny charm of which the elder Hawthorne was an unrivalled master—while, indeed, the atmosphere of " Garth " is " of imagination all compact "—not the less do the action and spectacle of the foreground—all its persons, incidents, dialogue—belong to the daylight world. Take, for instance, this portrait of Garth Urmson ; nothing could be more positive and substantial :

A broad built young fellow, about twenty-six years of age, but looking older, stands on the cloven threshold of Urmhurst, with his feet apart and his face bent downward, as though in revery. His eyes, however, are rather outlooking than introspective. * * Like most Urmsons, Garth is shorter than the average of men, but to make up for it he is chested like a bison, and vigorous and compact all over. His dress this morning differs little from that ordinarily worn by the New Hampshire farmer. His dark, shaggy hair pokes itself through the torn crown of a battered straw hat which he has clapped on the capacious back of his head. In his left hand is a tuft of maple leaves, the splendid scarlet of which causes his red flannel shirt to appear dingy by contrast. A rough sack coat (the pockets bulging with crimson and yellow apples) and corduroy trousers, tucked into cowhide boots, complete his costume.

Let not the æsthetic person be discouraged by this outward integument—Garth Urmson is in reality an artist, a painter; the more narrowly you observed him the greater would have been your doubt whether the agricultural element was really vital in him at all. His hands were certainly not those of a farmer; their form was at once powerful and elegant, and the texture of the skin was fine and soft. And where did he acquire that firm carriage of the shoulders and that easy precision of tread? Not, surely, from the plough and the scythe. And though his features seemed at the first glance rugged and almost harsh, they were in fact moulded with singular force and meaning, every part responding sensitively to his thought. "There was a flavor of distinction about him such as is only given by travel, thought, and conversation with the world. Admitting this, his quiet assumption or resumption of rusticity argued a freshness and independence of nature unusual in travelled youth nowadays."

But what is his present destination; for a man, especially a young gentleman of culture, does not plunge into pathless forests before breakfast for nothing? By way of answer to this question, and because we should like to offer the reader the kernel of the plot, as well as to illustrate a little more adequately the author's diction, we give one more citation:

Let us suppose, then, that while Garth was travelling in Europe he met a noble and lovely lady, who, like himself, was a stranger there. In the rich heart of the Old World they met, and neither knew the other, nor was it granted them ever to speak together, or to exchange a pressure of the hand ; but once, in a strange room, full of antique jewels and precious works of art, their glances had met in a crystal mirror, and had read in one another a mutual revelation. For one deep moment they gazed and knew they loved ; then time and space rolled between and parted them. But for years thereafter, as they moved along their separate paths, visions would rise before them of that unforgotten moment, until at length, by much dreaming over it, the event itself began to take on the semblance of a dream ; and Garth, returning home, pledged himself to another woman, and the lady promised, against her better instincts, to become the wife of another man. Shall our romance end here, or shall that picturesque providence which watches over her lovers only bring them once more together ere the last irrevocable steps that fix their destinies be taken ? Yes, let them meet, since all is imagination.

As we have said, the canvas covered by "Garth" is much broader and more amply peopled than that which Mr. James has chosen to fill in "The American." Yet the many and diverse figures here brought upon the stage all alike bear the impress of the creative faculty. They are men and women, each of them self-prompted and self-consistent, so that, given a particular situation, the clever reader should foretell unerringly what he or she will say or do. But such is the author's fertility of invention that the cleverest reader will seldom foresee the situation. We must add that one decisive distinction will hardly escape those who compare the two novels of which we have been speaking. However bright and fastidious may be the social world into which Mr. James inducts us, it is certain that we move throughout the narrative on a low intellectual plane. His most satisfactory persons, Madame de Cintré and her younger brother, winning as they are, seem of slight texture, narrow of brain, and weak of soul, while as for the titular character, we may esteem but cannot fervently admire him; his mental horizon is too contracted; he is too small a man. On the other hand, in Mr. Hawthorne's history, while we are not spared that admixture of baseness and infirmity which belongs to the mingled skein of life, yet in converse with at least three persons we are lifted above the common highway of existence to a level of thought and purpose on which it is good to dwell. Not that these characters are too flawless for human nature's daily food, for they are "spirits, too." And therefore it is that those persons who concede, not without regret, the truth of the picture which Mr. James has drawn, may find no small solace in the fact that Garth Urmson, being the descendant of a family planted in New England for two centuries, has also some claim to be considered a typical American.

I.

By his "Atalanta in Calydon," Mr. Swinburne secured a place of honor rarely accorded to the first essay of any poet. It was the peculiar good fortune of that poem to please scholars who were not artists, artists who were no scholars, and the general public, which is swayed mainly by the melody and emotional fervor of verse. It might have been better for his subsequent reputation had his first success been less signal. We are forced to attribute the publication of a later volume—the "Laus Veneris"—to a species of intoxication which conceived itself exempted from the operation of canons of cleanliness and decorum. Afterward, however, he produced "Erechtheus, a Tragedy," which was in no wise open to censure on the score of morality ; and for that and other reasons it went far to reinstate him in the position which on many grounds he may fairly claim, and which nothing but overweening self-confidence or supreme cynicism could have imperilled.

Since Swinburne has twice attempted to create a veritable Greek tragedy in the uncongenial medium of a modern and Northern tongue, we are prompted to consider the scope and purport of such a performance. Whether it falls within a right conception of poetic art, or is essentially a *tour de force,* and how far it has been paralleled in our literature, are questions that may deserve attention after a glance at the poet's general qualifications.

Few readers probably would concur in the indiscriminate eulogy bestowed on Swinburne by the little London coterie of which William Morris and the Rossettis were conspicuous members. His experiments have been too numerous and too divergent to admit of uniform success. His narrative poetry, for instance, while illumined with bits of vigorous painting, and enlivened here and there with bursts of exquisite melody, on the whole wants the swiftness, cohesion, and graduated evolution which distinguish "Jason," and the tales rehearsed in the "Earthly Paradise." Again, if we look at the etchings of character contained in the volume entitled "Laus Veneris," we find no lack of dramatic insight, or historical intuition—indeed a curiously accurate comprehension of certain morbid and anomalous types. But he fails to project his figures in crisp outlines, his hand missing the sure, clean touch which makes of Browning's *dramatis personæ* a gallery of sculpture. It is true that the poet's conception of Marie Stuart, which is wrought out at great length in "Chastelard" and "Bothwell," is distinct and telling. She is portrayed as one of those giddy, utterly godless and soulless women, combining rare accomplishments and vicious instincts, who were numerous enough at the Court of Catherine de Medicis, and are drawn scarcely less incisively in a few rough sentences of Brantôme than in Swinburne's elaborate portrait. But while, aside from the two Greek tragedies which ought to be ranked in a distinct category, and studied apart from the author's other writings, we cannot but recognize some material shortcomings in his power of characterization and consecutive development of theme, we are bound to say that his faculty of lyrical utterance seems unapproached by any living English poet. We might go further, for although there is no dearth of unconscious and fitful melody among English. singers, especially prior to Anne's miscalled Augustan age, Swinburne was perhaps the first to exhibit a conscious and decisive mastery of the English lyre, and to reveal capacities of music in our language before unsuspected or denied.

We are so unaccustomed to define the precise relations of poetry to music that the transfer of terms, in current criticism, from one art to the other is often ludicrously inapt. The smoothness and grace, for instance, which studious chiselling and metrical finesse impart to much of Tennyson's work is sometimes confounded with melody ; whereas the word might as appropriately be applied to the Odes of Horace, to which some of Tennyson's minor poems present perhaps the nearest English analogues. But the *Ars Poetica,* far from associating poetry with music, substantially identifies it with another art, since Horace obviously conceives the poet as a painter, manipulating words for pigments. Boileau, too, in his paraphrase of Horace's treatise, expands the same idea, and his theory of the poetic function and method has uniformly controlled the practice of his countrymen. What is more noteworthy, Lessing, in his "Laocoön," while scrupulously marking the boundary line between the province and the processes of poetry and those of painting and sculpture, appears to ignore its relations to music. So rigorously was the pictorial conception of the poet's art accepted in England throughout the eighteenth century, until Shelley and Byron resuscitated lyric verse, that it may be questioned whether works like Johnson's "London," or even Pope's "Epistles," could, in a Greek sense, be called poetry at all. Of lyrics, at all events, the Greek notion was very different. Tyrtæus, Pindar and the tragic poets in their choruses, were never conceived as carvers of form or manipulators of color, mediately evoking sentiment through the taste and the intellect, but as veritable singers or musicians, working directly on the emotions through the musical sense. For example, the famous prelusory burst in the "Agamemnon" has nothing specially pregnant or vivid about it, regarded as pictorial expression, but read aloud, even with our bastard and tentative pronunciation, it has almost the effect of a symphony. How, indeed, would it be possible to explain the traditional triumphs of Athenian lyric verse among the less cultivated Greeks of Dorian stock, the power of Tyrtæus's songs over the Spartans, or of the choruses of Euripides in the mouth of captives at Syracuse, except upon the theory that such poetry must have hit the senses like a trumpet blast or the tones of a flute?

Since, then, the fact could not be gainsaid that lyric verse, in one language at least, had been partially identified with music, to a certain extent sharing its aim and working through its processes, the obvious inference has been met by a plea in avoidance. Stress is laid on the supposed discrepancy between the Greek and English speech in respect of vowel and liquid sounds, and as regards the capacity of assonance in general. But the truth is that assonance has been nowhere more sedulously cultivated than in the rude poetry of those early English, whom Mr. Freeman will not permit us to call Anglo-Saxons ; and Swinburne has proved that it may be reinstated in modern English with effective and often delightful results.

Byron undoubtedly did something, and Shelley much more, toward restoring melody to English poetry ; the one, it would seem, unconsciously, obedient to an instinct of his ear, the latter deliberately approximating at times in aim and method to the Greek conception of lyric verse. To Swinburne, however, belongs the credit of continually and overtly recognizing that lyric poetry is meant for the voice and not the eye, that it is a creature of the spoken, not the written tongue ; whereas the diction of Dryden and Pope, like the classical Latin, was a dead literary language, scanned and conned in the closet, never alive upon the lips of men. It is, of course, unreasonable to condemn Englishmen of the last century for adopting a notion of poetic methods which to this day prevails in France, but after reading aloud some burst of

song from the " Atalanta," for example, " The hounds
of spring are on winter's traces," it is hard to control a
feeling of astonishment and disgust, akin to that provoked by a Chinese tom-tom, when we turn to our so-
called heroic couplet with its sorry click of pendulous
rhyme—mere epigrammatic prose in a metrical strait
jacket.

There is scope, unquestionably, for large variety in
rhyme. There are rhymes consecutive, alternate, periodic, intercalated; rhymes male, female and polysyllabic;
but while Swinburne seems to have mastered the whole
register, he has shown rhyme to be but one species of
assonance. He has aimed to supplement it with that
other species—consonance, we might call it—which consists in the identity of vowel sounds without regard to
the terminal consonant, and which is thought to
lend to Spanish poetry a robust and virile harmony.
There is still another sort employed by Swinburne, borrowed perhaps from the Anglo-Saxon (for Cædmon's
poem is full of it), where vowel sounds, not identical
but accordant, are so placed as to simulate the effect of
a chord in music. Add to this a right use of allitera-
tion, which is only undervalued by those who fail to
recognize its limits. The iteration of initial gutturals
is, of course, intolerable, and we rarely meet with it in
Swinburne's work, but the recurrence of liquids and
semi-liquids is a vital element in the melody of verse.

While we dwell on the fact, and credit Swinburne
with discerning it, that harmony must be kept steadily

in view as the essential vehicle of poetry, we cannot forget that the freightage must be worthy of the vehicle. Indeed, Wagner accounts all music worthless unless through sense it penetrates the soul, kindling high thought and generous emotion. On the whole, Wagner's conception of an opera accords more nearly with the idea of Greek tragedy as it existed in the mind of Æschylus, and as it was actually embodied at the Dionysia, than does our modern notion of a play. It is obvious that a large measure of lyric power and a right conception of its aim and processes are indispensable to the creation of dramas like the "Erechtheus." That so far Swinburne is better qualified than any living English poet to reproduce a lost drama of Euripides, will probably appear from the extracts we shall have occasion to make.

The argument of Erechtheus had been treated by Euripides in a tragedy no longer extant. The drama before us is presented by Swinburne, not avowedly but impliedly, as a substitute for the original play. It is only gradually, as we turn the pages of the volume, that we appreciate the audacity of his purpose. Can an English poet of our day seriously hope to transport the reader across the gulf of twenty centuries, behind the curtain of mediæval transformation and modern growth, beyond the Christian religion, Roman civilization, and all the pregnant events which have moulded the lives and minds of men, to a world whose horizon and atmosphere, creed, sympathies, ideals and aspirations were almost totally alien to the ideas and associations of the present day ? How will it be possible to avoid glaring anachronisms (Milton could not, as we shall see), or at all events those subtler but equally fatal incongruities of thought and sentiment inseparable from the poet's nurture and environment ? Suppose, however, the preliminary step gained, that the reader is able to approximate the mood of an Athenian at the high festival of the Dionysia, that he is seated in the great theatre from whose upper tier the eye sweeps across the Long Walls and Piræus to the blue Ægean and Salamis—yet to what a colossal task has the writer addressed himself ! For of what stuff is the play we are to hear ? Will it win the first prize, or the third ? Will it show touches of the masters' handi-work—a glimpse of the severe majesty of Sophocles, a poignant stroke from "Euripides, the human ;" or will it prove the botchery of some Ion or Iophon, surviving by a foolish chance the wreck of its co-progeny ? Clearly it is no light thing to borrow a theme from Euripides, and attempt to build upon it a Greek tragedy which must infallibly invite comparison with his. In such an undertaking absolute triumph is not possible, and whether Swinburne has relatively achieved success can be best determined after a glance at previous experiments in the same direction.

Without including transcripts of Greek plays like those which Browning has lately given us—although in his case vivid translation is supplemented by most incisive and helpful commentary—there would seem to be two ways of writing antique drama, or indeed of reproducing antique life in any literary form, the mosaic and the assimilative. Ben Jonson is an English example of the former method. His "Sejanus" and "Catiline" are so vigilantly pruned of anachronisms, and follow so studiously the text of Latin authorities, that Dryden said : "He so represents old Rome to us, that if one of her own poets had written the tragedies, we had seen less of her than in him." But as might be expected, where the mind is intent upon such microscopic work, the characterization is feeble, the plays want movement and cohesion, and possess about as much vitality as Becker's "Gallus." Racine, on the other hand, although he, too, in the "Britannicus" rather piques himself on a close adhesion to Tacitus, was careful to inform his plays with the modern spirit, making them hinge for the most part on the passion of love, which seldom formed the pivot of antique drama or played a conspicuous part in Greek existence.

Of the assimilative process, from which alone a presentation of antiquity, at once accurate and lively, could be looked for, we have an instance in Landor. It is the distinctive merit of his "Pericles and Aspasia" that while it contains scarcely a sentence which can be proved to have been uttered by an Athenian, there is hardly one which might not have been. Swinburne's method is identical with Landor's, and in many respects the younger poet reminds us of that impracticable man who was himself a living anachronism. The most

famous attempt, however, to rear the antique tragedy on
English soil—and that mainly by a process of assimilation, although direct translation is interjected here and
there—is the "Samson Agonistes." It may be interesting to note some of Milton's happy strokes and
shortcomings as we follow in detail the course of Swinburne's play.

The story of the Erechtheus is one of the simplest and
grandest of Greek myths. Athens, assailed by Eumolpus, son of Neptune and King of Eleusis, is menaced
with annihilation. Her King, Erechtheus, has been ap-
prised by the Delphic oracle that his country can only
be redeemed by the sacrifice of his virgin daughter. The
maiden consents, dies, and in the battle which follows
both Erechtheus and Eumolpus are slain and Athens is
saved. In a majestic type the myth incarnates the passion of patriotism, the strongest known to the Greek
breast while Greece was strong, and one, happily for the
modern poet who has based his play on it, which we are
able to comprehend. Greek patriotism, however, was
twofold. The love of race, of the whole Hellenic land
as opposed to the barbarian world, and especially to that
Asiatic empire which loomed above the eastern horizon,
was at certain periods fervent and fruitful, and to this
Euripides appealed in his "Iphigenia in Aulis." It is
the narrower but far profounder passion which Swinburne's play is supposed to address—the love of a Greek
for his own city—above all that of an Athenian for
Athens, of whose soil he believed himself autochthonous,

with whose glory and prosperity his personal happiness
and pride were indissolubly blended. Such a theme is
manifestly safer than that of his earlier drama, since it
was hardly possible to depict effectively the love of
Meleager for Atalanta without an infusion of modern
sentiment. It will be found that the tinge of romanticism which overlaid the classic structure of the former
piece is scarcely discernible in the present work.

Erechtheus *prologizes.* He is discovered alone, invoking
Earth, of whom tradition declared him son. In curt,
strong iambics, he discloses the imminent peril of the
State, and hints shudderingly at the remedy prescribed
by the Pythian message, and which has yet to be imparted to wife and child. Presently, however, he strikes
the key note of the piece, and rises above the gloom and
agony of the hour in a burst of unselfish resolution, which
voices ringingly the brave, proud spirit of Athenian
patriotism :

> Mother of life and death and all men's days,
> Earth, whom I chief of all men born would bless
> And call thee with more loving lips than theirs
> Mother,   •
> *   *   *   *   *   *   *
>   Lo, I stand
> Here on this brow's crown of the city's head
> That crowns its lovely body till death's hour
> Waste it,
> *   *   *   *   *   *   *
>   but now
> Would this day's ebb of their spent wave of strife
> Sweep it to sea, wash it on wreck, and leave

A costless thing contemned ; and in our stead
Where these walls were, and sounding streets of men
Make wide a waste for tongueless water-herds
And spoil of ravening fishes ; that no more
Should men say, Here was Athens.   This shalt thou
Sustain not, nor thy son endure to see,
Nor thou to live and look on ; for the womb
Bare me not base, that bare me miserable ;
To hear this loud brood of the Thracian foam
Break its broad strength of billowy-beating war
Here, and upon it as a blast of death
Blowing, the keen wrath of a pure-souled king
*   *   *   *   *   *   *
Eumolpus.   Nothing sweet in ears of thine
The music of his making, nor a song
Toward hopes of ours auspicious, for the note
Rings as for death oracular to thy sons,
Full of this charge laid on me, to put out
The brief light kindled of mine own child's life,
Or with this helmsman's hand that steers the State
Run right on the under shoal and ridge of death
The populous ship with all its fraughtage gone,
And sails that were to take the wind of time
Rent, and the tackling that should hold out fast
In confluent surge of loud calamities,
Broken, with spars of rudders and lost oars
That were to row toward harbor and find rest
In some most glorious haven of all the world,
And else may never near it.

While the king is speaking, the chorus of old men too
weak for war, " gray borderers on the march of death,"
has wound slowly across the stage, and now opens with

a doleful prelude contrasting the happy auguries which
had marked the city's birth with the impending cloud of
ruin, then drifting back to past calamities which had
stricken the royal house, and closing with a prayer. We
cite several strophes which illustrate the specific merits
of Swinburne's lyric style :

> A noise is arisen against us of waters,
> A sound as of battle come up from the sea;
> Strange hunters are hard on us, hearts without pity,
> They have staked their nets round the fair young city,
> That the sons of her strength and her virgin daughters
> Should find not whither alive to flee.
>
> *   *   *   *   *   *   *   *
>
> Let a third wave smite us not, father,
>   Long since sore smitten of twain,
>   Lest the house of thy son's son perish
>   And his name be barren on earth.
>
> Whose race wilt thou comfort rather
>   If none to thy son remain ?
>   Whose seed wilt thou choose to cherish
>   If his be cut off in the birth ?
>
> *   *   *   *   *   *
>
> But enough now of griefs gray-growing
>   Have darkened the house divine,
>   Have flowered on its boughs and faded,
>   And green is the brave stock yet.
>
> O father, all-seeing and all-knowing,
>   Let the last fruit fall not of thine
>   From the tree with whose boughs we are shaded
>   From the stock that thy son's hand set.

If now we glance at the "Agonistes," we shall find

Miltonic vigor in the opening iambics; but the utter indifference to melody and even rhythmic effect in the chorus of what purports to be a Greek play must appear unpardonable, and the more remarkable because the third book of his great epic abounds in choral passages, which, in his own phrase, " voluntary move harmonious numbers." The argument of his drama is of course familiar. Samson, captive, blind, and now in the prison of Gaza, on a festival day, in the general cessation of labor, comes forth into the open air, and while he bemoans his condition is visited by certain friends of his tribe, who form the chorus. In their prelude, by the way, occur such incongruities as " *Chalybean* tempered steel," and a reference to the fable of Atlas, paralleled later by allusions to Circe, Tantalus, the Phœnix, and other Hellenic mythical persons or legends, which have a strange sound in the mouths of primitive Hebrews. We quote a few lines from Samson's prologue, and from the prefatory chant which follows :

> A little onward lend thy guiding hand
> To these dark steps a little further on ;
> For yonder bank hath choice of sun or shade;
>   *   *   *   *   *   I seek
> This unfrequented place to find some ease,
> Ease to the body some, none to the mind
> From restless thoughts that like a deadly swarm
> Of hornets armed, no sooner found alone,
> But rush upon me thronging, and present
> Times past, what once I was, and what am now.
> Oh, wherefore was my birth from heaven foretold

Twice by an angel ?   *   *   Promise was that I
Should Israel from Philistian yoke deliver ;
Ask for this great deliverer now, and find him
Eyeless in Gaza, at the mill with slaves.
Himself in bonds under Philistian yoke.

Chorus.

This, this is he; softly a while,
Let us not break in upon him;
Oh, change beyond report, thought, or belief;
See how he lies at random, carelessly diffused,
With languished head unpropped
As one past hope, abandoned,
And by himself given over
In slavish habit, ill-fitted weeds
O'erworn and soiled.

Returning to Swinburne's tragedy, we find that during the chanting of the chorus, Praxithea, the wife of Erechtheus, has come upon the stage. In the dialogue which ensues, her husband's reluctance to communicate the oracle, engenders a species of mystification, where the rapid interchange of sententious single lines may remind the reader of Euripides :

Prax. What portent from the mid-oracular place
      Hath smitten thee so like a curse that flies,
      Wingless, to waste men with its plagues? Yet speak.
Erech. Thy blood the gods require not; take this first.
Prax. To me than thee more grievous this should sound.
Erech. That word rang truer and bitterer than it knew.
Prax. This is not, then, thy grief to see me die?
Erech. Die! shalt thou not yet give thy blood to death?
Prax. If this ring worse I know not; strange it rang.
    5*

At length Erechtheus reveals the truth, and because he cannot bear the sight of his wife's first anguish, leaves her alone, to be joined, however, presently by Chthonia, the destined offering. Meanwhile the chorus bemoans the destiny of both :

He hath uttered too surely his wrath, not obscurely nor wrapt as
    in mists of his breath:
The master that lightens not hearts he enlightens, but gives them
    foreknowledge of death.
As a bolt from the cloud hath he sent it aloud and proclaimed it
    afar,
From the darkness and height of the horror of night hath he shown
    us a star;
Star may I name it and err not, or flame shall I say,
Born of the womb that was born for the tomb of the day?

O, Night, whom other but thee for mother, and Death for the
    father—Night,
Shall we dream to discover, save thee and thy lover, to bring such
    a sorrow to sight?
From the slumberless bed for thy bedfellow spread and his bride
    under earth
Hast thou brought forth a wild and insatiable child, an unbearable
    birth.
Fierce are the fangs of his wrath, and the pangs that they give;
None is there, none that may bear them, not one that would live.

There is nothing in the play more moving than the scene that now begins. The mother's mouth cannot shape the words that are to acquaint her child with death, and she implores counsel of the chorus, "all honorable and kindly men of age," but they are dumb.

At last waveringly, but gaining heart, as she depicts
the public danger, and the splendid guerdon of the
appointed sacrifice, Praxithea speaks :

    *   *   *   *   *   *   *

Now this third time the wind of wrath has blown
Right on this people a mightier wave of war
Three times more huge a ruin;   *   *.
*   *   *   *   Yet not here,
Here never shall the Thracian plant on high
For ours his father's symbol.   *   *   *
And if this be not I must give my child,
Thee, my own very blood and spirit of mine,
Thee to be slain.   Turn from me, turn thine eyes
A little from me ; I can bear not yet
To see if still they smile on mine or no,
If fear make faint the light in them, or faith
Fix them as stars of safety.   Need have we,
Sore need of stars that set not in mid storm,
Lights that outlast the lightnings ; yet my heart
Endures not to make proof of thine or these,
Nor yet to know thee whom I made and bare
What manner of woman ; had I borne thee man
I had made no question of thine eyes or heart
Nor spared to read the scriptures in them writ,
Wert thou my son ; yet couldst thou then but die
Fallen in sheer fight by chance and charge of spears
And have no more of memory, fill no tomb
More famous than thy fellows in fair field   .
Where many share the grave, many the praise ;
But one crown shall one only girl, my child,
Wear, dead for this dear city.

We pass over several subsequent scenes, which are

occupied partly by the chorus in melancholy retrospection and foreboding, and partly by a dialogue of the choral spokesman, and afterward of Erechtheus with the herald of Eumolpus, the purport of which is to announce the final and impending battle. Presently the stage is again untenanted, save by the chorus (which of course never leaves it), and Praxithea enters with her daughter robed for sacrifice. Their farewell, the species of responsive invocation between the chorus and Chthonia, which reverberates like a solemn litany, and the virgin's death song, appear to us to be fraught with so much beauty, that we are impelled to quote again. We shall mark, at all events, in this Athenian maid, none of that faltering and whimpering which are thought to belittle the "Iphigenia" of Euripides.

Chthonia.

That I may give this poor girl's blood of mine
Scarce yet sun-warmed with summer, this thin life,
Still green with flowerless growth of seedling days,
To build again my city; that no drop
Fallen of these innocent veins on the cold ground
But shall help knit the joints of her firm walls,
To knead the stones together and make sure
The band about her maiden girdlestead,
Once fastened and of all men's violent hands
Inviolable for ever, these to me
Were no such gifts as crave no thanksgiving.
*   *   *   *   *   But my heart
That leaps up lightened of all sloth or fear
To take the sword's point, yet with one thought's load

Flags and falls back broken of wing that halts
Maimed in mid flight for thy sake and borne down,
Mother, that in the places where I played
An arm's length from thy bosom and no more
Shalt find me never, nor thine eye wax glad
To mix with mine its eyesight, and for love
Laugh without word, filled with sweet light and speak
Divine dumb things of the inward spirit and heart
Moved silently ; *   *   *   *   Yet set this thought
Against all edge of evil as a sword
To beat back sorrow, that for all the world
Thou broughtst me forth a saviour who shall save
Athens; for none but I from none but thee
Shall take this death for garland; and the men
Mine unknown children of unsounded years,
My sons unrisen shall rise up at thine hand
Sown of thy seed to bring forth seed to thee
And call thee most of all most fruitful found
Blessed ;   *   *   *   *   *

Praxithea.

Farewell, I bid thee; so bid thou not me
Lest the gods hear and mock us ;   *   *
     *   *   *   *   Thee, O child,
I help not, nor am holpen; fain, ah fain,
More than was ever mother born of man,
Were I to help thee; fain beyond all prayer,
Beyond all thought fain to redeem thee, torn
More timeless from me sorrowing than the dream
That was thy sister ;   *   *   now but once
I touch, but once more hold thee, one more kiss
This last time, and none other evermore
Leave on thy lips and leave them.
*   *   *   *   This breast once thine

Shall rear again no children ; never now
Shall any mortal blossom born like thee
Lie there, nor ever with small silent mouth
Draw the sweet springs dry for an hour that feed
The blind, blithe life that knows not; never head
Rest here to make these cold veins warm, nor eye.
Laugh itself open with the lips that reach
Lovingly toward a fount more loving :		*	*
 *	 *	 *	 *	 *	 *

Then follows a heart-shaking interchange of invocations between the gray-headed men of the chorus, and the girl who gives her life for them and their fair city.

Chthonia.

O city, O glory of Athens, O crown of my father's land, farewell.

Chorus.

For welfare is given her of thee.

Chthonia.

O Goddess, be good to thy people, that in them dominion and freedom may dwell.

Chorus.

Turn from us the strengths of the sea.

 *	 *	 *	 *	 *	 *	 *

Chthonia.

O crown on the world's head lying
 Too high for its waters to drown,
Take yet this one word of me dying,
 O city, O crown ;
Though land-wind and sea-wind with mouths that blow slaughter
 Should gird them to battle against thee again,
New-born of the blood of a maiden thy daughter,
 The rage of their breath shall be vain.

> For their strength shall be quenched and made idle,
> And the foam of their mouths find a bridle,
> And the height of their heads bow down
> At the foot of the towers of the town.
> Be blest and beloved as I love thee
>   Of all that shall draw from thee breath;
> Be thy life as the sun's is above thee:
>   I go to my death.

We cannot follow the progress of the play—we will not stay to recall the affecting picture of the maiden's sacrifice, the túmultuous storm song of the chorus which surges between hope and doubt while the distant battle is waging, or the ultimate triumph announced by a herald, and his account of Erechtheus's death, which ranks among the most forceful descriptions within our knowledge. We have space only for the closing words of Athena, which aim to comfort the desolate queen, and for the concluding choral song. In order that the reader may appreciate the worth of Swinburne's work in the difficult field of antique drama, we will once more place him side by side with Milton.

The finale of the " Agonistes " is commonly accounted the strongest portion of the work. Samson is dead, and with him half the nobles of Philistia. The edifice where all were met to see him, the blind hero pulled down upon their heads and his own. The closing words are put in the mouth of Manoah, his father:

> Come, come ! no time for lamentation now,
> Nor much more cause ; Samson hath quit himself

Like Samson, and heroically hath finished
A life heroic, on his enemies
Fully revenged, hath left them years of mourning
And lamentation to the sons of Caphtor
Through all Philistian bounds; to Israel
Honor hath left and freedom, let but them
Find courage to lay hold on this occasion.

   *   *   *   *   *   *

Chorus.

All is best, though we oft doubt
  What the unsearchable dispose
Of highest wisdom brings about
  And ever best found in the close.
Oft he seems to hide his face
  But unexpectedly returns
And to his faithful champion hath in place
  Bore witness gloriously ; whence Gaza mourns
And all that band them to resist
  His uncontrollable intent ;
His servants he with new acquest
  Of true experience from this great event
With peace and consolation hath dismissed
  And calm of mind all passion spent.

And now let us see how our younger poet concludes a
tragedy :

Athena.

Hear, men that mourn, and women without mate,
Hearken : ye sick of soul with fear, and thou
Dumb-stricken for thy children ; * * *
  * * *   I Pallas bring thee word,
I virgin daughter of the most high god
Give all you charge and lay command on all

The word I bring be wasted not ; for this
The gods have 'stablished and his soul hath sworn
That time nor earth nor changing sons of men
Nor waves of generations, nor the winds
Of ages risen and fallen that steer their tides   .
Through light and dark of birth and lovelier death
From storm toward haven inviolable, shall see
So great a light alive beneath the sun
As the aweless eye of Athens ;   *
     *   *   *   In thine hand
Shall time be like a sceptre, and thine head
Wear worship for a garland ; nor one leaf
Shall change or Winter cast out of thy crown
Till all flowers wither in the world ; thine eyes
Shall first in man's flash lightning liberty,
Thy tongue shall first say freedom ; thy first hand
Shall loose the thunder terror as a hound
To hunt from sunset to the springs of the sun
Kings that rose up out of the populous East
To make their quarry of thee, and shall strew
With multitudinous limbs of myriad herds
The foodless pastures of 'the sea and make
With wrecks immeasurable and unsummed defeat
One ruin of all their many-folded flocks
Ill shepherded from Asia.   *   *   *

Chorus.

From the depth of the springs of my spirit a fountain is poured of
    thanksgiving,
  My country. my mother, for thee,
That thy dead for their death shall have life in thy sight and a
    name everliving
  At heart of thy people to be.

In the darkness of change on the waters of time they shall turn
    from afar
To the beam of this dawn for a beacon, the light of these pyres for
    a star ;
They shall see thee who love and take comfort, who hate thee
    shall see and take warning,
  Our mother that makest us free ;
And the sons of thine earth shall have help of the waves that made
    war on their morning,
  And friendship and fame of the sea.

The reader will now determine for himself whether
the re-creation of Greek tragedy in an alien and awkward speech should be scouted as a chimera, or be accounted a legitimate work of art. In æsthetic questions,
the conclusive test and seal of legitimacy is victory. It
appears, at all events, indisputable that certain themes
of universal and perennial power—the conception of
self-devotion for humanity or kindred embodied in the
"Prometheus" or the "Agonistes," and that of self-
immolation for country portrayed in the "Erechtheus"
—in spite of the strange and ill-intelligible treatment
exacted by the conditions of antique drama, the obscure
myths, metaphors, points of view, and turns of thought
inseparable from its texture, somehow contrive to hit
the heart. The latest experiment of Swinburne presents
no unworthy semblance of a Euripidean play. It has,
at least, demonstrated the possibility of suggesting to
the modern eye and ear, by example more forceful than
the most eloquent description, what manner of work it

was which knit the heart of Greece to the Attic stage, what and how those

> Lofty, grave tragedians taught
> In chorus or iambic, teachers best
> Of moral prudence with delight received
> In brief, sententious precepts ; while they sang
> Of fate, and chance, and change in human life,
> High actions and high passions best describing.

II.

THE lyric poems collected under the title of *Songs of the Springtides* cannot fail to signally enhance Mr. Swinburne's reputation. Both as regards form and contents, they constitute a splendid and conclusive voucher for his claim to the foremost rank among contemporary English singers. In view of these exquisite compositions, no one henceforth, we imagine, will challenge the author's right to occupy a place of honor which Shelley alone is entitled to share with him among the modern masters of the English lyre.

That Mr. Swinburne has carried the development of rhythm and melody to a pitch of elaborate refinement and manifold beauty, not only unattained but unconceived before in English verse, had been already demonstrated by his previous performances. But there have been signs in certain quarters of an attempt at subtle disparagement by a perfunctory recognition of his skill in the technics of assonance and metre, coupled with the implied suggestion that higher and more spiritual gifts were less adequately attested in his poetry. Such vague, insinuated slurs were somewhat hard to meet, because although abundant proof of profound insight and of the strongest sweep of the imagination could be drawn from his works, there were also, undoubtedly, scattered through his writings, snatches of song which touched the strings of merely fugitive emotion, and which did not aim to strike the deeper chords of feeling or to sound the wells of thought. Most of the lyrics, however, presented in this volume are fraught of larger, richer, more enduring tissues ; they are weighted with great thoughts, and instinct with high passions ; they breathe a purity, an elevation, a nobility of sentiment which, without pedantic exaggeration, may at times be termed Pindaric. Whatever may be said of some earlier and shorter flights by which the author tried his wing, there is no question here of voluptuous tinklings and soft Lydian airs, of carnal hankerings and gross delights ; the song is lifted far above the paltrinesses and the impurities of earth, and poises with steady plume in the cool empyrean. In a word, the beauteous body which Swinburne's poetry always had is here informed with a soul.

By far the loftiest strains which have come for many a year from any English singer are to be found in the " Birthday Ode " addressed to Victor Hugo, which fills a considerable part of the present volume. It is this remarkable work to which we would especially direct notice, but before scrutinizing it in some detail we would pause a moment over two of the charming lyrics inserted in another poem, "The Garden of Cymodoce." The first is a description, or rather an invocation, of the Island of Guernsey, which the poet calls "the loveliest thing that shines against the sun," set, as it is, "midmost of the murderous water's web, all round it stretched and spun," and which "laughs reckless of rough tide and raging ebb." Only the artist in metre is likely to appreciate the consummate mechanism of this composition, but every ear attuned to music can feel the beauty of the rhythmic beat and the charm of an assonance subtler than that of rhyme.

> O flower of all wind-flowers and sea flowers,
>   Made lovelier by love of the sea
> Than thy golden own field-flowers, or tree-flowers
>   Like foam of the sea-facing tree !
> No foot but the sea-mew's there settles
>   On the spikes of thine anthers like horns,
> With snow-colored spray for thy petals,
>   Black rocks for thy thorns.
>
> Was it here, in the waste of his waters,
>   That the lordly north wind, when his love
> On the fairest of many king's daughters
>   Bore down for a spoil from above,
> Chose forth of all farthest far islands
>   As a haven to harbor her head,
> Of all lowlands on earth and all highlands,
>   His bride-worthy bed ?

Presently the poet reminds us that this fairest of islands hung like a "flower or jewel on the deep soft breast of the sea," was for long years the home of one whom he has elsewhere called "the greatest exile, and therefore the greatest man, of France ;" of that patriot poet, proscribed after the crime of December, and whose "God-like, banished gaze turned," we are told, "from its goal of natural days and homeward hunger for the clear French clime toward English earth." In a second song, which voices the associations suggested by the refuge which Guernsey gave to Victor Hugo, the author returns to a scheme of melody, an example of which he published fifteen years ago, under the name of "Rococo." After apostrophizing the island as "throned with the world's most perilous sea for throne, and praised from all its choral throats of thunder," he continues thus :

> Yet one praise hast thou holier,
>   Than praise of theirs may be,
> To exalt thee, wert thou lowlier
>   Than all that take the sea
> With shores whence waves ebb slowlier
>   Than these fall off from thee :
>
> That One, whose name gives glory,
>   One man whose life makes light,
> One crowned and throned in story
>   Above all empire's height,
> Came, where thy straits run hoary,
>   To hold thee fast in sight.

The ode written for the anniversary festival of Victor Hugo, February 20, 1880, is a work of extended scope, containing five hundred and twenty lines, and whether

we regard it from an artistic or intellectual and moral
point of view, must be counted among the performances
by which Mr. Swinburne will longest be remembered.
As regards structure, it is framed with the nicest accuracy on the most admired Greek models, but so sure yet
delicate is the author's touch, so close are the joinings,
so felicitous the breaks, so apparently spontaneous the
transitions and recurrences, that the reader's recognition
of the study and effort implied in the artificial arrangement is not awakened for a moment. So smooth and
limpid is the current of the verse, so naturally do its
bend and gush seem to obey the changeful impulse of
emotion, that not one reader in a hundred is likely to
detect the technical super-excellence of the work, or real-
ize that beneath the even and lustrous surface lies a vast
amount of tireless experiment and matchless skill; that
we have here, in fact, a marvel of dexterity in the transfer to an alien and reluctant tongue of the most intricate
and perfect metrical product transmitted by the Hellenic
masters. That the substance of the poem is worthy of
its garb will probably be demonstrated to the reader as
we transcribe a series of passages in which the central
motive or individual charm of Victor Hugo's multitudinous creations is succinctly outlined. We shall confine
ourselves to the poet's allusions to the dramas and ro-
mances with which the American readers of Victor Hugo
are most familiar.

Here, for instance, the pivotal situation of Hernani is
painted in four lines :

> Before the storm-blast blown of death's dark horn
> The marriage moonlight withers, that the morn
> For two made one may find three made by death
> One ruin at the blasting of its breath.

The next four sketch the groundwork of "Marion de Lorme," who, in the first copy of the piece, was made to say that "*L'amour m'a réfait ma virginité;*"

> Clothed with heart's flame renewed
> And strange new maidenhood,
> Faith lightens on the lips that bloomed for hire
> Pure as the lightning of love's first-born fire.

In the following the reader will recognize the root idea of "Le Roi s'amuse," that ghastly tragedy in which the jester Triboulet, thinking to wreak a frightful chastisement on Francis I., finds his own hand has murdered the beloved child whose seduction he intended to avenge :

> Wide-eyed and patient ever, till the curse
> Find where to fall and pierce,
> Keen expiation whets with edge more dread
> A father's wrong to smite a father's head.

In the six lines which succeed Mr. Swinburne alludes, of course, to that strong drama of "Marie Tudor," which is to Tennyson's treatment of the same theme as is red wine to water :

> As red the fire-scathed royal Northland bloom
> That left our story a name
> Dyed through with blood and flame
> E'er her life shriveled from a firier doom

> Than theirs her priests bade pass from earth in fire
> To slake the thirst of God their Lord's desire.

In the two lines that ensue, namely :

> As keen the blast of love-enkindled fate
> That burst the Paduan tyrant's guarded gate,

there is an obvious reference to the drama of "Angelo," animated and illumined by the striking figure of "La Tisbé." With like incisive brevity the poet indicates the wretched fate of the luckless Esmeralda :

> As sad the softer moan,
> Made one with music's own,
> For one whose feet made music as they fell
> On ways by loveless love made hot from hell.

Next the author outlines, in few words, the culminating situation of Ruy Blas, when, after frustrating the vile project of Don Salluste and saving the honor of the Queen, the hero of the piece seeks the one refuge left from a fatal complication :

> But higher than these and all the songs thereof
> The perfect heart of love,
> The heart by fraud and hate once crucified
> That dying gave thanks, and in thanksgiving died.

Although it is seldom acted, there is no doubt that what may be called the trilogy of "The Burgraves" is one of the most massive and precious works of Hugo. The stage is crowded with strong types, from the august figure of Barbarossa to the slave woman who has nursed

6

the dream of vengeance through two generations. What reader, too, is not impressed by the sharpness with which the author has brought out the swift decadence of German society in the thirteenth century through the concrete examples of grandsire, sire, and son ? . Hardly less striking is the felicity with which Hugo has relieved the strain upon the sterner emotions by introducing an idyl of youth and love whose mild gleams flicker in the shadow of sombre and ferocious passions. On "The Burgraves" Mr. Swinburne dwells at greater length :

> Above the windy walls that rule the Rhine
> A noise of eagles' wings
> And wintry war-time rings,
> With roar of ravage trampling corn and vine
> And storm of wrathful wassail dashed with song ;
> And under these the watch of wreakless wrong,
> With fire of eyes anhungered ; and above
> These, the light of the stricken eyes of love,
> The faint sweet eyes that follow
> The wind-outwinging swallow,
> And face athirst with young wan yearning mouth .
> Turned after toward the unseen all-golden south,
> Hopeless to see the birds back ere life wane,
> Or the leaves born again ;
> And still the might and music mastering fate
> Of life more strong than death and love than hate.

We come now to the terse, thought-laden lines in which, as in a bejeweled catalogue, Mr. Swinburne enumerates the studies of human life that, under the form of novel or romance, Victor Hugo has given to the world. Here, again, a line or two expresses the quintessence of the thing described. We may take for example the reference to "Notre Dame de Paris," which we cannot but esteem a nearly perfect realization of that almost impossible ideal, the historical novel :

> Higher than they rose of old,
> New builded now, behold
> The live great likeness of our Lady's towers,
> And round them like a dove
> Wounded, and sick with love.
> One fair ghost moving, crowned with fateful flowers,
> Watched yet with eyes of blood-red lust
> And eyes of love's heart broken and unbroken trust.

The next allusion is to the broad canvas of "Les Misérables," which portrays so many of the characteristic features and propounds so many of the problems of our modern civilization :

> Nor less the weight and worth
> Found even of love on earth
> To wash all stain of tears and sins away,
> On dying lips alit,
> That living knew not it
> In the winged shape of song with death to play;
> To warm young children with its wings
> And try with fire the heart elect for God-like things.
> For all worst wants of all most miserable
> With divine hands to deal
> All balms and herbs that heal
> Among all woes whereunder poor men dwell,
> Our Master sent His servant Love to be
> On earth His witness.

In the lines which immediately follow the poet marks
the psychological subject treated by Victor Hugo in the
" Toilers of the Sea."

> But the strange, deep sea,
> Mother of life and death inextricate,
> What work should Love do there to war with fate ?
> Yet there must Love to keep
> At heart of the eyeless deep
> Watch, and wage war wide eyed with all its wonders.
> Lower than the lightnings of its waves, and thunders
> Of seas less monstrous than the births they bred ;
> Keep high there heart and head,
> And conquer : then for prize of all toils past
> Feel the sea close them in again at last.

The lines that succeed outline the central thought
embodied in " L'Homme qui rit : "

> A day of direr doom arisen thereafter
> With cloud and fire in strife
> Lightens and darkens life
> Round one by man's hand masked with living laughter,
> A man by men bemonstered, but by love
> Watched with blind eyes as of a wakeful dove
> And wooed by lust, that in her rosy den
> As fire on flesh feeds on the souls of men.
> To take the intense impure
> Burnt offering of her lure,
> Divine and dark and bright and naked, strange
> With ravenous thirst of life reversed and change,
> As though the very heaven should shrivel and swell
> With hunger after hell.

> Run mad for dear damnation, and desire
> To feel its light thrilled through with stings of fire.

And here we see interpreted the dominant, abiding impression left on the reader's mind by the latest of Victor Hugo's novels—" Quatre-vingt-treize :"

> Above a windier sea,
> The glory of Ninety-three
> Fills heaven with blood-red and with rose-red beams
> That earth beholding grows
> Herself one burning rose
> Flagrant and fragrant with strange deeds and dreams,
> Dreams dyed as love's own flower, and deeds
> Stained as with love's own life-blood, that for love's sake bleeds.

In words equally succinct and searching, quivering with a like sympathy and suffused with the same glow of passionate admiration, Mr. Swinburne runs over the whole list of Victor Hugo's remarkable achievements. Looking back at last over the expanse, so wide as to seem incredible of " one great man's good works," and beholding in him not alone the many-sided prince of letters, but a leader in the advance of men made better through harsh trial and steadfast aspiration, he sums up what he deems the august significance of such a life in terms of noblest eulogy. He calls him " the mightiest soul,"

> That came forth singing ever in man's ears
> Of all souls with us, and through all these years
> Rings yet the lordliest, waxen yet more strong,
> That on our souls hath shed itself in song,

> Poured forth itself like rain
> On souls like springing grain
> That with its procreant beams and showers were fed
> For living wine and sacramental bread;
> Given all itself as air gives life and light,
> Utterly, as of right;
> The goodliest gift our age hath given, to be
> Ours while the sun gives glory to the sea.

The ode from which we have made these quotations ends with an apostrophe whose simplicity and dignity fall on the reader's ear like the deep notes of a diapason. If we except the invocation to Athena, which concludes the tragedy of Erechtheus, we must discern in the lines which follow a conscious majesty, coupled with a heart-thrilling reverence, without a parallel in the poetry of our time. They constitute the fitting capstone of an incomparable monument:

> Our Father and Master and Lord,
> Who hast thy song for sword,
> For staff thy spirit, and our hearts for throne;
> As in past years of wrong,
> Take now my subject song,
> To no crowned head made humble but thine own;
> That on thy day of worldly birth
> Gives thanks for all thou hast given past thanks of all on earth.

We cannot take leave of this volume without noting the stern words in which Mr. Swinburne utters his individual protest against the projected interment of the son of Napoleon III. in Westminster Abbey. With what

undying hate republicans should regard that Second
Empire which has proved an accursed blight to France,
and how little it behooves the sons of liberty-loving
England to bestow misplaced honor and a sickly sympathy on any of the brood of Bonaparte the poet had
pointed out in "The Garden of Cymodoce," from which
we quote a specially pertinent passage :

> But when our master's homeless feet were here,
> France yet was foul with joy more foul than fear,
> And slavery chosen, more vile by choice of chance
> Than dull damnation of inheritance
> From Russian year to year.
> Alas fair mother of men, alas my France,
> What ailed thee so to fall, that wert so dear
> For all men's sake to all men, in such trance,
> Plague stricken ? Had the very gods that saw
> Thy glory lighten on us for a law,
> Thy gospel go before us for a guide,
> Had these waxed envious of our love and awe?
> Or was it less their envy than thy pride
> That bared thy breast for the obscene vulture claw,
> High priestess, by whose mouth Love prophesied.
> That fate should yet mean freedom ? Howsoever,
> That hour, the helper of men's hearts, we praise,
> Which blots out of man's book of after days
> The name above all names abhorred for ever.

It is not strange that the author of these lines should
feel himself irresistibly impelled—in view of the anomalous distinction offered to the hereditary representative
of Bonapartist plots and crimes by the Dean of West-

minster—to relieve his conscience from a sense of public
duty in the following sonnet :

> "Let us go hence."   From the inmost shrine of grace
>   Where England holds the elect of all her dead
>   There comes a word like one of old time said
> By gods of old cast out.   Here is no place
> At once for these and one of poisonous race.
>   Let each rise up from his dishallowed bed
>   And pass forth silent.   Each divine veiled head
> Shall speak in silence with averted face;
> "Scorn everlasting and eternal shame
> Eat out the rotting record of his name
> Who had the glory of all these graves in trust
>   And turned it to a hissing.   His offence
> Makes havoc of their desecrated dust
>   Whose place is here no more.   Let us go hence."

Such are the accents of austere truth and compressed
scorn with which a republican poet denounces the pro-
posed desecration of Westminster Abbey by the erection
of a monument to the son of Napoleon III.   Such an act
Mr. Swinburne would denounce as "an insult at once to
contemporary France, and to the present only less than
to past generations of Englishmen."

III. MARY STUART.

IN the tragedy called *Mary Stuart* by Algernon Charles
Swinburne, we have the concluding member of the tril-
ogy of which the preceding parts were "Chastelard" and
"Bothwell," and in which the author has undertaken to

depict one of the most enigmatic and interesting persons that have lived upon this earth. That this play, like its predecessors, was not intended for the theatre is sufficiently obvious, though we would not venture to affirm that if its long speeches underwent the process of lopping and pruning to which Victor Hugo's "Burgraves" was subjected, it might not be presented effectively upon the stage. No part, however, of this dramatic poem was written, we may be sure, with a view to any such mutilation ; the play was intended to be read, not seen, like "Philip Van Artevelde," or Browning's essays in the field of dramatic poetry. The author has sought, as we have said, to render lifelike and intelligible, one of the strangest figures in the strange sixteenth century ; to interpret at once the fascinations and the short-comings of one who embodied all the weaknesses and all the charms of the Renaissance, who united an admirable alertness of the intellect to an exquisite sensitiveness to all forms of beauty, but in whose consummate egoism there seems to have been no place for altruistic sentiments or for the moral sense. Those who are conversant with the private lives of high-placed men and women in the Italy of the fifteenth and the France of the sixteenth century, know that characters quite as problematic as that which Mr. Swinburne has portrayed in the Scottish Queen were continually encountered at those epochs. Mary Stuart's mother-in-law and sister-in-law, Catherine de Medicis and Marguerite de Valois, were women of the same type, and there is no indication in the me-

6*

moirs of Brantome and other contemporary writers that
the fusion of supreme attractiveness and total heartless-
ness exhibited in those instances was regarded as anything exceptional.   There was about the court of
Francis I., of his son, and of his grandchildren, an atmosphere of self-indulgence and moral obliquity such as
Mr. Mallock would have us think will again pervade the
higher sphere of society, should agnosticism succeed in
displacing religion.

In the trilogy which ends with the present poem, Mr.
Swinburne has performed a remarkable achievement by
putting an end to the idle controversies touching the
criminality of the Queen of Scots—controversies raised
for the most part by persons who have known little of
the influences under which Mary Stuart was brought up
—and by assisting us to understand the apparent incon-
sistencies of her conduct, the crimes and the acts of
baseness at which she must be held to have connived,
and the inexhaustible devotion which she inspired to
her last hour.   This task, which was carried far toward
completion in "Chastelard" and "Bothwell," and
which exacted an immense amount of antiquarian research, directed and illuminated by a poet's insight,
and by what Comte chose to call the historical conscience, is finished in this tragedy.   The author has also
aimed in the play before us to tell the truth about Elizabeth, to show the so-called maiden Queen as she was
known to her contemporaries, to strip her of the preposterous attributes with which her flatterers endowed her,

and which have been transmitted to our day through the hero-worship of Charles Kingsley and other light-headed enthusiasts. It is, by the way, a curious fact that Swinburne's veracious portrait of Elizabeth should have appeared almost at the same time with a careful study of the Queen's character based on contemporary correspondence. We refer to the series of papers entitled "Les Projets du Mariage d'une Reine d'Angleterre," written by M. Hector de la Ferrière for the *Revue des Deux Mondes.* Nothing could be more grotesquely unlike the popular impression of Elizabeth, or more thoroughly consonant with Mr. Swinburne's conception, than the picture drawn by M. de la Ferrière, in which we are made to see the selfish, peevish, vain, jealous, amorous daughter of Henry VIII., as she really appeared to courtiers and ambassadors. What is more extraordinary, the letter supposed to have been written by Mary Stuart, and whose delivery to Elizabeth causes the tragic culmination of this play, has been shown by M. de la Ferrière to be actually extant in the archives of the Marquis of Salisbury. We can perhaps demonstrate in no better way the historical accuracy of Mr. Swinburne's portrait of Elizabeth than by prefacing some extracts from the poem, with an account of what is actually known about the letter on which the action is made to turn.

It is well known that Catherine de Medicis endeavored to bring about a marriage between the Queen of England and one of her sons, and that after Charles IX. and

Henri III. had been successively rejected by Elizabeth, she sought to substitute their younger brother François, commonly known as the Duc d'Alençon, but who, on the accession of his brother Henri to the throne, became Duc d'Anjou. M. de la Ferrière shows us that François entered eagerly into his mother's scheme, and in February, 1575, sent an envoy to England to press his suit. For this purpose he selected the master of his wardrobe, one Jean de Simier, whose origin seems to have been obscure (and who is therefore aptly designated in the letter as the Duke's "knave"), but who, according to a contemporary writer, was "un courtisan raffiné qui avoit une exquise connoissance des gaîtés d'amour et attraits de la cour." It is certain that Simier gained Elizabeth's favor, and that his relations with her became so intimate as to occasion great scandal at the English court. When, a few months afterward, the Duc d'Anjou came to England, it was observed that Elizabeth had a room prepared for him next her own, and that she frequently passed her days and evenings alone with him, the Duc not leaving her private chamber until two hours after midnight. It was the conduct of Elizabeth with the Duc and with his envoy Simier on which Mary Stuart dilated in a letter which she penned in an hour of ungovernable anger, and which Mr. Swinburne supposes to have been delivered at a critical moment when Elizabeth was hesitating to sign the warrant for her rival's execution. In this letter, according to M. de la Ferrière, Mary Stuart rebuked

Elizabeth for her vices, in language which he thus translates, and which will be found to justify the expressions used by Mr. Swinburne: "Je prends Dieu à témoin que la Comtesse de Shrewsbury m'a dit que vous aviez engagé votre honneur avec un étranger, allant le trouver dans la chambre d'une dame là où vous le baisiez et usiez avec lui de privautés deshonnêtes, mais aussi lui révéliez les secrets de royaume, trahissant vos propres conseillers avec lui." In the same letter wherein Mary thus taunts Elizabeth with her intimacy with Simier, she denounces her similar indiscretions with Simier's master, the Duc. Her words are thus reproduced in French by M. de la Ferrière: "Vous vous êtes déportée avec lui de la même dissolution qu'avec Simier; une nuit vous l'avez rencontré à la porte de votre chambre, n'ayant que votre seul chemise et votre manteau de nuit, et vous l'avec laissé entrer, et il est demeuré avec vous pres de trois heures." We are told by M. de la Ferrière that this letter was copied by Prince Labanof from the original, which is in the handwriting of Mary Stuart, and is now in the possession of the Marquis of Salisbury, who has, of course, inherited the papers of Elizabeth's chief counsellor, Lord Burleigh. This document, plainly, suggests a very different conception of Elizabeth's character from the popular notion to which Shakespeare gave utterance when he discoursed on the high-souled virgin whose days were passed "in maiden meditation, fancy free." We shall see, as we proceed with Mr. Swinburne's poem, that Elizabeth's rage on reading the letter above mentioned wants the accent of virtuous indignation, and reveals rather the fury and spite of an unmasked hypocrite who discovers that her secret vices are known to a bitter enemy, and who hastens to suppress an inconvenient witness.

In the present play we have the closing scenes of Mary Stuart's life, beginning with Babington's conspiracy, and ending with her trial and execution for complicity in the intended murder of Elizabeth. This plot was peculiarly formidable because it was formed among the gentlemen in immediate attendance on the English Queen, and was aimed not merely at her deposition, but at her life. The drama opens at the moment when their plans are ripe, and Babington has convoked his accomplices at his lodgings. The words in which Babington announces the prompt fulfilment of their purpose are obviously suggested by the language which Shakespeare puts into the mouth of the Duke of Gloster :

Babington.   Welcome, good friends, and welcome this good day
That casts out hope and brings in certainty
To turn raw spring to summer.   Now not long
The flower that crowns the front of all our faiths
Shall bleach to death in prison; now the trust
That took the night with fire as of a star
Grows red and broad as sunrise in our sight
Who held it dear and desperate once, now sure,
But not more dear, being surer.

Babington, as the event proved, was an imaginative but weak-hearted braggart, who, when subjected to torture, tried to lay the guilt of the conspiracy on the shoulders of his comrades. He was one of Mary Stuart's many tools, unconsciously made such by her incomparable fascination. The species of witchery which she could exercise at will is revealed in the following passage, in which he justifies the heat he displays in her service :

Look you, sirs,

This is no new thing for my faith to keep,
My soul to feed its fires with, and my hope
Fix eyes upon for star to steer by; she
That six years hence the boy that I was then,
And page, ye know, to Shrewsbury, gave his faith
To serve and worship with his body and soul
For only lady and queen, with power alone
To lift my heart up and bow down mine eyes
At sight and sense of her sweet sovereignty,
Made thence her man for ever ; she whose look
Turned all my blood of life to tears and fire,
That going or coming, sad or glad—for yet
She would be somewhile merry, as though to give
Comfort and ease of heart her servants, then
Weep smilingly to be so light of mind,
Saying she was like the bird grown blithe in bonds
That if too late set free would die for fear,
Or wild birds hunt it out of life—if sad,
Put madness in me for her suffering's sake,
If joyous, for her very love's sake—still
Made my heart mad alike to serve her, being
I know not when the sweeter, sad or blithe,
Nor what mood heavenliest of her, all whose change
Was as of stars and sun and moon in heaven.

Several of the persons in this opening scene are skilfully discriminated, and Mr. Swinburne makes us see that the soul of the plot is not the romantic and self-vaunting Babington, but a Jesuit priest, who, when the conspirators are arrested, refrains from cowardly accusations of his companions, and, like Iago, goes silently to his doom. In the remainder of the first act the scene is shifted from London to Chartley, where the Queen of Scots is a prisoner under the ward of Sir Amyas Paulet. Just as Mr. Swinburne sought to show us from the lips of Babington what Mary Stuart seemed to be, so now we are helped to see her as she really was through her unguarded communings with her tirewoman. The latter, Mary Beaton, is the link which binds this play to the first member of the trilogy, for she has never forsaken the Queen through the long years of captivity, while, on the other hand, she has never forgotten Chastelard, and has more than once been tempted to avenge him. The instrument of vengeance is in her hand, for the letter in which Mary Stuart had taunted Elizabeth with her dishonorable passion for Simier and the Duc D'Anjou had been given to Mary Beaton. Subsequently Mary's prudence led her to regret this hasty and perilous step, and she ordered it to be burned. Mary Beaton, however, keeps it, and being wrought, as we shall see, to uncontrollable indignation and anger by the pitiless egoism of her mistress, and by the proof that the very name of Chastelard is forgotten by the woman for whom he died, sends the fatal document to Elizabeth at

a moment when the life of Mary Stuart hangs on a
thread. In this first scene at Chartley Mary speaks as
follows of Elizabeth, and alludes to the letter she supposes to be destroyed :

> I am yet some ten years younger than this queen,
> Some nine or ten ; but if I die this year
> And she some score years longer than I think
> Be royal-titled, in one year of mine
> I shall have lived the longer life, and die
> The fuller-fortuned woman.   Dost thou mind
> The letter that I writ nigh two years gone
> To let her wit what privacies of hers
> Our trusty dame of Shrewsbury's tongue made mine
> Ere it took fire to sting her lord and me ?
> How thick soe'er o'er curfed with poisonous lies,
> Of her I am sure it lied not ; and perchance
> I did the wiselier, having writ my fill,
> Yet to withhold the letter when she sought
> Of me to know what villainies had it poured
> In ears of mine against her innocent name :
> And yet thou knowest what mirthful heart was mine
> To write her word of these, that had she read
> Had surely, being but woman, made her mad,
> Or haply, being not woman, had not.   Faith,
> How say'st thou ? did I well ?

In the same scene there is another characteristic reference to Elizabeth by Mary, who hints that she believes
not only the scandals reported by the Countess of Shrewsbury, but the other current rumor which imputed sterility to her rival. Mr. Swinburne seems to accept both
stories as not inconsistent with each other, and perhaps

they are not, either on physiological or psychological
grounds :

> *Mary Stuart.* I would not be so tempered of my blood,
> So much mismade as she in spirit and flesh,
> To be more fair of fortune.   She should hate
> Not me, albeit she hate me deadly, more
> Than thee or any woman.   By my faith,
> Fain would I know, what knowing not of her now
> I muse upon and marvel, if she have
> Desire or pulse or passion of true heart
> Fed full from natural veins, or be indeed
> All bare and barren, all as dead men's bones
> Of all sweet nature and sharp seed of love,
> And those salt springs of life, through fire and tears
> That bring forth pain and pleasure in their kind
> To make good days and evil, all in her
> Lie sere and sapless as the dust of death.
> I have found no great good hap in all my days
> Nor much good cause to make me glad of God,
> Yet have I had and lacked not of my life
> My good things and mine evil : being not yet
> Barred from life's natural ends of evil and good
> Foredoomed for man and woman through the world
> Till all their works be nothing and of mine
> I know but this—though I should die to-day,
> I would not take for mine her fortune.
>   *Mary Beaton.*   No ?
> Myself perchance I would not.
>   *Mary Stuart.*   Dost thou think
> That fire-tongued witch of Shrewsbury spake once truth
> Who told me all those quaint foul merry tales
> Of our dear sister that at her desire
> I writ to give her word of, and at thine

Withheld and put the letter in thine hand
To burn as was thy counsel ?

After dwelling on the offensive details of the letter in language substantially accordant with the quotations above given from the version of M. de la Ferrière, Mary Stuart concludes by saying that she believes the slanders, and had made her belief manifest to the reader of the letter :

God wot,
Had she read all, and in my hand set down,
I could not blame her though she had sought to take
My head for payment : no less poise on earth
Had served, and hardly, for the writer's fee ;
I could not much have blamed her ; all the less,
That I did take this, though from slanderous lips,
For gospel and not slander, and that now
I yet do well believe it.

The act closes with the abrupt removal of Mary from Chartley to Tixall, and her detention in the latter place while her papers are ransacked for proof of her connivance at Babington's treasonable project against the life of Elizabeth. No documents are found, but her secretaries, being arrested and put to torture, acknowledge that they wrote at her dictation some letters which implied full knowledge of his purpose. The proof, however, is incomplete, and both for this reason and because instinct tells Elizabeth that the trial and public execution of a queen is a dangerous precedent, she is minded to put her rival out of the way privily, and sounds one of her council, Walsingham, touching the expediency of assassination. Walsingham at heart cares more for the supremacy of English laws than for the theory of royal dignity and immunity, and insists that Mary Stuart shall be tried for treason against the realm of which she is a resident. The spiteful and treacherous character of Elizabeth is indicated by some subtle and acrid strokes which we would willingly reproduce. But we must confine ourselves, for the most part, to the scenes in which Mary Stuart and the agent of retribution, Mary Beaton, personally figure. In the second act we see them both again at Chartley, to which they have returned, and Mary Beaton is informed by their jailer, Sir Amyas Paulet, of her mistress's approaching trial and too probable condemnation. Left alone for a few moments, Mary Beaton reveals in a soliloquy the key to her action in the tragedy. We quote her words at length, as exhibiting the pivotal motive of the drama :

> Here looms on me the landmark of my life
> That I have looked for now some score of years
> Even with long-suffering eagerness of heart
> And a most hungry patience. I did know,
> Yea, God, thou knowest I knew this all that while,
> From that day forth when even these eyes beheld
> Fall the most faithful head in all the world,
> Toward her most loving and of me most loved,
> By doom of hers that was so loved of him
> He could not love me nor his life at all
> Nor his own soul nor aught that all men love,
> Nor could fear death nor very God, or care
> If there were aught more merciful in heaven

Than love on earth had been to him.   Chastelard,—
I have not had the name upon my lips
That stands for sign of love the truest in man
Since first love made him sacrifice of men,
This long sad score of years retributive
Since it was cast out of her heart and mind
Who made it mean a dead thing; nor, I think,
Will she remember it before she die.

*   *   *   *   *   *   *

Yet my soul
Knows, and yet God knows, I would set not hand
To such a work as might put on the time
And make death's foot more forward for her sake;
Yea, were it to deliver mine own soul
From bondage and long-suffering of my life,
I would not set mine hand to work her wrong.
Tempted I was—but hath God need of me
To work his judgment, bring his time about,
Approve his justice if the word be just
That whoso doeth shall suffer his own deed,
Bear his own blow, to weep tears back for tears,
And bleed for bloodshed ?

*   *   *   *   *   *   *

Tempt me not, God.   My heart swelled once to know
I bore her death about me ; as I think
Indeed I bear it.

In the third act takes place the trial of Mary Stuart
in Fotheringay Castle.   In his account of the trial Mr.
Swinburne adheres closely to the extant records of that
remarkable proceeding in which, as is well known, Mary
Stuart bore herself with admirable dignity, and, al-

though unprovided with legal assistance of any kind, defended herself with great ability. She begins by excepting to the jurisdiction of the court, and then proceeds to sift and comment on the evidence alleged against her. But notwithstanding the skill which Mary exhibited in her defence, and the want of any decisive evidence in her own handwriting, the judicial commission found her guilty of treason, and sentenced her to death. It was still uncertain, however, whether Elizabeth would sign the warrant for her execution, and in the fourth act her counsellors try in vain to secure her signature. She remembers, doubtless, that while sovereigns had more than once been removed by clandestine means in England, yet none had ever publicly suffered the death penalty for the violation of English laws. Nor will it probably be disputed that Charles I. would never have been tried and executed but for the precedent which Elizabeth had countenanced in the case of the Queen of Scots. Mr. Swinburne makes it manifest that the arguments of Burleigh and Walsingham—based, as they were, on the assumption, extremely distasteful to a Tudor, that the laws of the realm were binding even upon a sovereign—served rather to intensify than overcome the reluctance which Elizabeth intuitively felt. The English queen falls back again on her scheme of assassination, and an agent is sent to Fotheringay to work upon Sir Amyas Paulet, who proves, however, no less intractable on this head than Walsingham. It is at this time that Mary Beaton learns of Elizabeth's hesitation, and how improbable it is that the warrant will be signed. At such a juncture it is evident that the letter in her possession will turn the scale, but before sending it she is prompted by a merciful impulse to ascertain whether her mistress feels any twinge of remorse for her treatment of Chastelard, for having suffered him to die when a word from her might have saved him. Curiously enough, Mary Stuart is represented as remembering some words uttered by Chastelard in loving but solemn warning, yet when Mary Beaton tries to lead her mind back to their author it turns out that she has forgotten even his name.

> *Mary Stuart.* I know not : yet
> Time was when I remembered.
> *Mary Beaton.* It should be
> No enemy's saying whom you remember not ;
> You are wont not to forget your enemies ; yet
> The word rang sadder than a friend's should fall
> Save in some strange pass of the spirit or flesh
> For love's sake haply hurt to death.
> *Mary Stuart.* It seems
> Thy mind is bent to know the name of me
> That of myself I know not.
> *Mary Beaton.* Nay, my mind
> Has other thoughts to beat upon : for me
> It may suffice to know the saying for true
> And never care who said it.

For a time Mary, dwelling on the past, glances at other incidents, but presently her mind returns to Chastelard's prediction, which, though uncoupled with a name, still

lingers in her memory. When again pressed by Mary
Beaton to recall the author, she opines that it might have
been David Rizzio :

> Friendship ? I should have died I think long since,
> That many might have died not, and this word
> Had not been written of me nor fulfilled,
> But perished in the saying, a prophecy
> That took the prophet by the throat and slew—
> As sure I think it slew him.   Such a song
> Might my poor servant slain before my face
> Have sung before the stroke of violent death
> Had fallen upon him there for my sake.
>   *Mary Beaton.*   Ah !
> You think so ? this remembrance was it not
> That hung and hovered in your mind but now,
> Moved your heart backward all unwittingly
> To some blind memory of the man long dead ?
>   *Mary Stuart.*   In sooth, I think my prophet should
>   have been
> David.
>   *Mary Beaton.* You thought of him ?
>   *Mary Stuart.*   An old sad thought :
> The moan of it was made long since, and he
> Not unremembered.
>   *Mary Beaton.*   Nay, of him indeed
> Record was made—a royal record : whence
> No marvel is it that you forgot not him.

By this Mary Beaton is well nigh resolved to rid the
world of a woman who, as Chastelard once said, was born
without a heart.   Her mistress asks her to sing, and she
sings a little French song which Chastelard had made

and sung to Mary Stuart in the days when she loved him
as well as she could love any one.   This tender ditty,
Mary Beaton thinks, shall furnish the supreme test.   If
Mary Stuart recognizes it, and finds it in her heart to
say but one gentle word of the unhappy writer, the letter
shall be destroyed, and the Queen's life will be saved.

> *Mary Beaton.*   Give me leave
> A little to cast up some wandering words
> And gather back such memories as may beat
> About my mind of such a song, and yet
> I think I might renew some notes long dumb
> That once your ear allowed of.   [*Aside.*]   I did pray
> Tempt me not, God ; and by her mouth again
> He tempts me—nay, but prompts me, being most just
> To know by trial if all remembrance be
> Dead as remorse or pity that in birth
> Died and were children in her ; if she quite
> Forget that very swan song of thy love,
> My love that wast, my love that would'st not be,
> Let God forget her now at last as I
> Remember, if she thinks but one soft thought,
> Cast one poor word upon thee, God thereby
> Shall surely bid me let her live ; if none,
> I shoot that letter home and sting her dead.
> God strengthen me to sing but these words through
> Though I fall dumb at end for ever.   Now—
>   [*She sings.*
> > Après tant de jours, après tant de pleurs,
> > Soyez secourable à mon âme en peine.
> > Voyez comme Avril fait l'amour aux fleurs ;
> > Dame d'amour, dame aux belles couleurs,
> > Dieu vous a fait belle, Amour vous fait reine.

7

> Rions, je t'en prie ; aimons, je le veux.
> Le temps fuit et rit et ne revient guère
> Pour baiser le bout de tes blonds cheveux
> Pour baiser tes cils, ta bouche et tes yeux ;
> L'amour n'a qu'un jour auprès de sa mère.

Mary Stuart. Nay, I should once have known that song, thou
　　say'st,
And him that sang it and should now be dead :
Was it—but his rang sweeter—was it not
Remy Belleau ?
　Mary Beaton. (My letter—here at heart !)　[*Aside.*
I think it might be—were it better writ
And courtlier phrased, with Latin spice cast in,
And a more tunable descant.

The letter is forwarded to London, and the scene
shifts to Greenwich Palace, where Walsingham's secretary, Davison, who has been intrusted with the deadly
missive, comes for the last time to ask Elizabeth's signature to the warrant. He is reluctant to produce the
letter, for he is shrewd enough to know that the Queen
will scarcely forgive either Walsingham or himself for
having perused its contents. At first, therefore, he
essays to gain his end by dwelling on the reasons of
state which make Mary's death essential to the security
of England, but to these considerations he finds Elizabeth more obdurate than ever. Unable to meet Davison's
arguments, she pleads finally a sentimental reluctance
to take life, and produces a petition, lately addressed to
her by Mary from Fotheringay Castle, which Elizabeth

pretends drew tears from her.   Then it was that Davison, appreciating the woman with whom he has to deal, has recourse to his last weapon, the letter written years before by Mary Stuart, and now transmitted secretly by Mary Beaton.

> *Davison.*   Sure it is
> This Queen hath skill of writing : and her hand
> Hath manifold eloquence with various voice
> To express discourse of sirens or of snakes,
> A mermaid's or a monster's uttering best,
> All music or all malice.   Here is come
> A letter writ long since of hers to you
> From Sheffield Castle, which for shame or fear
> She durst not or she would not thence despatch.
> Sent secretly to me from Fotheringay,
> Not from her hand, but with her own hand writ,
> So foul of import and malignity
> I durst not for your Majesty's respect
> With its fierce infamies afire from hell
> Offend your gracious eyesight: but because
> Your justice by your mercy's ignorant hand
> Hath her fair eyes put out, and walks now blind
> Even by the pit's edge deathward, pardon me
> If what you never should have seen be shown
> By hands that rather would take fire in hand
> Than lay in yours this writing.   [*Gives her a letter.*
> *Elizabeth.*   By this light,
> Whate'er be here, thou hadst done presumptuously,
> And Walsingham thy principal, to keep
> Aught from mine eyes that being to me designed
> Might even with most offence enlighten them.
> Here is her hand indeed.

* * * * * * * *

Davison.　　　　　　　　　　Your Grace
Shall but defile and vex your eyes and heart
To read these villainies through.
　　Elizabeth.　　　　　　　God's death, man ! peace :
Thou wert not best incense me toward thine own,
Whose eyes have been before me in them.　What !
Was she not mad to write this ?　*　*　*

　　　*　　　*　　　*　　　*　　　*　　　*

　　　　　　　　　Give me again
That warrant I put by, being foolish ; yea,
Thy word spake sooth—my soul's eyes were put out—
I could not see for pity.　Thou didst well—
I am bounden to thee heartily—to cure
My sight of this distemper, and my soul.
Here in God's sight I set my hand, who thought
Never to take this thing upon it, nor
Do God so bitter service.　Take this hence :
And let me see no word nor hear of her
Till the sun see not such a soul alive.

The scene of the last act is Fotheringay Castle, where Mary Stuart is to die.　We scarcely need to say that the execution does not take place upon the stage, but it is witnessed from a window of the gallery where Mary Beaton (who had seen Chastelard go to his death, and even then vowed to avenge him), and another of the Queen's tirewomen, Barbara Mowbray, have remained. There are few things finer in the dramatic poetry of our time than the concluding passage, in which Mary Stuart, though she may have lived basely, resumes her queenhood and dies like the great ones of the earth, and in which

Mary Beaton, like a new Electra, is now racked by the agonies of compassion and remorse, and anon seems to tower before us with the mien of a retributive angel. In this culminating scene, at all events, Mr. Swinburne has struck with no feeble or uncertain hand the master chords of fear and pity, and speaks to us, as the great teachers of tragic truth have spoken. We make a final extract from the drama :

> *Barbara.*   Yea, I see
> Stand in the mid-hall the scaffold black as death,
> And black the block upon it all around.
> Against the throng a guard of halberdiers,
> And the axe against the scaffold rail reclined,
> And two men masked on either hand beyond,
> And hard behind the block a cushion set,
> Black, as the chair behind it.
> *Mary Beaton.*   When I saw
> Fallen on a scaffold once a young man's head,
> Such things as these I saw not.   Nay, but on :
> I knew not that I spake : and toward your ears
> Indeed I spake not.
>   *   *   *   *   *   *   *   *
> *Barbara.*   Not a face there breathes of all the throng
> But is more moved than hers to hear this read,
> Whose look alone is changed not.
> *Mary Beaton.*   Once I knew
> A face that changed not in as dire an hour
> More than the queen's face changes.   Hath he not
> Ended?   *   *   *   *   *   *   *
> *Barbara.*   And now they lift her veil up from her head.
> Softly and softly draw the black robe off,

And all in red as of a funeral flame
She stands up statelier yet before them, tall,
And clothed as if with sunset ; and she takes
From Elspeth's hands the crimson sleeves, and draws
Their covering on her arms, and now those twain
Burst out aloud in weeping ; and she speaks :
Weep not : I promised for you.   Now she kneels ;
And Jane binds round a kerchief on her eyes :
And smiling last her heavenliest smile on earth,
She waves a blind hand toward them, with *Farewell,*
Farewell, to meet again : and they come down
And leave her praying aloud, *In thee, O Lord,*
I put my trust : and now, that psalm being through,
She lays between the block and her soft neck
Her long white peerless hands up tenderly.
Which now the headsman draws again away,
But softly too : now stir her lips again—
Into thine hands, O Lord, into thine hands,
Lord, I commend my spirit : and now—but now,
Look you, not I, the last upon her.
   Mary Beaton.   Ha !
He strikes awry; she stirs not.   Nay, but now
He strikes aright, and ends it.
   Barbara.   Hark, a cry.
   Voice below.   So perish all found enemies of the Queen !
   Another voice.   Amen.
   Mary Beaton.   I heard that very cry go up
Far off long since to God, who answers here.

THERE is only one French novelist who it seems can hope just now to divide with the author of "L'Assommoir" the attention of the Parisian public, and there is only one theme left to the political satirist comparable in pungent and wide-reaching interest to Zola's caustic picture of the imperial régime. Since 1870 the Legitimist party have gained not a little in importance and prestige at the expense of the partisans of the Bonaparte dynasty, and have infected a majority of the reactionary classes with Bourbon principles and sentiments. We need not say that the abortive *coup d'état* projected by the De Broglie ministry and countenanced by the Marshal-President was organized in the interest of the White Flag and the Lilies, and in this quarter, if anywhere, the new republic has had cause to recognize a danger. For the present, however, there is no ground to apprehend overt hostility, and the moment, therefore, seems propitious to frustrate the clandestine efforts of the Legitimist propaganda by ridicule, the most deadly weapon known to French polemics. This is what Alphonse Daudet has undertaken to do in his novel called "Les Rois en Exil." What sort of men are these kings, whose foreheads wear the aureole of majesty, whose functions are deemed consecrate by the grace of God to a benignant stewardship of the nations, and whose misfortunes have the privilege of evoking the blind fervors of an undying loyalty and the poignant homage of self-sacrifice ? What are they, stripped of the illusions which veil and glorify a throne, thrust down from their superb and lofty isolation into the crowded walks of common life and left naked in the searching and pitiless light of indigence, of impotence, and exile ? Can the lingering faith in an unselfish, high-aiming, and paternal kingship find no ray of truth and fact in the lives of disinherited princes, or must the sole gleam of large resolve and aspiration, the one flash of dignity and grandeur, be looked for in the generous impulse of a woman or the frail promise of a child ? Such is the thesis which M. Daudet has debated in this volume with an acrid and relentless disclosure of the true characters and veritable careers in exile, of these dethroned types of royalty which the events of the last twenty years have consigned to private life.

This novel is dedicated to Edmond de Goncourt, and there is no doubt that the influence of the brothers Goncourt is traceable in Daudet's style. As regards their conception of the novelist's function they were realists, but they had mixed, it is said, a good deal with painters, and were as fond as that unswerving idealist, Gautier, of painting with the pen. It was they, too, who, in a feverish recoil from commonplace phraseology, introduced the use of abstract terms, saying, for instance, "a cat's blackness," instead of "a black cat." From them Daudet, who in his early stories wrote with simplicity, has caught a good many affectations, among others, the whimsical idea, distinctly exhibited in the book before us, of representing the whirl and throb of Paris existence by a nervous, jolting, breathless diction. Moreover, although Zola himself has treated Daudet with much respect, it is certain that the latter commits one sin against a fundamental canon of realism, that, namely, of sympathizing with his characters instead of dissecting them with the icy, passionless firmness of the surgeon or biologist. Thus he will doubtless be arraigned by headlong partisans of the new school for the species of tenderness with which he depicts the raptures and self-abnegations of unreasoning loyalty; and we may add that some republicans will scarcely think the author has atoned by the unflinching truthfulness of his framework for the pathetic tincture of his picture, by his merciless exposure of royal baseness and futility for the unconscious sigh of pity and regret with which he chronicles the wreck of fine enthusiasms and the unfruitful outcome of inflexible devotion. Nor is the wavering and divided feeling with which the reader lays down this book, notwithstanding the dominant tone of irony and satire, the sole artistic fault of this remarkable performance. Although cast in the form of a novel, and compacted with a certain reference to cumulative effect and climax, " Les Rois en Exil" has no true plot, but is rather a congeries of situations, adjusted with a view of evolving the main characters and demonstrating the intrinsic sterility and absurdity of the Legitimist idea, as

7*

well as the deplorable misdirection and waste of energies entailed upon its votaries. In a word, Daudet's new performance must be classed, not with such perfected and satisfying works of art as "Jack" and "Froment Jeune," but rather with the essays of a propagandist whose controlling aim is less æsthetic than political. Such another book was "Le Nabab," in which the former secretary of the Duc de Morny held up to scorn the garish splendors of the Second Empire, though there, too, he was withheld by the delicate and sympathetic side of his talent from emulating Zola's sweeping and brutal strokes. We may add that both "Le Nabab" and "Les Rois en Exil" seem open to further criticism even on realistic grounds ; for if we go so far as to concede that realism means photography, it is at least clear that the photographs must be anonymous, otherwise the narrative becomes biography and ceases to be a work of art. It is true that this definition might be repudiated by Zola, whose "Son Excellence, Eugene Rougon" is obviously a portrait of Eugene Rouher, the stalwart champion of Napoleon III.

The number of real personages who figure in the foreground, or float, like shadows, in the perspective of this picture, is indeed very large, and those who care more for piquant disclosures of royal delinquencies than for artistic merit may find some amusement in tracing Daudet's characters to their originals. There is, however, a perfunctory and faint effort at disguise, not merely through a transparent change of titles, but by an intentional entanglement of dates and confusion of dynastic relationships, as well as of personal attributes. The ex-King and Queen of Illyria and Dalmatia are, of course, Francis II. of the two Sicilies and his wife, the high-spirited Bavarian Princess who, by her resolute defence of Gaeta, sought to save at least the honor of the Neapolitan crown. So, too, the ex-Queen of Palermo is plainly the Grand Duchess of Parma, who was, however, not the cousin, but the sister-in-law of the Queen of Naples. It is equally manifest that the Duchess of Malines is intended for the Duchesse D'Alençon, though here, too, the relationship is purposely misstated, the Duchess being, we need not say, a sister of the Empress of Austria and Queen of Naples, but in no wise a kinswoman of the Grand Duchess of Parma. In the Queen of Galicia it is easy to recognize Isabella of Spain, though her son is depicted rather with the coarse and tawdry lineaments of Don Carlos, than with the mild and common-place features of Alphonso II. The blind King of Westphalia will at once be identified with the ex-King of Hanover, while it is equally palpable that Prince d'Axel has been drawn from that brutish stigma upon royalty, the late Prince Henry of Orange. But with the exception of the ex-King and Queen of Naples, and of the Prince of Orange, introduced to mark, as it were, the ditch into which the weak and frivolous Francis II. was to fall, the regal exiles are mere phantoms without the faintest influence on the action of the narrative. Scarcely more may be said for the Marquis de Hezeta, in whom the curious may discover a well-known Carlist conspirator; or for the Duc de Rosen, in whom the traits of a certain Neapolitan noble are not exaggerated, including his meek willingness to accept the dishonor of a daughter-in-law, on the ground that his royal master had an indefeasible right to amuse himself with one of his servants; or for the Duc de Fitz-Roy, apropos of whom the allusion to dull historical compends, whose sole readable chapters had been stolen, indicates the author's intention to suggest the Duc de Broglie. So much for such figures in this story as are labelled and ticketed with sufficient distinctness to insure their recognition without a very profound study of the "Almanach de Gotha."

So far as this new work of Daudet's has artistic rather than political aims, they are concentrated on the diverse development of two characters—those, namely, of Francis II. and Queen Maria of Naples, under the sinister pressure of dethronement and impoverishment, amid a narrow, shabby, and degrading environment, in which the single bracing, saving, ennobling element is the presence of an honest royalist by instinct and conviction, a man of the people, who, nevertheless, believes in the divine mission of kings, the son of a poor weaver, whose splendid talents and quenchless enthusiasm had procured him the appointment of tutor to the heir of the exiled monarch. Here we may point out that in the character of this low-born, but incomparable exponent of the royalist faith, as well as in that of the proud, upright, and resolute nature of the Neapolitan Queen, Daudet has evinced the same willingness to reproduce the outlines sketched by a more creative hand, which he betrayed even in his masterpiece of "Fromont jeune et Risler ainé." Just as Madame Risler in that novel was a refined but weakened copy of Flaubert's Madame Bovary, so the ex-Queen of Illyria, in the present book, though her physical and some of her moral traits are copied from those of the Queen of Naples, is in the fundamental conception of her attitude between a worthless consort, wasteful of dignity and opportunity, and a magnificent embodiment of natural kingship in the person of a humble follower, an almost perfect analogue to the royal mistress of "Ruy Blas." It is worth noting that the heroine of Victor Hugo's play, Doña Maria de Neubourg, was, like the Queen of Naples, a Bavarian princess. The coincidence is significant, indicating that artistic instinct compels a resort to Teutonic lineage for the fast-fading type of conscientious, beneficent, and majestic royalty. Certainly it is a fact that with one exception the only dynasties which retain a hold on the respect and affections of their subjects are of German stock, and that the most firmly planted is precisely that which, on the whole, has most distinctly recognized and faithfully fulfilled its duties : namely, the line of Hohenzollern.

The relation of the tutor Méraut to the ex-Queen of Illyria corresponds in all essentials to that occupied by Ruy Blas to the Bavarian Queen of Spain, and if the son of a French weaver does not become Prime Minister, like the Spanish lackey, it is because the exiled Princess has no such post to offer.   As it is, he is the soul of the royalist conspiracies organized to bring about the speedy reinstatement of the disinherited monarchs; conspiracies, by the way, which the reader who remembers the experience of Alphonso II. will not by any means regard with indifference or derision.   Indeed, the state of things which existed in Spain after the flight of Isabella, has been transferred by the novelist to the southern provinces of Italy; while the intrigues of Bourbon partisans in the Spanish Cortes during the short reign of Amadeus and the succeeding years are but thinly cloaked in the imaginary proceedings of the Diet of Leybach.   Moreover, the abdication of Isabella, which was indispensable to the success of the Bourbon cause in Spain, is reproduced in the act of renunciation imposed upon the ex-King of Illyria by the solemn and unflinching demand of Méraut, who, at this crisis, stands forth as the spokesman of the Queen, as the teacher and inspirer of the heir apparent, and as the vindicator of outraged royalty and a tarnished crown.   We may add that these unflagging and precious services rendered to the monarchical cause by a liegeman of humble birth, are by no means the only points in the narrative which recall Victor Hugo's drama.   Like Ruy Blas, Méraut has the gift of a flaming, infectious, irresistible eloquence, and it is while listening to an outburst of steadfast faith, dauntless purpose, and soaring aspiration, from which the shallow and conventional spirits of her attendants turn away in perplexity and something like disgust, that the Queen

awakens to the true nature of the sentiment which this
base-born savior of empires has kindled in her breast.
It is needless to point out how forcibly we are here reminded of that scene in "Ruy Blas" where from an
alcove of the council chamber Doña Maria overhears the
scorching rebuke administered by Ruy Blas to the knot
of thievish Ministers, and his superb apostrophe to the
shade of the Emperor Charles :

> Charles Quint, dans ce temps d'opprobre et de terreur
> Que fais tu dans ta tombe, O puissant Empereur !
> O lève toi ! viens voir !   Les bons font place aux pires ;
> Ce royaume effrayant, fait d'un amas d'empires,
> Penche—il nous faut ton bras—au secours, Charles Quint !
> Car l'Espagne se meurt, car l'Espagne s'éteint.

We are also made to remember how Spain's German
Queen, mindful with a proud humility of how powerless
she is, wedded to the semblance of a king, to bestow an
adequate guerdon on the single-armed upholder of a
crumbling realm, gives him for recompense only the one
word " merci," but in that one word she puts her heart.

Not only has Daudet borrowed something from Victor
Hugo as regards the humble birth and rearing and the
self-effacing posture of Méraut, the born apostle and unapproached protagonist of the legitimist faith, but in
the physical aspect and intellectual traits of this great-
hearted loyalist we cannot but recognize a well-known
historical personage.   In the flaming southern blood and
vehement gesture of Méraut, in his massive vitality,
coupled with the swift, acute vibrations of his nervous

system, in his leonine head, with its tossing mane and flashing eyes, in his visage, seamed with lines, not of age, but of emotion, and in the rushing, sweeping flow of his spontaneous eloquence, we can see that the author means us to recognize Mirabeau, not as he was, but as he might have been but for the bruises and storm-stains of a tempestuous life, and but for the stubborn, fatal reluctance of Marie Antoinette to accept the one defender who might have saved the monarchy. Those who bear in mind how utterly Mirabeau's intellect was the slave of his instincts and sentiments, and how far he recoiled in the last months of his career under the impulse of a dormant loyalty, quickened by the tardy appeal of a high-souled queen and woman, will acknowledge that in Méraut the author has reproduced the great orator of the States-General, only diverging so far from history as to enlist him on the side to which his traditions and inherited proclivities would have inclined him. Like Mirabeau, Méraut is a prophet rather than a philosopher, an evangelist rather than an expounder ; his spacious intellect is the servant, not the master of his heart, and responds, like some well-attuned and far-resounding instrument, to the touch of deep emotion ; he does not scrutinize his axioms, but accepts them blindly, and bends his puissant energies to the propagation of principles he has never stopped to weigh. Like Mirabeau, too, he is mighty rather in the spoken utterance than with the written word, because his large and lusty faculties seem to need the bounding impulse of an upright posture, of swelling lungs and brandished arms, and, above all, the electric animation shot forth from the eyes of a wrapt audience.

This figure of Méraut is, beyond comparison, the most virile and majestic that Daudet has ever aimed to draw ; and, although the outlines may be familiar, the coloring and movement are so vigorous that there is ample room for eulogy of the author's talent. Neither is it easy to speak with merely temperate encomium of the companion portrait—the wronged, insulted, disappointed, and disillusionized princess, who sees the volatile nature of her Neapolitan husband sink lower and lower in the depths of Paris debauchery, until the lustre of the crown and the honor of the gentleman are alike befouled and lost. There is something heroic in the constancy with which this high-hearted daughter of Suabian dukes, amid the cruel shipwreck of her conjugal aspirations and the thousand petty stings of unaccustomed poverty, clings to her belief in a sublime, irrevocable mission of kingship, in the fixed sanctity of a crown, despite its transient defilement on the brows of an unworthy wearer, and to the faith that her son, nourished with her own pure aims, and uplifted by the teachings of Méraut's lofty genius, will yet redeem a sullied and seemingly hopeless cause.

Side by side with these unwavering, austere, majestic figures, the heroes and martyrs of a shattered faith, Daudet portrays the listless, heedless, unstable comportment of its titular standard bearer, its official representative, the despicable ex-King of Illyria. We see him accepting, without protest, the spurious prestige won through the pious lie by which the wife transferred to her worthless husband the credit of her own gallantry at the siege of Gaeta ; debauching the daughter of his most devoted partisan, and outraging the decencies of life by giving the queen a rival in her own household ; stealing the crown jewels, and pawning them to pay his debts at cards ; reeling home drunk and witless at an hour when a deputation of his subjects representing a majority of the national Parliament were waiting to concert measures for his restoration ; ready to sell for money, in order to appease the importunities of a courtesan, the dynastic rights transmitted from his ancestors, and which he held in trust for his own son ; and only hindered, at the last moment, from signing an instrument to that effect by the threat of suicide on the part of the distracted queen, a menace which he could not doubt would be straightway executed. So, too, when a project of counter-revolution has been matured, and his friends, embarked in the expedition which is to kindle the uprising, are expecting their prince to lead them, he is coaxed aside by the ignoble bait of a new intrigue, and leaves them to die alone. And, finally, after running through the whole gamut of dissipation, from the elegant vices of the self-esteeming sensualist, to the crapulence and lewdness of the dance hall and the gutter, we find him guilty of a baseness to which even the comrade of his orgies had been a stranger. It could at least be said of the Prince d'Axel, in whom, as we have said, the late Prince of Orange is depicted, that in whatever slough of animalism he might wallow, he had at least accepted the stain of his own ignominy. When, therefore, the ex-King of Illyria imputes to his friend and boon companion a crime of which a court of justice is about to take stern cognizance, we cannot but feel that the bold cynicism with which Prince d'Axel takes the offence on his own shoulders clothes him with a kind of respectability compared with the liar and the dastard. But although in the end the king's character undergoes such complete deterioration, the steps of the descent are graduated with much art; as if the author meant to show us that the normal type of royalty differs in no wise from an ordinary person, being, so far as inherited disposition is concerned, neither much better nor much worse than the mass of men about us—than the sons of railroad contractors and pork-merchants, who succumb by scores every year to the seductions of Paris. Indeed the ex-King of Illyria has rather more than the usual good humor and attractiveness remarked in shallow natures. He likes to see people cheerful about him, and is willing enough to spare others suffering or annoyance, provided he can do so without the sacrifice of habit or caprice. He is conscious, too, of his grotesque incompetence for the august requirements of his royal rôle. He knows the idol of his loyal Illyrians is a sorry piece of brittle clay ; he does not want to be a king ; he wants nothing but a bank account and the opportunity of free living without the irksome exactions of official duties and the oppressive consciousness of rank. His experience has taught him how incongruous and absurd is the position of a king in exile, and how futile is the effort to uphold his titular dignity by the mockery of etiquette and ceremony.

The contrast between royalty as it is in the person of "Christian II.," and royalty as it seems to be in the eyes of fervent zealots; between the intrinsic worthlessness of the object venerated and the immense devotion called forth on its behalf; is strikingly emphasized by a scene in the French Academy, where, among the prizes distributed, the highest is awarded to an eloquent monograph of the siege of Gaeta, published as the composition of the Prince de Rosen, though, in fact, the hand of Méraut had penned every line. The monarchical coterie, we are told, had profited by the occasion to organize a sort of moral demonstration against the republican government, under the pretext of applauding the heroic conduct falsely attributed to the King of Illyria by the self-effacement of his wife, and grandly chronicled by Méraut in his memorial of the siege. It was understood that the Duc de Fitz-Roy, who was to read a report on the works crowned by the Academy, would turn to particular account the ardent passages of the fine pamphlet, and thus record one of those sly protests against the existing state of things in which the Academy indulged itself, even under the Second Empire, and of which it has been especially lavish under the republic. This scene is drawn with so much care, and there is such a manifest intent on the part of the satirist to photograph in its minutest details the academical ceremony, that we may permit ourselves to glance at the interesting proceedings.

Premising that at this species of ovation offered him, by reason of the spurious reputation for gallant conduct which his queen had managed to create for him, the King of Illyria, by way of appreciative recompense, had placed his mistress in a box opposite to that occupied by his wife and son, we will proceed to note one or two of the incidents which followed the opening of the session. It was the noble Duc de Fitz-Roy, as we have said, who read the report on this occasion, and everybody, says the novelist, was constrained to admire the way in which he rose, moved forward, and set his papers in order on the regulation green table. Stooping, spindle-shanked, round-shouldered, he looked like a man of seventy, though he was in reality a score of years younger. On his ill-made shrunken body wagged a puny head with unformed features and a complexion suggesting the hue of parboiled flesh, the whole framed in ragged side whiskers and a few tufts of hair. To the women, however, he seems distinguished-looking, for they cannot forget he is a Fitz-Roy; and it was the same lustre of his long genealogy, in which knaves and blockheads have not been wanting, that procured him admission to the Academy much more than his historical writings, meagre, sapless compilations, among which the first volume

only had some real value. It is true that this particular volume was written by somebody else ; and could the
noble Fitz-Roy recognize in the rear of the Illyrian
Queen's box the broad and luminous forehead which
gave birth to his best work, perhaps, says the author, he
would not gather up the sheets of his discourse with
that air of supreme and disdainful mastery, or begin his
lecture with that haughty sweeping glance which sees
nothing, yet dominates the whole assembly. In a pale,
labored, flaccid style the Duc begins a pompous eulogy
of the so-called Memorial, written, so he tells his audience, by the young Prince Herbert de Rosen, "who
handles the pen as he does the sword," and then passes
to a panegyric of the hero who inspired the monograph
"of that chivalrous Christian II., in whom meet the
grace, the nobility, the strength, and captivating charm
invariably encountered on the steps of the throne."
Now and then, amid these empty, commonplace, bombas-
tic periods sounds a true, ringing note, some quotation
from Méraut's text, for which the queen had furnished
all the documents, everywhere substituting, however,
the king's name for her own. The crowd applauds
with an instinctive discernment the citation of strong
words breathing a proud and careless valor, the story of
heroic acts performed with a superb simplicity, and told
by Méraut in a bounding, figurative prose that called to
mind the epics of old times ; and the result is that, observing the rapturous welcome given to such extracts,
the noble Fitz-Roy, who is no fool, shuts off his own

literary outgivings, and contents himself with turning over the finest pages of the pamphlet. Roused by the accents of conviction to a genuine enthusiasm, the whole audience springs to its feet, breaks into loud acclaims, salutes the incarnation of monarchy, vanquished yet glorious, in the wife and child of Christian II., the last of knightly sovereigns. The little prince, intoxicated, like all children, by the uproar, applauds, too, in his naïve way, while the queen, drawing a little back, feels herself swept away by this explosion of electric sympathy, and yields her worn heart to the blissful illusion of the moment. She has succeeded then, she thinks, in clothing with an aureole this spectre of a king behind whom she has been masked, in gilding with fresh lustre that Illyrian crown her boy shall one day wear, with a lustre, too, that no one, not even his father, can besmirch. How trivial now seem all the pangs of exile, betrayal, insult, in this dazzling moment which has drowned all the surrounding shadow. Suddenly she turns, remembering to pay due homage for her joy to him, who, standing behind her, obscure, unknown, unthought of, his head pressed against the wall, and his eyes fixed upon the sky, has listened to those magic phrases unmindful that they are his own, has looked on at this brave triumph without a sneer or a sigh, without bethinking himself an instant that he has been robbed of all this glory. Like those monks of the middle ages who grew old in rearing anonymous cathedrals, the weaver's son is content to do his work like a workman,

to see it rise firm and massive, and towering in the sun-
light.	And for all Méraut's abnegation, for the self-
immolation of his smile, for the soul which she knows
vibrates in kinship with her own, the wife of Christian
II. can only put out a white hand with a soft *"merci—
merci!"*

Another scene is fraught with illusions no less radiant,
though fated to be as transient, that, namely, in the
modest apartments of the queen, where the pledge of
abdication extorted from the shuffling monarch is form-
ally carried out.	As the crown, dishonored by the
father, is set upon the innocent brows of a child already
sensitive to noble admonitions, and destined, it appears,
to reward with proud fruition the mother's hopes and
prayers, Méraut's faith in the future of royalty, in the
mission of kings on earth, which at times had flickered
and grown faint, blazes up once more with the old fer-
vor.	But how precarious seem the prospects of a cause
whose triumph hinges on a filament so slender as an in-
fant's life or health.	Is it well to risk the welfare of a
people on a chance so hazardous, to stake on such a venture the anxious lives and willing deaths of men like
Méraut, to waste the splendid powers of their capacious
intellects on an anachronism, a mirage, a dream ?	Such
is the lesson which Alphonse Daudet enforces with the
cogency of veracious portraiture, and the mordant irony
of example in "Les Rois en Exil."

WHATEVER shortcomings and limitations may be ascribed to Longfellow's genius, it is certain that no contemporary poet, not even Tennyson, has been so universally and cordially welcomed by the English-speaking race. Neither has any Englishman since Byron approached so nearly to a world-wide reputation, for there is scarcely any country of Europe where some acquaintance with Longfellow's writings is not accounted an essential element of culture. If, moreover, he had never written a line of original verse, his reproduction of the Divine Comedy would have challenged respect for its author and his country, since perhaps no man has more nearly satisfied Dryden's well-known definition of right translation, " true to the sense but truer to the fame."

It is obvious that the favor of contemporaries constitutes a letter of credit which posterity may decline to accept at its face value. Circumstances, of course, may foster, as well as depress, an author ; and it is conceivable that the consummate adjustment of his work to the taste and sentiment dominant in his age and country might assure to a given poet such ardent sympathy that the task of cold and rigorous analysis would be gladly remitted to another generation. How inflexibly that function is then executed, and how vainly isolated gems appeal to the niggard hand which is incessantly weeding the roll of honor, is demonstrated by the permanent eclipse of Pope's reputation and the precipitate decline of Moore's, no less than by the crescent fame of Wordsworth.

It is probable that Longfellow received in his lifetime as much praise as he may fairly claim, and there seemed to be a tacit agreement on the part of reviewers and other arbiters of opinion to postpone the estimate of his merits to a later day. Even by English critics he was for many years treated with peculiar gentleness, while at home, if we except the assault by Edgar Poe, which was discredited by its excessive acerbity, he can hardly be said to have been criticised at all. And yet the precise appraisement of Longfellow's performances, as well as the inquiry into the ground and nature of the popularity which he unquestionably enjoys, cannot well be neglected by one who would comprehend the historical development and the actual status of our native literature.

It would be difficult to guess the characteristic stamp and natural scope of Longfellow's genius from a catalogue of his works, for he has tried his wing in many directions. Nor is it at all surprising to find the conscious possession of artistic power unaccompanied by any clear perception of its specific quality and compass. Painters, it is true, seem willing enough to confine their labors within a particular province ; but poets are slow to recognize limitations, which, nevertheless, are inexorably demonstrated by the very efforts made to evade them. What was effected, for instance, by Byron's reiterated essays in dramatic verse, beyond the exposure of his curious weakness in characterization; and how incredibly ponderous and flat is Milton's attempt to portray, with lyrical grace and lightness, the domestic joys of Eden. The truth is that the old division of the poetic field by the river Loire went deeper than distinctions of race and language, and the special qualities of the story-telling *Trouvère,* who touched something like epic grandeur in the *Roland,* and half forestalled in the *Roman de la Rose* the social photography of the modern novel, were resumed for Englishmen in Chaucer, while Burns continued the very different traditions of those Provençal Troubadours, whose fitful lays seldom interpreted any broader theme than the raptures and disquietudes of love. To whichever of these schools a man belongs, in whichever province, whether narrative or lyric, his poetic talent more willingly exerts itself, it is evident that his work lies there, and that he will gain no substantial credit by excursive experiments. Thus it might not be difficult to show that Longfellow's forte is lyric verse; that whenever he is signally felicitous it is in this direction; that in the ratio of his divergence from it his failures are more or less decisive; and that the compulsory employment of his energies in wholly uncongenial tasks is chargeable with some productions by no means worthy of his reputation.

The first volumes published by Longfellow were largely made up of translations, and his selection of subjects for reproduction revealed the bent and quality of his mind. It was plain that he was instinctively attracted by the Spanish and German song-writers, and especially by utterances of their more serious and pensive moods. With Uhland in particular he discovered a sympathy so intimate, and assimilated so thoroughly the delicate aroma of his model's verse, that poems like "The Beleagured City," "Nuremberg," the "Belfry of Bruges," and "Walter von der Vogelweide," can scarcely be discriminated from the work of the German balladist. Indeed, the attitude of Uhland's mind, and the strange, haunting charm of his melody, were curiously congenial to the temper of cultivated New England people at the date of Longfellow's début. The anti-slavery movement had not yet shocked men into earnestness and compelled their energies to the business of the hour. While, moreover, political questions awakened but a languid interest, what scope was there for scholastic or æsthetic expansion within the contracted bounds of a provincial civilization, where books were not abundant and travelled men were few, where not a single fine picture or statue, nor a vestige of noble architecture, could be found? Uhland, too, though for somewhat different reasons, was profoundly dissatisfied with his surroundings. He had a keen eye for the shortcomings of the present, and beholding the past through a mist which magnified outlines and obscured blemishes, he was half persuaded that Germany had retrograded since the days of the Minnesingers. Of course, an accurate knowledge of mediæval life would be a positive nuisance to those who love to dwell among the legends and romantic lore of chivalry ; and accordingly ballad makers of Uhland's school prefer to veracious illumination the light that never was on sea or shore, and are accustomed to steep their work in sentiment which would be pleasing enough, were it not an anachronism. Regarded as reflecting in any sort the texture and colors of actual life in bygone times, such poetry is the mere cloud-work of a dream, the beautiful but preposterous mirage conjured up by weary and yearning eyes.

Had Longfellow contented himself with mirroring the fantastic predilections and tentative dilettanteism of a particular class, his audience might have been as esoteric as Matthew Arnold's. But in the collection entitled, " Voices of the Night," were two or three short poems, and notably the " Psalm of Life," pitched in a key manifestly alien to the writer's prevailing mood, but well calculated to win the ear and engage the suffrages of plain people. We have heard the above-named little lyric gravely cited as a compendium of wholesome ethics, when plainly the whole philosophy of the " Psalm" consists in a vehement begging of the question, in the clever marshalling and burnishing of almost Tupperian commonplaces. No doubt the author often smiled to find his good-natured attempt to emphasize some odds and ends of current rhetoric rated by not a few of his readers as the captain jewel of his carcanet.

It would be absurd to suppose that a reputation like

our author's was built upon nothing more enduring than the charm of a broad culture, the dexterous reproduction of the pseudo-mediæval ballad, or those vigorous exhortations to be "up and doing," which divide with "Excelsior" the applause of our common schools. His popularity, doubtless, has many elements, but one is of a very sterling sort, and to this he may reasonably look for durable and fond remembrance. We refer to that remarkable series of household lyrics which appeared during the first ten years of the poet's literary life. They are not very numerous, but are to be found scattered through the earlier volumes, shrinking bashfully behind some elaborate paraphrase from the Swedish or Gascon—a score, perhaps, in all. Their dress is of the plainest, and they seem in a measure like waifs or changelings, as if the author had forgotten to affix his private mark. It was not long, however, before these tender and touching outgivings—"The Rainy Day," "The Bridge," "Maidenhood," "Daybreak," and kindred songs—found a home by every fireside in America and England, and like the south wind or the carol of spring birds, proved as welcome to the palace as to the cottage. And very likely had Longfellow been born in Scotland, and grown up, like Burns, in obscurity and poverty, he might have sung always thus. It is certain that in the pathos and simplicity of these modest, naïve creations we touch the high-water mark of his achievement, for they remain to this day more widely known and warmly cherished than any of his later, more ambitious and sustained performances. Nor can the judgment well be accounted harsh which, while questioning the success of his experiments in some directions, recognizes Longfellow's claim to a high place in the choir of which Burns is a leader and Shelley an ornament.

While we can give no praise to Longfellow's management of narrative verse, except in the instance of "Evangeline," we need not now dwell at any great length on his comparative miscarriage in that field. It may be said that the stories rehearsed at the "Wayside Inn" were for the most part "twice-told tales," and could hardly be expected to stimulate the languid appetites of modern readers, glutted as they are with piquant novelties. Under an artist's hand, however, the old, faint outlines should have been made to retreat behind the finished picture—the limpid current of the narrative, the crisp, strong characters encountered, and the breezy atmosphere inhaled combining to displace the earlier versions precisely as the shapes and colors of waking life exorcise the shadows of a dream. But the fact that Longfellow could see no misnomer in the term "romance" as applied to his "Hyperion" was of itself a sufficient indication that he would almost always fail to apprehend, or to observe, the fundamental laws of story-telling.

When Longfellow directed his attention to the legendary treasures of America, it is plain that he had the great opportunity of his life, and it is almost equally clear that, through the inherent weakness of the particular theme which he elected to interpret, he substantially renounced it. But aside from the meagreness of its subject matter, "Hiawatha" fails in other ways to answer the requirements of a narrative style. No doubt the landscape painting is often charming, and the facile grace which marks Longfellow's compositions is still discernible through the gyves of an awkward and artificial metre. But the pictures of Indian manners, although painstaking, are not vivid, the incidents are few and unimpressive, and the threads of connection slight. The characterization is particularly faint, Hiawatha and Minnehaha being rather phantoms than persons, and the general result is a congeries of crude materials instead of an organic, vital poem. The book was received on its first appearance with considerable enthusiasm; but it is now read with the same listless interest as Southey's "Thalaba," and seems likely to be consigned to the same oblivion.

Neither can the "Courtship of Miles Standish" be considered a felicitous exhibition of the author's powers. There is not much briskness in the movement of the story, and the characters are scarcely adapted to elicit sympathy. There are certain homely themes which can be safely treated only with the rugged, honest realism of which George Eliot had the secret, and any attempt to idealize and exalt them is apt to end in something like burlesque. The captain of a corporal's guard, whose warlike exploits are limited to brow-beating half a dozen timid savages, is not a very heroic figure, except in the sense that a child's terrors in the dark may be accounted tragical. People forget what the Spaniards had been doing throughout the previous century when they talk of the Mayflower's voyage as something calling for exceptional fortitude, and seek to invest with epic dignity the somewhat prosaic privations which her pilgrims encountered on a peaceful shore. The services of Miles Standish were doubtless of some value to the Plymouth colony; but, perhaps, the rude sincerity of "Gulliver" would have depicted them more faithfully than Longfellow's pensive hyperbole.

Against these less successful productions it is fair to set "Evangeline." There is so much sweetness and beauty in this poem, such exquisite tenderness and poignant pathos that we are well content to overlook the looseness of its construction and surrender ourselves again and again to its soft spell. The choice of subject was most happy, for English colonial annals present few incidents fraught with so much sadness and so responsive to the gentle melancholy which pervades Longfellow's verse as the fate of Acadie. To this day the western coast of Nova Scotia, blessed as it is in a mild climate and fertile soil, discovers many traces of the patient industry which made of this district a French Eden. Religion has often had her voluntary exiles, but it was loyalty which controlled those simple *habitans*, who might easily have kept their pleasant farms by a formal oath of allegiance, but whose integrity rejected even that shadow of compromise with principle because, as one of them put it, "he might swear with an English mind, but his heart would still be French." The unswerving constancy and meek resignation of this singular people are accented in the figure of Evangeline, which, though it may lack some human touches and seems hardly a denizen of earth, is securely niched in the affections of very many, and nobly embodies their purest aspirations. But it must be said that Evangeline alone, of all the characters Longfellow has aimed to draw, stands forth in the memory of his readers with some distinctness of outline.

It may be questioned whether a novel and elaborate metre was suited to the artless narrative of a village girl's misfortunes. Until it has been more completely naturalized in English, the hexameter line must always in some degree divert attention from the thought to the mere vehicle of expression. At present it cannot be properly pronounced by those who are not classical scholars. Moreover, in the conduct of a metrical experiment it is well to follow closely the fundamental scheme of your model, and not perplex the scholar's ear by a license of variation scarcely sanctioned by authority. Now, the sluggish and ponderous effect produced by the use of a spondee in the fifth place, is twenty times more frequent in "Evangeline" than in Ovid or Virgil. And, again, since nine-tenths of our English poetry has preferred the iambic movement, an author writing dactylic verse cannot safely make the first foot a spondee, for an English ear will instinctively mistake it for the beginning of an iambic line. These slips might be easily avoided, but neither vigilance nor practice would enable us to reach the comparative grace and airiness of German hexameters, a multitude of monosyllabic words, and that division of compound verbs by which the prefix is thrown to the end of a sentence, giving that language a decisive advantage. No English adventure in this direction has approached the smoothness of Voss's Homeric translations.

One other example of Longfellow's descriptive manner deserves brief mention—the "Building of the Ship." So far as the poem chronicles, in a vein half lyric half pictorial, the varied phenomena of the ship-yard, it is nervous and effective, but the attempt to enliven the narration with a little character-drawing wholly fails. Instead of the short, sharp strokes which might have shown us the virile, rough-hewn lineaments of the man, we are asked to imagine a Yankee shipwright, while engaged in fashioning the model of a vessel, running over in his mind the absurdities of Tudor naval architecture. Presently, too, when he smokes his evening pipe, the old man is made to indulge in some curious reminiscences worth quoting, because they exemplify the not infrequent vagueness of our author's imagery, and his random use of geographical names. Thus he portrays the "magic charm of foreign lands : "

> Where the tumbling surf
> O'er the coral reef of Madagascar
> Washes the feet of the swarthy Lascar
> As he lies alone and asleep on the turf.

The phenomenon of turf growing on a reef below high water mark is certainly suggestive of "magic ;" but what business has an East Indian Lascar to be asleep on a South African Island ? And yet we have heard these identical lines adduced in perfect seriousness to illustrate the "weird" music of Longfellow's verse.

It is clear that any deficiency in the power of consecutive movement and distinct characterization, essential to success even in Chaucer's vein, would make itself more fatally conspicuous in the field of dramatic poetry. Nevertheless, Mr. Longfellow has several times adopted a dramatic form, in the " Spanish Student," for instance, and the " Golden Legend." Of the former it is enough to say that it is a comedy without actors, neither the student nor his Gitana sweetheart being competent to impress us with the reality of their existence. Two or three songs, however, intercalated in the piece, have been plucked from their cumbrous setting, and placed among our household treasures.

We were informed by the local critics who stood sponsors to the latter poem that it must be esteemed an important American contribution to those mystical, metaphysical outgivings of which Faust and Manfred are types ; and a number of ingenious parallels were instituted tending to exalt the psychological profoundness and ethical worth of the " Golden Legend." Thereupon the docile American public straightway ranked it with the books which nobody reads, but everybody concedes to be worth reading. What a brave, robust, and trustworthy thing was our native criticism between the years 1830 and 1850, and what a ruthless eye it had for shallow sentiment and flimsy thinking ! Is it possible to imagine any spectacle more ridiculous than the attitude of those provincial wiseacres cocking their ears to catch a fancied echo of Gœthe's Titan song, and sniffing doubtfully at those modest lyrics upon which, in spite of the reaction here and there provoked by foolish eulogy, Longfellow has built a real and lasting fame.

If we examine the fundamental texture and essential quality of this writer's work, we find nothing in it distinctively American. It never occurs to us to say of his performances, as we are continually impelled to say of Bryant's or Whittier's, this or that verse could only have been penned by one born and bred in the atmosphere of the New World. Neither have Longfellow's productions an English flavor ; indeed, it would be difficult to name an English poet the cast and temper of whose mind reveal any strong affinities with his. Few men have been more catholic in their sympathies, more cosmopolitan in their range of study, and we seem to trace in him at different epochs a half-conscious surrender to the influence of three distinct foreign schools. But while these have tinged and shaped the larger part of his creations, his inquisitive and assimilative intellect has rambled into more sequestered fields, and delicate flowers from Provence and Portugal, as well as hardy plants from Sweden and Gascony, have proved obedient to his transplanting hand, and learned to thrive and

blossom in his garden.   Take for instance the following
from the Swedish of Bishop Tegner :

Love among mortals

Is but an endless sigh !   He longs and endures and stands waiting,
Suffers, and yet rejoices, and smiles with tears on his eyelids ;
Hope, so is called upon earth his recompense, Hope, the be-
    friending.
Does what she can, for she points evermore up to Heaven, and
    faithful—
Plunges her anchor's peak in the depths of the grave, and be-
    neath it
Paints a more beautiful world, a dim but a sweet play of shadows.

Add to this a single familiar stanza, which seems to
exhibit the perfection of translation, from Malherbe's
famous consolatory epistle :

> But she was of the world which fairest things exposes
>   To fates the most forlorn,
> A rose, she too hath lived as long as live the roses,
>   The space of one brief morn.

To appreciate the finish of work like this we should
set the original beside it :

> Mais elle était d'un monde où les plus belles choses
>   Ont le pire destin,
> Et rose, elle a vécu ce que vivent les roses,
>   L'espace d'un matin.

Excursions of this sort, however, were only the episodes of a long literary career, and it is chiefly from Calderon and Lopez de Vega, from Dante, Petrarch, and
Tasso, but above all from those Germans balladists like

Bürger, Wieland, and Uhland, who have aimed to resuscitate in a sublime and dainty form the romantic rhapsodies of the Minnesingers, that Longfellow has drawn his inspiration. It will be noted that all these writers, however distinct their rank in the poetic hierarchy, and however divergent the direction and character of their work, have yet one trait in common, a certain gravity and solemnity, a pervading sense of the seriousness of life, and a profound acquaintance with human sorrows. In most of them there is scarcely a trace of humor, but their power over the stronger emotions is extraordinary, and they are the sovereign masters of pathos.

Now it has doubtless been remarked by every reader that in the wide range of Longfellow's poetry there is absolutely nothing to evoke a smile, much less a laugh, while, on the other hand, no English singer has more frequently commanded the homage of moistened eyes. It is not only that his verse abounds in moving incidents recommended to sympathy by a delicate and patient art, but he has subtle pathetic touches, peculiarly his own, which stir the heart we know not why, and affect us with a mysterious, inexplicable sadness. As illustrations of that vague, tristful manner we might cite "My Lost Youth" with its dreamy refrain :

> The voice of that wayward song
> Is singing and saying still :
> A boy's will is the wind's will,
> And the thoughts of youth are long, long thoughts.

Or again, in a slightly different key, the two final stanzas of "The Open Window." It is, of course, the last four lines to which we would direct attention :

> The birds sang in the branches
>   With sweet, familiar tone,
> But the voices of the children
>   Will be heard in dreams alone.
>
> And the boy that walked beside me
>   He could not understand
> Why closer in mine, ah, closer,
>   I pressed his warm, soft hand.

So, too, in the introduction to "Hiawatha," there are a dozen lines steeped in the same mild melancholy. We may add that this is one of those instances where the porch is finer than the temple. The following is the passage :

> Ye who sometimes in your rambles
> Through the green lanes of the country,
> Where the tangled barberry bushes
> Hang their tufts of crimson berries
> Over stone walls gray with mosses,
> Pause by some neglected graveyard
> For a while to muse and ponder
> On a half-effaced inscription,
> Writ with little skill of song-craft ;
> Homely phrases, but each letter
> Full of hope and yet of heart-break,
> Full of all the tender pathos

> Of the Here and the Hereafter ;
> Stay and read this rude inscription,
> Read this song of Hiawatha.

It is impossible to think of Longfellow, and especially of his efforts in this direction, without recalling " Evangeline," which may well be ranked among the superlative exhibitions of pathetic power. The poem, indeed, may be said to traverse the whole gamut of tender emotion, from the deep-drawn sigh of resignation to the passionate sob of yearning and hope deferred ; but there are certain moments and certain scenes wherein the exquisite features of the heroine seem transfigured with intensity of feeling. Thus in the earlier years of her long pilgrimage we find Evangeline's mood shadowed in the words which suggested the well-known picture :

> Something there was in her life incomplete, imperfect, unfinished ;
> As if a morning of June, with all its music and sunshine
> Suddenly paused in the sky, and, fading, slowly descended
> Into the east again, from which it late had arisen.
> Sometimes she lingered in towns till urged by the fever within
>   her,
> Urged by a restless longing, the hunger and thirst of the spirit,
> She would commence again her endless search and endeavor,
> Sometimes in churchyards strayed, and gazed on the crosses and
>   tombstones,
> Sat by some nameless grave, and thought that perhaps in its
>   bosom
> He was already at rest, and she longed to slumber beside him.

Years glide on, and the wandering maiden is seen in

strange and distant places till at length the fruitless
search is given over.   Yet

Gabriel was not forgotten.   Within her heart was his image,
Clothed in the beauty of love and youth, as last she beheld him,
Only more beautiful, made by his death-like silence and absence ;
Over him years had no power, he was not changed but transfigured;
Patience, and abnegation of self, and devotion to others,
This was the lesson a life of trial and sorrow had taught her ;
So was her love diffused, but like to some odorous spices,
Suffered no wasten or loss, though filling the air with aroma.

She finds at last the lover of her youth, in a hospital,
friendless and dying, and kneels by his bedside :

Vainly he strove to whisper her name, for the accents unuttered
Died on his lips, and their motion revealed what his tongue would
    have spoken.
Vainly he strove to rise ; and Evangeline kneeling beside him
Kissed his dying lips, and laid his head on her bosom.
All was ended now, the hope and the fear and the sorrow ;
All the aching of heart, the restless, unsatisfied longing,
All the dull, deep pain and constant anguish of patience ;
And as she pressed once more the lifeless head to her bosom,
Meekly she bowed her own and murmured, " Father, I thank thee!"

And then we listen to the concluding strophes, which,
like the faltering strains of some sad symphony, breathe
the requiem of the faithful lovers :

Still stands the forest primeval, but far away from its shadow,
Side by side in their nameless graves, the lovers are sleeping ;
Under the humble walls of the little Catholic church-yard,
In the heart of the city they lie, unknown and unnoticed.

Daily the tides of life go ebbing and flowing beside them ;
Thousands of throbbing hearts where theirs are at rest and forever,
Thousands of aching brains where theirs no longer are busy,
Thousands of toiling hands where theirs have ceased from their
    labors,
Thousands of weary feet where theirs have completed their journey.

And now one word respecting that proneness to imitation, and to the occasional assimilation of others' thoughts and images, which have been ascribed to Longfellow. Doubtless with him, as with all men of ripe culture, certain ideas and even forms of expression may be traced to this or that extraneous source. But the simple test of an author's right to borrow is this : Is he able to lend ? There is no question that the stumbling Pegasus of many an ill-provisioned bard has been fed at Longfellow's crib. We confess ourselves a little tired of this charge of plagiarism preferred so glibly by those who, when they try to purloin on their own account, behave like the Italian thief, who, as the author of " Hudibras " averred, never robs but he murders to prevent discovery. No man was ever more open to accusations of this sort than Ben Jonson, and it is well to bear in mind what Dryden said of that writer : " He invades authors like a monarch, and what would be piracy in others is only victory in him.".

I.

THERE is a writer who at this moment is the most striking, positive, and original personage among French men of letters, and who yet was long almost wholly unknown, except by name, to English readers. Whether our tastes or our convictions prompt us to side with those who praise, or with those who scout him, the fact is beyond dispute that Emile Zola has attained a measure of success seldom paralleled in our generation, and that his themes and his style, his aims, methods, and performances have provoked the widest attention and the liveliest discussion throughout Europe. The truth is that the author of the series of novels, grouped together under the generic title of *Les Rougon-Macquart* is a phenomenon that invites at once the study of the artist, the scientist, and the politician. As regards subject and treatment, Emile Zola incarnates an æsthetic revolution, while in his social and political leanings he represents the literary side of the great upheaval which followed the collapse of the second empire. Still more curious and suggestive is his deliberate application of Darwinism to literature, his portrayal of life and character under the strict conditions of the evolutionary theory, namely, heredity and atavism on the one hand, with environment and natural or sexual selection on the other. These are Zola's credentials, and such a man deserves to be scanned, if not with sympathy and approval, at all events with respect as the type of an epoch.

M. Zola would probably contend that his distinctive attitude as a student of human life is mainly due to physical causes, including, of course, hereditary aptitudes. He would not repudiate, however, the influence exercised by intellectual ancestors, whose works by virtue of a subtle affinity, or of long contact at an impressionable age, may have tinctured, developed, or directed his mind. He is not unwilling to be counted the successor of writers who have recognized more or less distinctly the same aims—as the latest exponent of a school whose origin may be traced back for a century. He himself calls Rousseau the founder of realistic narrative in France, having in view, of course, the *Confessions,* and not the *Nouvelle Héloise* as some of his critics have imagined. But Rousseau only suggested the tremendous force that lies in naked veracity, and it was Balzac who first carried out the process of ruthless vivisection on a great scale. The wonderful minuteness with which the individual characters of his persons were projected by the author of the *Comédie Humaine,* and the painstaking accuracy of the surroundings in which he placed them, sharply distinguished his treatment from Victor Hugo's exaggerated coloring on the one hand, and from George Sand's pursuit of abstract types upon the other.   But although Balzac diverged at once from romantic and from classical models, he did not always evince the scrupulous, and, so to speak, mechanical fidelity of the modern naturalists.   He was no mere photographer, a strangely fecund fancy and an irresistible instinct of generalization not seldom forcing him to transform individuals into veritable types, as in the case of *Rastignac*, or *Lucien de Rubempré*, or *La Femme de trente Ans*.   After Balzac's death realism in literature lost its hold on the French world for almost a generation.   Something, it is true, was done by the co-workers Erckmann-Chatrian within a restricted provincial horizon, something by Emile Gaboriau in the almost unworked field of the judicial and detective novel, and something on a wider canvas by the brothers Goncourt. But if we except some of Gaboriau's stories, which ran through numerous editions, the works of the realists failed to please the artificial, jaded society of the second empire, and were eclipsed not only by clever adepts in the classic conventions like Octave Feuillet, but even by the wretched imitators of the elder Dumas, who spun out serial sensations for the daily newspapers.   And even Zola's veritable master, Gustave Flaubert, whose *Madame Bovary* and *L'Education Sentimentale* are consummate examples of novel writing conceived as a form of natural history where the methods of scientific scrutiny are applied with perfect cynicism, never won anything beyond the esteem of a narrow circle.   Certainly a man of his temper was scarcely fitted to be the pet of the

Tuileries, or to become, like Feuillet, the arbiter of festivals and charades at Compiègne, or, like Proper Merimée, the literary mentor of the frivolous personage whom caprice and accident had made Empress of France.

With the empire fell a vast scaffolding of spurious or fragile reputations in art and literature, which had helped to prop the political structure. What has become of Houssaye and Bélôt, who made a sumptuous living by the portrayal of vice and scandal ? What has paralyzed the pen of Gustave Droz, whose quaint admixture of sentiment and sensuality had the piquancy of a new sauce ? What has come over the public which used to flock by tens of thousands to buy *Camors*, but which now turns with indifference, almost with contempt, from the listless elegance and refined vapidity of Feuillet's latest works ? So, too, the cunning affectations and pungent epigrams of the accomplished Genevese, Cherbuliez, seem to have lost much of their savor, if we may judge from the waning vogue of his performances at home. And if Theuriet has so far escaped the general submergence of former favorites, it is solely due to his descriptions of natural scenery, where, of course, a novelist's special qualifications do not come at all in question. The real sovereigns of the French reading public at this time, as attested by the conclusive voucher of unapproached success, are Zola and Alphonse Daudet. The latter began as an idealist, and his *Lettres de mon Moulin* and *Tartarin de Tarascon* are charming examples of the sentimental school ; but it was only when he joined Zola in accepting Flaubert for a master, and under his impulse produced *Fromont Jeune, Jack,* and *Le Nabab* that he attained a great reputation. Yet it is a curious fact that the orthodox realists are not quite willing to class Daudet in their ranks. They admit that the persons of his recent books are human beings of very complex character about which it is not easy to pronounce an absolute opinion, but in their judgment he makes the mistake of sympathizing with his heroes, and giving too much scope to poetry and feeling. Moreover, his style wants, they say, the simplicity and translucency with which the more austere realist seeks to efface his personality and mirror with crystalline distinctness the object of his portraiture. He has borrowed, seemingly from the brothers Goncourt, a somewhat affected diction, loaded with florid ornament and far-fetched metaphor, and at the same time rugged and precipitous in movement, as if the novelist meant to suggest to the ear the headlong current of Paris life. The French naturalism of our day finds, as we have seen, its perfect model in Flaubert's *Madame Bovary,* but that wonderful anatomist of vicious instincts wanted industry or fecundity, and only once returned to the task of impassive, implacable reproduction. Accordingly his mantle has fallen on Zola's shoulders, who not only undertakes the function of dissection without the faintest sign of conventional shudder or rebuke, but avows his purpose of disclosing in all his personages the physiological causes of their actions.

What is the object contemplated by the author of the Rougon-Macquart novels? It is, as we have said, to trace the natural and social history of a family which by one or another of its offshoots shall represent every class of French society. The better to define his purpose and enforce the essential unity of his design, the author has prefixed to one of his volumes, *Un page d'Amour*, a genealogical tree, which, exhibiting the origin of the lineage, marks its early bifurcation into two main trunks sharply distinguished in physical traits, which, however, are sometimes softened, sometimes accented in their various ramifications. The remarkable virility of a peasant progenitor is transmitted through two channels, legitimate and illegitimate, and according to the greater or less influence of the female lines, is transformed in his descendants into diverse forms of moral and intellectual energy or weakness. Under felicitous conditions of admixture and environment, this ancestral vigor rises to the heights of heroism, of creative genius, or of consummate executive ability, while in untoward circumstances it engenders dexterous knavery or desperate crime. In one of the main branches there is an hereditary taint amounting to a disease of the nervous system, which in some of the offspring is sublimated to the sensitive organization of the poet, or the mystical fervor of the priest, while in others it breeds a frantic excitation of the appetites, conducting in the end, perhaps, to imbecility. In the case of every individual whose career is made the object

9

of special study, we are put in possession of all the physiological facts which a materialist might deem indispensable to a just sentence upon his conduct. We are told about his parents and his grandparents; we know what passions, proclivities, sensibilities he brought with him into the world; how far these congenital tendencies have been encouraged, lulled, or supplanted by his surroundings, until, when he is launched into a given medium, we can almost forecast his behavior. As with each new volume a new problem in human life is laid before us, we approach its solution with a conviction that at least the statement of its terms has been exhaustive, that none of the springs of motive, so far as these are physical or social, have escaped the author's scrutiny. You are impressed also by the glacial impartiality of the narrative, as if the worst extremes of sin and suffering and the divinest soarings of self-sacrifice and virtue were alike referred to the inexorable workings of natural law. In Zola's indifference, however, there is nothing galling: there is no trace of malicious satisfaction as in Flaubert's cynicism—it recalls rather the profound, far-gazing serenity of an Assyrian statue, the inflexible, inscrutable tranquillity of a sphinx. It is not to be supposed, meanwhile, that because Zola never blames or applauds his characters, that the reader's sympathies are equally unstirred. Such is often the power of his trenchant strokes, such the vitality of certain figures, that you quite lose sight of the artist's unconcerned, impassive temper, and fix your eyes with an eager, poignant intentness on the canvas. Curiously, too, this man, who handles like a surgeon the most delicate fibres of the human heart, discovers the effusive tenderness of a poet when he turns to outward nature. It is as if the materialist were blended with the pantheist in his philosophy; as if the God whom he had lost in the labyrinth of physiology, were found again in the play of light and motion, the infinite beauty and suggestion of the inanimate world.

It is true that M. Zola eschews psychological analysis, that he is satisfied with an outward portrayal of people, and that for this reason their soul escapes him. We say of his creations, Yes, they are most lifelike, we might have passed them but now in the street; on the other hand, we know no more of them than if we had passed them in the street. We may con, if we choose, a catalogue of the physiological causes for their feelings and actions. But in real life we never use such data; we only see them transformed in sentiment and motive, and it is the transformations which kindle interest and constitute originality. To which M. Zola might reply that if the soul has escaped him, perhaps it was not there. That he knows very well what judges, and juries, and law-makers, and, for that matter, novelists, have been wont to look at; that it is a question, however, not of what we are accustomed to study, but of what we ought to study. If we seem to know less intimately the men and women to whom Zola has introduced us, than we know the impressive or exquisite types created by other masters of fiction, the author of " L'Assommoir," would probably remind us that types do not exist in nature, that what we call our knowledge of such figments is a delusion, that nothing is known but physiology, and that the transmutation of food into thought is still a mystery. Moreover, it is not quite fair to compare Zola's characters to the stranger that brushes us in the street ; we understand them quite as thoroughly, after all, as we understand our acquaintances, or indeed, our personal friends, for we can foretell their conduct with rather more precision. We shall never probably in this world know so much of any human being as we know of certain personages in the works of Fielding, Thackeray, or George Eliot. Now, is it the business of a novelist to draw figures of which we shall say, these are men and women, ordinary, every-day folk, neither better nor worse; or figures in which you shall recognize winning and noble types sufficiently individualized for you to caress the dream of their possible incarnation ? That is the question at issue between the realist and the idealist, and Zola, for his part, does not hesitate to accept the former conception of the function undertaken by the writer of prose fiction.

A word as to the crudities and vulgarities which disfigure many of Zola's pages. Those who have read only " L'Assommoir" or " Le Ventre de Paris," and who are accustomed to the carefully pruned diction of Octave Feuillet are naturally shocked to stumble upon words belonging to the unprinted vocabulary which exists in

every language. The truth is that when this thorough-
going realist essays to describe a particular stratum of
society, he does not purpose to put you off with his impression, but means to paint it precisely as it is, and let
you form impressions for yourself. He insists that if
this principle is anything but a pretence, if the truth is
really to be shown in its native rawness and squalor, then
the author must reproduce without squeamishness or
euphuism the idiom of the class and calling he has elected
to depict; otherwise we miss the master key to its intellectual and moral attitude. Of course, those who do
not care to study at first hand the factory and the grog
shop need not read " L'Assommoir," but they should not
go the length of supposing that the same language is employed to photograph very different phases of society.
When, for example, the author sketches the home circle
of the Tuileries or the Ministerial vicissitudes of the
second empire, we can assure the reader that M. Zola's
style is not unequal to the occasion, although his pen is
not by any means that of a courtier. In a word, Zola's
novels are like the world. If your ears cannot bear the
coarse and brutal phrase by which vulgar folk are wont
to drive an idea home, you must pick your company.
There will be scope enough for dainty discrimination in
these twenty volumes.

There is something almost colossal in the proportions
of Zola's undertaking, yet it is already well nigh completed. He purposes, as we have said, to leave behind
him a complete panorama of French civilization under

the social and political conditions of the second empire. In "La Fortune de Rougon" he has unfolded the circumstances of provincial life and the characteristic features of the mercantile calling in the petty commerce of a rural town. "La Faute de l'Abbé Mouret" is a study of the Church, and especially of the privations, compensations, experiences, and temptations incident to the clerical vocation. In "Le Ventre de Paris" the author studies the method of provisioning Paris, while in "L'Assommoir," he depicts the burdens, blunders, vices, and the redeeming virtues, the shabby, the revolting, and the honorable sides of a workman's life in the Faubourg St. Antoine. In "Son Excellence Eugene Rougon," we have a portrait of Eugène Rouher, the famous ex-Minister of the empire, so curiously minute in its biographical details that almost every incident and personage in its pages can be identified. In another number of the series, "Un Page d'Amour"—which by the way is accessible in an English version under the name of "A Love Episode"—Zola opens to us those minor professional circles of the Parisian community which embrace the households of notaries, of physicians in moderate practice, of Government employees below the grade of heads of bureaus, in fact all that stratum of society which in England would be ranked just below the top of the lower middle class. In succeeding novels the army, journalism, the magistracy will by turns occupy the field of his camera. Zola contemplates also a volume on the Commune, that is to say, on the artisan in his political aspect.

Whatever may be thought of the fundamental principles of realism in art and literature—a discussion into which we will not just now enter—it is manifest that Zola's immense accumulations will prove of singular value to the future student of France under the social conditions of our day. It is probable that hereafter the young bachelor of arts, returning from his sojourn in the Quartier Latin, and pressed to account for his wide knowledge of Paris—instead of replying like his fathers, "I have read Balzac, and that suffices"—will point to "Les Rougon-Macquart" as the exhaustless treasure house of vicarious observation.

II.

It may be thought that the theories of realism received a sufficiently crude embodiment in "L'Assommoir" and "Le Ventre de Paris," but the scope of those works at least embraced something besides sheer animalism. They purported to be exhaustive transcripts of the life of workshop and market, and, accordingly, types of industry, sobriety, and kindliness were interspersed, as we see them every day, amid illustrations of sloth, viciousness, and shame. They attested, too, such a profound comprehension of the mechanism of society in the particular strata portrayed, of the rude necessities and coarse devices, of the promptings, pressures, contagions amid which the tinge and fibre of individual character is acquired, that our respect for the observer modified our judgment of the artist. The student of social science seemed so signally to obscure the novelist that we were scarcely more disposed to quarrel with a raw phrase, or an offensive fact, than we should be to insist on a surgeon's performing vivisection in immaculate kid gloves. Yet, even in those cases, the suspicion must not seldom have crossed us that this unshrinking, all-embracing scrutiny of human life belonged to the methods of science, rather than the processes of art; that the uncompromising purpose of telling the whole truth, in the most literal and unvarnished words, would preclude the exercise of the artistic faculty in the selection, disposition, and accentuation of materials. In proportion as the inquirer's purpose should be fully carried out, as his eye should be keen, his hand firm, and his tongue fearless, his work, it was suggested, must inevitably pass out of the category of artistic composition, and be classified with the raw material of history. Unassorted, unwinnowed, and unchastened with any reference to æsthetic emphasis and significance, the record of his observations would be, at best, a photograph and not a picture, a diary and not a novel, a chapter of biography, a cross-section of real life. Heretofore, however, none of the champions of realism, neither Flaubert, nor the brothers Goncourt, nor Zola himself, had been perfectly unswerving and unscrupulous in the application of their theory. Zola, for instance, in "La Faute de l'Abbé Mouret," actually reverted, for a moment, to the idyl and the parable. His latest work, "Nana," on the other hand, is the most extravagant result of the doctrine that anything which is true may be printed, and that nothing human, though it reek with the foulness of a worse than bestial humanity, is foreign to the purpose of the student of manners and the painter of society.

The aim of "Nana" is to depict the sexual vice in its most rabid and noisome exhibitions, and the place chosen for study is Paris, in the year just preceding the collapse of the Second Empire. The principal figure of the book is intended to recall, in many phases of her career, a person at one time sufficiently notorious under the name of Cora Pearl. Like the latter, Nana contrives to ruin three men at once, each of whom may be identified with a well-known personage of the Parisian world. Like her, too, she has at one epoch of her changeful existence a little palace betwixt court and garden, from which she, also, one day decamps, leaving a million francs' worth of debts behind her ; and again, like Cora Pearl, Nana displays her charms to the community at large in one of those burlesques constructed to permit a close approach to nudity in the feminine performer. There are numerous other incidents, which are obviously reproduced from the edifying record of the English adventuress. Nana, however, is not English ; she is French, as truly and intensely French as the mud of Paris from which she sprang. She is the daughter of Gervaise, the story of whose pitiful deterioration is recited in "L'Assommoir." In the last part of that narrative we caught a glimpse of Nana which is worth recalling, for it discloses the early surroundings of the woman whose more brilliant years are chronicled in the book before us. One night, we are told, just as Gervaise and her drunken husband were going to bed, they heard a rap on the door. It was their daughter Nana, all rags and dirt, who came to ask if she could sleep there. She might come in, they said, or stay out, just as she pleased, provided she kept the door shut. So Nana came in, devoured a crust of dry bread, and fell asleep with a part of it in her hand. This sort of thing continued for some time; the girl coming and going like a will o' the wisp, sometimes in rags, and sometimes well dressed. Only one thing exasperated Gervaise now, and that was when her daughter appeared with a bonnet and feathers and a train. This she could not endure; and one night when the dearly-bought finery had created a great stir in the house, Gervaise reproached her daughter violently for the life she led, and finally, in her rage, took her by the shoulder and shook her. "Hands off," cried the girl; "you are the last person to talk to me in that way. You did as you pleased, why can't I do the same?" "What do you mean?" stammered the mother. "I have never said anything about it," the girl continued, "because it was none of my business; but do you think I did not know where you were when my father lay snoring? Let me alone. It was you who set me the example." Gervaise, the author tells us, turned away pale and trembling, while Nana composed herself to sleep again.

After dwelling two or three years in the lowest strata

of Parisian vice, and acquiring in this forcing house a certain ripeness of physical comeliness, Nana attracts the attention of the manager of the Variétés, and, at the time when this story opens, is on the point of making her début at that theatre. The piece is named "The Blonde Venus," and she fills the title rôle. The girl has an air to sing and a few lines to speak, but she has not the slightest pretension to be ranked as either actress or singer. She is depicted, however, as an extremely seducing creature, a Phryne of the stage. One effect of her pyramidal triumph, for that is the phrase by which a lubricous journalist struggles to indicate her success, is the conquest of a certain financier, in whom the reader familiar with the second empire will probably recognize the quondam head of the Credit Mobilier. Approved and supported by this protector of talent, we find her presently installed in a handsome apartment, and the mistress of a country seat, to which she retires in moments of sentimental expansion, when the game of cheating an old man for the sake of a dozen young men has grown somewhat stale. Here she carries her child, a sickly infant of unknown paternity, and it is striking to observe how even expressions of maternal affection become grotesque and loathsome in the mouth of this sorry creature. Equally repulsive is the transient semblance of disinterested affection, which, on one of these visits, she contracts for an innocent youth, whose appetites, prematurely quickened, ultimately drive the poor wretch to suicide. By way of ironical comment on the nature of the sentiment experienced, the intrigue with this foolish boy, which is the one pastoral feature of the book, and is indeed strongly tinctured with the pseudo-idyllic flavor relished by the admirers of "Traviata," is immediately followed in this novel by Nana's headlong flight from her sumptuous surroundings, not for the boy's sake but to live with a filthy low comedian, for whose grimaces and antics she had conceived a morbid and insatiate admiration. A species of surfeit with the relative splendors and decencies of her station on the heights of vice is represented as periodic, Nana returning at stated intervals to wallow in the mire, as if obeying the imperious dictate of congenital instincts. After divers self-entailed vicissitudes, she disappears from Paris altogether, and returns, in the last chapter, to die of the small-pox in a chamber of the Grand Hotel. Her death takes place on the memorable evening when the Corps Législatif has ratified the declaration of war against Germany, and a knot of her wretched comrades, collectively representing the virus and spume of Paris, are seated about the corpse, recounting their projects and abusing Bismarck, while from beneath the window surges upward the roar, "To Berlin—to Berlin !" from the throats of an excited and deluded populace.

In Zola's narrative Nana, and the class of coveted hetairæ which she typifies, is conceived as some fair ogress, into whose yawning and fatal cave multitudes of men in hurried and endless procession descend and are engulfed. There is room for all grades and ranks of the social hierarchy, from the Prince of Wales, who figures in the tale under the thin disguise of the Prince of Scotland, to the rudest athlete or contortionist whose salient muscles have provoked a moment's caprice. It is merely indispensable that each shall bring an offering of some kind in his hand. He that cannot defray the charge of the establishment may pay the dress-maker; another shall furnish pin money, another trinkets and bouquets. There is a certain breadth and grandeur in her insatiate greed and comprehensive harlotry; her net drags great and small; she seems to have infected a whole city. Zola regards her triumph as a kind of hideous retribution inflicted by the crushed, mud-stained rabble, from which she sprang, on the sumptuous and insolent plutocracy. She had grown like a rank weed, he says, amid the garbage of the Parisian pavement; she has the gorged luxuriance of a plant whose turgid leaves betray the compost bed; with the superb curves of her soft flesh she avenges the beggars and outcasts who gave her birth. With her, the cesspool which "L'Assommoir" had shown us fermenting among the poor strikes upward and permeates the social mass, befouling and cankering the idle and affluent. She becomes a malignant force of nature, a pestiferous yeast, tainting and disintegrating Paris, turning it sour like curdled milk. In one chapter she is compared to a gold-spangled horse-fly, spawned from ordure, hovering above the carrion that lies rotting by the way-side, sucking venom from its putrescence, and poisoning the wayfarer, whose cheek it brushes with its fetid wing.　Elsewhere in the volume she is pictured in her gorgeous dwelling, heaped with aimless, tasteless riches, as standing erect, arrogant, sphinx-like, with a drove of worshippers rooting, swine-like, at her feet.　Like those antique monsters, says the author, whose redoubtable domain was strewn with bones, her heel rested upon skulls, and catastrophes environed her.　At length the task of ruin and death is completed; wretchedness has spent its store of venom; Nana has exacted blood money for her bruised and smarting kindred; the beggar and the outcast are avenged.　She has made her house like the place of which Ruskin has written, "A loathsome centre, the smoke of its sin going up into the face of Heaven, like the furnace of Sodom, and the pollution of it rotting and raging through the bones and the souls of its frequenters as if it were a volcano whose ashes break out in blains upon man and beast."

It should be manifest to the reader that this latest book of Zola's cannot be literally translated into English. In this country we are not in the habit of locking up our bookcases, or of prohibiting our daughters from turning over volumes on the counters of reputable booksellers. It is true that the narratives of Defoe may be found in most gentlemen's libraries, and that the great English realist has treated a theme analogous to that dealt with in this volume.　But "Roxana" is relatively cleanly and austere, because while the incidents of a vicious woman's life are therein reported faithfully and crudely enough, the novelist has not thought it needful to transcribe the shocking impurities of her language. In this respect Defoe is far less brazen and unflinching than is Zola, who lets us hear the kind of speech uttered amid the garish splendors and spurious refinement of opulent Parisian lewdness. There is a vein, too, of enigmatical and anomalous depravity for which the English language has no name, and which cannot be excised, because it winds through the whole action, and curls about the pivots of the story.

There is another reason why Nana is not presentable in an English version. To expurgate the foul language put in the mouths of certain characters, to soften and disguise the crapulence of certain incidents—in a word, to emasculate the work—would infuse a taint into the performance. It would give us a lascivious semi-disclosure for Zola's relentless and freezing nudity; it would transform a repulsive into a libidinous picture. Zola's ethics are different from Burke's : he believes that vice becomes tenfold more hurtful and contagious when it is shown divested of its essential grossness. He does not expect young women to read his books, and he would be the first to concede that even the most severe and icy survey of certain themes is incompatible with innocence. He writes for men, but not after the manner of too many of his fellow authors, with the aim of tickling and exciting them. He holds, with Flaubert, that an absolutely veracious exhibition of vice in its nakedness is rather repellant than attractive. No man has read

"Madame Bovary" without carrying away a profound impression of loathing and abhorrence for the sins against continence which so many novelists have essayed to dignify. And just as Flaubert, in his master-work, has pilloried the adulteress, so Zola has foreseen, in the book before us, that he should make the modern Lais offensive and sickening by painting her exactly as she is. Through all the smudge and obscenity heaped upon his truthful canvas, the essential cleanliness of his purpose never wavers and is never frustrated. We rise from the perusal of his narrative without one sting of appetite, one twinge of sympathy, but sick and faint as from the retchings of some violent emetic.

The appearance of this novel, in which Zola's point of view and characteristic method are projected with peculiar emphasis, naturally suggests comparison with that work of Balzac's in which a like subject has been handled upon distinct principles, and with a widely different result. Balzac, it will be remembered, designed to offer to posterity in his "Comédie Humaine," just such a conspectus of French society in the third decade as Zola means to furnish for the seventh decade of our century. In the former's comprehensive survey, the kaleidoscopic phases of Parisian vice and crime were by no means overlooked; indeed, they have been thought to occupy more than their due proportion of his teeming canvas. In "Les Splendeurs et Misères des Courtisanes," Balzac attempted a broad and faithful portrayal of their lives, a review of their abrupt and inexorable vicissitudes from affluence to indigence. So far as the mere framework, accessories, and stage properties, the situations, incidents, and motives of his narrative were concerned, Balzac's genius for observation has seldom been more potently exerted. The nurture and surroundings of Esther Gobseck, her congenital instincts and habitual practices, her degraded past and remediless future, are etched with a mordant veracity that bites into the bone. But when the scene is ready and the girl herself is brought upon the stage, an extraordinary metamorphosis comes over the spirit of the tale. Instead of a frigid study in morbid anatomy, we have a flight of rhapsody ; the surgeon gives place to the poet. What began like an autopsis of bestiality, ends in the apotheosis of a pure and selfless love. In his portrait of the typical courtesan, as in so many of his works, Balzac the dreamer and creator effaces Balzac the observer. He has put himself into the picture, discarding realities, pursuing an ideal. He starts with the monstrous incongruity of giving Ésther, the courtesan *par excellence*, a poet for a lover, and thenceforth bends the energies of his incomparable talent to proving her worthy of a poet's devotion. He invests this offspring of the gutter and tenant of the slums (whom her old associates had given the suggestive sobriquet of La Torpille—the cramp-fish), with Miranda's candor and Imogen's sweetness, with Helen's docility, Cordelia's spirit of self-sacrifice, and Isabel's horror of impurity. Of course such a being commands sympathy, and not detestation ; her life appears a tragedy, and not a shabby farce. In a word, her story has become, in Balzac's hands, a masterpiece of idealization ; a work of art, and not at all a work of nature. A being who is drawn thus lovable, admirable, almost celestial in the height of her self-abnegation, has obviously ceased to have anything in common with the class which Balzac assumes to study. Far from being a type, she is not even a possible anomaly, for it may safely be affirmed that no such creature could exist in the given environment. The glorification of the courtesan thus begun by Balzac has, we need not say, been pushed *ad nauseam* by later novelists. It reached the acme of absurdity in Dumas' "Dame aux Caméllias," from which, happily for the morals of the youthful reader, the reaction has been sudden and profound. At last a harlot has been stripped of her counterfeit idealism, and exposed in her genuine foulness by Emile Zola, the moral influence of whose books can no more be likened to that exercised by Balzac and the younger Dumas than the function of a chemist can be compared with a procurer's.

To purge the passions, we are told on high authority, is the aim of tragedy ; but Aristotle is far from affirming that the methods of the dramatist and those of the physician should be identical. It is one thing to watch, rapt and awestruck, on the stage of an Athenian theatre those who have sinned in the high places, a Thyestes, a Clytemnestra, caught in the meshes of an irrevocable doom. It is another thing to track the fetid course of a lewd woman from pinchbeck magnificence to hopeless squalor, from the lazaretto to the morgue. For his part, however, Zola cares but little about the abstract conceptions of beauty and sublimity, and he snaps his fingers at æsthetic canons, no matter how potent the names which may have sanctioned them. He is a Jacobin in politics, an iconoclast in literature ; he prefers the dissecting room to the studio, and is perfectly willing to be refused the title of artist, provided you will concede to him the useful name of physiologist. Certainly the works of Zola will be accounted valuable material by the future student of nineteenth century society. What the writings of Apuleius and Petronius Arbiter are for the resolute inquirer into Roman civilization that Zola's "Nana" may be found when another generation shall seek to comprehend the social decomposition and political catastrophe of France under the second empire.

WE are favored from time to time with ingenious theories to account for the non-appearance of the American drama or novel. For the composition of those desiderated works, the one thing lacking, probably, is brains. We can hardly escape this conclusion, since the social asperities and crudities supposed to cramp the play of fancy in general should be specially discouraging to poetry; yet it so happens that we possess a poet who is distinctively, even curiously, American. We refer, of course, to John G. Whittier. This earnest and useful man, who is likewise a punctilious and painstaking artist, owes nothing to class or coterie, to the atmosphere of partial praise and mutual admiration. His reputation has grown like a forest tree, and may reasonably expect the life of one. In the evening of his days, a modest singer, who seems never to have sought prestige by cunning ways, and whose merits were long eclipsed at home by the transient glitter of other names, finds himself grown dear to a whole country and very generally accepted as one of its truest lyric representatives.

Mr. Whittier is a very voluminous, and therefore inevitably an unequal, writer. In the attempt to form an estimate of a given poet in our day, when the trick of correct metrical expression seems to be easily learned, we are confronted on the threshold by the question, what precise distinction have we in mind when we talk of *vers de société,* " occasional verses," and the like, as something discriminated from genuine poetry, and hesitate to accord the name of poet to such masters of charming rhyme as Praed, Thackeray, and Wendell Holmes ? Some clear notion of this difference is indispensable for grading and classifying the work even of the greatest artists, since the field of their achievements is commonly too broad to admit everywhere the theory of irresistible vocation, much less of impulsive utterance. Not even these men sang as the birds sing, of if they sometimes did, not always or often. Obviously where the range of theme is wide, and the treatment exacted various, the chemic heat of strong emotion must many times be wanting, and the cold chisel of the mechanical crafts-man, toiling to keep body or reputation alive, will not seldom leave its marks.

The truth is, apparently, that all canons of intelligent criticism may be deduced from the ancient difinition (which shuts out, by the way, didactic verse), that a poet's single aim is to rouse the emotions, and his instrument the pictorial power of the quickened imagi-nation, coupled with the musical effects of song. But since the wells of profound feeling must be sought about the roots of humanity, in the fundamental relations of men to one another and to their surroundings, rather than in the surface contrasts of artificial life, it may happen that one writer mistakes the proper field of poetry, and so produces something trivial or occasional —*vers de société*, in a word—while another, aiming shrewdly enough, may yet through native frigidity or temporary miscarriage fail to fire the reader's fancy, and the result is merely rhythmic, lacquered prose.

Inherent inertness and clumsy workmanship are seldom overlooked, and each generation may be trusted to deal with the latter class of poetasters. Kirke White, Montgomery, Alexander Smith, and our American Percival were brought to judgment by their contemporaries. But those accomplished gentlemen who masquerade in verse, and use the sonnet as Congreve did the drama, to embalm the sentiment of high society, whose shortcomings are principally due to a narrow and superficial theme, and whose *genre* pictures often evince considerable imagination and a remarkable command of rhythmic mechanism, carry it bravely enough for a season, and sometimes in England have been thought worthy of the laurel. Moreover, as these pleasant, tempered voices have their moments of genuine fervor, and strike now and then some chord of universal sympathy, while on the other hand the strongest works of the great singers are marred by intervals of languor and remissness, discrimination in certain cases becomes a question of averages which is willingly left to later times.

Mr. Whittier can afford to own that he has sometimes failed to rise above the level of the verse-maker, and perhaps only those who, like Gray, lead a semi-claustral life, are able to practise that wise reticence which assures unqualified approval. A writer who celebrates the events of the passing hour must expect the lustre of some performances to fade with the interests which called them forth, and in the mass of Mr. Whittier's productions, representing as it does the fruitage of a long and busy life, there is much, undoubtedly, of an ephemeral character. But there is an abundance of durable work of a peculiar and rare quality, and there are certain themes which, by right of discovery, this writer has made his own. On the whole, his distinctive merit is to have detected beneath the rugged surface of New England life a romance and beauty of whose existence many of us were sceptical; and with respect to his achievements in this direction we are naturally led to contrast him with Longfellow.

The first metrical essays of Longfellow and of Whittier were published about the same time, but the former's success was far more prompt and signal. His "Voices of the Night," and those still earlier poems now forgotten, were written in the same tristful minor key to which his most characteristic later utterances instinctively adjust themselves. It is the voice of an elegant Jeremiah bewailing the rudeness of his environment, gazing hungrily outward and backward to lose in other lands and times the homely spectacle of hard-working, hard-featured New England, and turning to the face of nature, not with cheery, spontaneous homage, as to the goodly frame of a blithe

world, but with a sigh of sentimental satisfaction,
because

No tears
Dim the sweet look that nature wears.

Hawthorne's attitude toward his own country was
much the same, and the limited sale of his novels measured the numerical strength of the cultivated class which
shrank from the rawness and austerity of a provincial
civilization, and sympathized with that spirit of plain-
tive isolation and dainty estrangement from the actual
world which imparts to Longfellow's verse its individual
flavor. If any one desires to gauge the mediocrity of
New England culture just before the period when a knot
of young people made the " Dial " their voice and began
to found a sterling native literature, let him examine
the curriculum of Harvard College at that date, and note
what a slender outfit was suffered to pass muster for a
liberal education. The fact that Mr. Longfellow was
master of a correct and graceful English style was of itself extraordinary distinction, and some metrical translations from the Spanish and German were accepted in
perfect good faith as the credentials of exceptional
scholarship. There is no pride like the pride of poverty,
and the spirit which prompts the Highlander to exaggerate the prowess of clansmen, was at once enlisted in behalf of an author who had some tincture of cosmopolitan
thought and could write fluently without lapsing into
dialect.

Whittier's initial performances were of a different kind.

The aroma of scholarship was not conspicuous in them, although the writer was a scholar, and has since evinced a range of culture by no means inconsiderable. But his first productions were racy of the soil, and their savor was pungently American. For this reason they were dealt with somewhat cavalierly by the censors of our nascent literature, and were substantially left to find an audience for themselves. We need not say that readers were nevertheless forthcoming, and it was not long before his household lyrics gave Whittier such a hold on the popular heart as made him later, in the anti-slavery agitation, a veritable power in the land. The songs and ballads which formed the bulk of his earlier volumes were pitched in a key wholly distinct from that of Longfellow's verse, being adjusted with intuitive precision to the average sentiment and intelligence of that great body of readers to whom recondite learning is a stumbling block and hyper-refinement foolishness. Naturally, an author who contrived to dignify the inexorable bleakness of existence under the conditions of New England climate and soil, and to cast a halo of high purpose about that scramble for warmth and food which summed the life of the majority, was, in the end, hailed with delight by thousands to whom the suave music of Longfellow's " Prelude " and the pensive charm of the " Coplas de Manrique " were wasted breath. Far from aiming to bestow felicitous embodiment on an evanescent mood of our higher society, the naïve, impersonal creations of the Quaker poet were conspicuously

10

wanting in that adroit reminiscence and dainty allusion which infuse an exotic sweetness and evolve a classic atmosphere. In them we catch for the first time the voice of a genuine New England bard, the accents native to a homely yet tender spirit, not cramped by any half-conscious imitation of foreign styles and methods, or strained by the deliberate effort to sustain ambitious song. We need not quote from works which are familiar to almost every reader, and we will merely name such legends of New England history as "Cassandra Southwick," "Mary Garvin," "The Witch's Daughter," "Skipper Ireson's Ride"—those "Songs of Labor," which found means to ennoble the most commonplace vocations—and, in another vein, "Maud Muller," "The Playmate," "Memories," and "The Old Burying Ground."

How tawdry beside some of these artless lyrics appear the finesse and glitter, for example, of Moore's Melodies, admirably attuned, no doubt, to the drawing-room or to the simulated simplicity of *fêtes champêtres,* but which do not rise to the lips unbidden beside a cradle or a grave. There would seem to be two roads to Parnassus, and probably the slow-growing affection of plain folk bestows a more enduring guerdon than the prompt applause of the cultivated few. Who, in our day, reads the "Fairy Queen" because he loves it ? and yet how many simple ballads, penned by nameless contemporaries of Spenser, are counted among our household treasures. We do not forget that our other poet, Longfellow, has written not a few sweet songs, but they seem to want in some degree the directness and spontaneity of Whittier's best work, and sometimes betray a kind of labored homeliness which jars on a sensitive ear.

While Mr. Whittier's lyrical reputation was slowly but solidly taking root, he made more than one venture in the field of narrative poetry. There was plainly a presumption against his success in that direction. There are singers and makers in the guild of poets, and not often are the diverse talents which speak in narrative and song united in the same mind. The capacity, in fact, of strong lyrical utterance seems to imply a temporary fusion of the whole emotional nature in a univocal mood, coupled with a partial suspension of the critical faculty. Now, is it probable that where a habit of facile self-surrender to transitory moods has been contracted, the fancy can safely be intrusted with the evolution of a coherent symmetrical work of considerable length ? Under such circumstances, should we not expect the essential conditions of narrative to be misconceived or impulsively ignored ?

Certain shortcomings of Whittier—and we may add, of Longfellow—in this direction are rendered salient by comparison with the master *raconteurs.* Doubtless the Canterbury Tales, the lays of Scott, and that cycle of legends set forth in the "Earthly Paradise" will be accepted as models. From Chaucer's "Knight's Tale," for instance, we learn the scope and processes of narrative verse. The poet means to tell us a story in the most straightforward and effective way, and, therefore, while glimpses of fair landscapes, fitful bursts of melody, and even pious homilies are not wanting, these are merely accessories everywhere subordinate to crisp characterization and the swift development of plot. Accordingly, it is not the rhythm or the diction, but just the story which holds the ear. A like directness of aim lends vigor to Scott's verse ; and for this reason, even children, who are impatient of digressions, and only perplexed by the more subtle graces of a poetic style, love Marmion and Rokeby. It is true that we are also indebted to Scott for some of the finest minor lyrics in our language, and so far he may seem to have furnished a precedent to Longfellow and Whittier ; but Sir Walter did not postpone until after years of song writing his essays in a form of poetry which demands protracted, deliberate evolution. On the contrary, his first serious performance was a sustained, resolute flight, and his abandonment to the lyric mood seems to have been merely episodical, and perhaps wore to him the aspect of relaxation from more circumspect and continuous labor.

There is no doubt that the latest successful weaver of tales in rhyme is a zealous student of Chaucer's manner. Indeed, Morris has somewhat estranged the sympathies of a modern reader by the curious felicity with which he has caught the mediæval tone and attitude of his master. He has even carried a fondness for Chaucer's diction to unreasonable length, reproducing words and turns of phrase, long obsolete, and laying violent hands on our present pronunciation, notably by accenting the present participle of many verbs on the last syllable instead of the penult. But we could cheerfully forgive any man such aberrations who would approach, as Morris does, the symmetry, briskness, and energy of the Canterbury Tales. His descriptions of outward nature, though vivid, are effected by short, random strokes, and his melody, like Chaucer's, is not suffered to drown the narrative in long strophes of lyrical expression, but modestly blends with it like the accompaniment of a lute. In short, he addresses himself to the business of a story teller with simplicity and self-repression.

In Whittier's " Tent on the Beach " and Longfellow's " Tales of a Wayside Inn " our American poets have tacitly invited a comparison with Chaucer. In the latter experiment a party of travellers weather-bound in a country tavern, and in the former a knot of friends encamped on the seashore in the heats of midsummer, agree, like the Canterbury pilgrims, to beguile the time with tales, and an attempt is made to preface their narratives with sketches of their several characters. But the etching is pale and irresolute and we miss the cunning touches, the nervous drawing, and bright tints which make the parson, the prioress, the clerk of Oxenford, and other guests of the " Tabard " as lifelike as the portraits of near friends. Moreover, in the tales themselves there is a deficiency of point, of progressive movement to a culmination, and they do not easily fix themselves in the memory.

Again, when Whittier and Longfellow in other narratives directed attention to the legendary treasures of America, their choice of theme was not specially felicitous.   How could they overlook, for instance, and abandon to alien hands that portion of the scheme of the "Earthly Paradise," which involved the portrayal of the Inca and Aztec civilizations, a subject steeped in that romance and mystery which poets go so far to seek ? What possible scope or stimulus could be afforded by the meagre annals of those savage red men, whose virtues are mainly mythical and whose simplicity is a snare, contrasted with the massive outlines of Montezuma's empire, or with the blended mildness and sagacity of that Peruvian State whose penal code recognized few offences, but chief among them ranked the lie.   To an American artist, apparently, it should have been a labor of love to illumine the fading record of those moribund races and to fuse the scattered data which lie sterile in the chronicler's page into shapes of life and beauty.   It scarcely seems a loftier or worthier task to dignify the crooked ways of lazy, treacherous nomads, and emphasize the mendacious features of Cooper's impossible Indian.

We should have liked to glance at the "Voices of Freedom " and other contributions to the anti-slavery cause, of which Whittier was as truly the laureate as Lloyd Garrison was the protagonist; but we must pass these for the present, as well as those national lyrics or "Songs in War Times," which are perhaps the best known of the poet's works. There is one aspect, however, of Whittier's verse which we would not overlook, and that is the singular purity of his moral influence.

There is no room in this case for the too frequent conflict between the feeling of grateful admiration which prompts us to exempt an accomplished artist from moral accountability, and the instinctive demand of the public conscience that the verse whose sweetness wins the ear shall likewise be clean and wholesome. Willingly would Chaucer in his last days, if the final paragraph of the so-called "Parson's Tale" is authentic, have stricken from the "Canterbury Tales" the lewdness and ribaldry which disfigure them; but there is not a line or a word in the wide range of Whittier's work whose suggestion of impurity the writer need wish to blot. Here, at all events, is a poet who can read Sidney's Defence of Poesy without a twinge or a sneer, who may affirm that kindly and upright living has been the constant burden of his song, and that he has faithfully, within the compass of his talent, fulfilled the genial function which, in Sidney's words, "not only shows the way but giveth so fair a prospect into the way as will entice any man to enter into it."

In that philosophy which refers all that is generous and lofty in the human heart to the operation of sympathy, we may doubtless find the key of Whittier's ethics. So far as his unobtrusive voice may be said to preach anything, it preaches the gospel of altruism, and we can only gauge aright the merit of such teaching by recalling what different lessons were put forth by a school of poetry which dominated at the outset of his career, as well as by another whose vigorous development has partially overshadowed its close. The philosophy of Byron, of Heine and De Musset exhibited that less repulsive form of egotism, the offspring of a half-reluctant atheism, which surveys its own isolation with a kind of horror, and whose defiance not seldom borrows the accents of despair. On the other hand, Morris and Swinburne appear to acquiesce with entire satisfaction in the dreariest corollaries of materialism, and the one with euphuistic refinement, the other with cynical sincerity set forth the rapture and the wisdom of selfish, sensuous existence. Perhaps in no way can the benignant spirit which makes Whittier's poetry a potent instrument of healthful education be more nicely discriminated than by contrast with the atmosphere which enfolds the " Earthly Paradise."

We need not stigmatize Morris's poetry as heathen, for that would raise an unnecessary question. We may even allow his premises, and still except to the bleak philosophy he rears on them ; and while we yield to the charm of his melody, repudiate his scheme of happiness. For admitting that life is bounded by the grave and that earth is the only paradise men's eyes are like to see, it by no means follows that all the joys of existence must be summed in a short decade of lusty youth, while the long vista of our later years is to be darkened with vain repining and regret. There would be truth in the picture if egotism could be trusted to serve the purpose even of Epicurus, since selfishness dwells in the passions and their heyday is indeed brief. But that common sense of mankind which is content to accept without too curious dissection the record of its impressions, finds sympathy at the root of its profoundest joys, and accordingly recognizes the affections as the veritable ministrants of happiness. Now it is a singular fact that of those affections whose office it is to wish and further another's welfare or delight, there is scarcely a trace in that Earthly Paradise to which Morris would conduct us. It is true he veils with exquisite tact and delicacy the grosser aspects of physical passion, but, although his lovers do not smite with eyes, or scorch with hot, fierce lips, or gripe with hard embraces, as Mr. Swinburne's sometimes do, they obey the same animal instinct, and seem unable to conceive of an affection that should outlive desire. Stripped of its demure accents and dainty dress, what is this but the philosophy of the sty? Surely, not even a shrewd materialism could be held responsible for these deductions, much less such atheism as Shelley's, whose pure and lofty ethics dignified the human nature on which he based them.

Had Whittier been moved to concentrate his energies upon the drama, it would have been incumbent on him to portray the passions, since they supply the shadows of life ; but, as a lyric bard, by impulse and habit, he had a right to ignore them and constitute himself the laureate of the affections. Scarcely any poet of our day, if we except Wordsworth, has touched with more honest reverence and loving tenderness the relations of friendship, of marriage, of parent and child. Whittier, in brief, is truly, in Sidney's sense, a homilist. Those winning pictures of a peaceful home, its innocent joys, and sweet contentment, which Jeremy Taylor loved to draw, are not more wholesome and serene than his, while no manual of noble living can hit the springs of motive and mould the character like the subtle influence of song.

THAT a new novel by the author of "Lothair" should have been simultaneously offered to American readers by no less than three publishers bears witness to the interest and curiosity which the remarkable career of the Conservative leader awakened on this side of the Atlantic. We do not mean, of course, that many of those who eagerly peruse "Endymion" care to trace in it the writer's political principles, or seek to evolve from its random allusions to public events the secret of his political success. But everybody appreciates the social triumphs of Lord Beaconsfield; everybody feels that this man's life constitutes, in its social aspects, a romance more gorgeous and extravagant than any he himself has penned. There is another reason why his portrayal of what are commonly regarded as the highest spheres of English society was certain to be scanned with exceptional avidity. There is nothing which the British middle class, or, for that matter, the majority of well-to-do Americans, regard with such keen inquisitiveness as the English aristocracy. The habits, manners, tastes, modes of thought, and modes of speech of that brilliant and envied caste are made the objects of unremitting inquiry and imitation. Books that purport to deal with what is vulgarly called high life, start with weighty credentials, as is proved by the simple test of sale. Experienced publishers will doubtless bear us out in asserting the superior attractions of this theme from a commercial point of view. But the majority of works intended to gratify the popular craving for enlightenment on this head, and assuming to photograph the best English society, are discredited by grave doubts of the author's competence. The middle-class reader, whose naïve and confiding attitude was a source of perpetual merriment to Thackeray, is now beset by a lurking apprehension that these glowing delineations of partrician existence are not instructive transcripts of reality, but delusive and useless products of a plebeian's imagination. For a too often victimized and justly suspicious audience it is plain that a novel written by a Knight of the Garter must have an incomparable charm. On the hints and examples gleaned from his authentic pages, the patient student of good manners, the ardent amateur of modish talk and genteel behavior, may build as on a rock. Indeed, Lord Beaconsfield's social studies are sure to be distinguished by a far more minute and instructive realism than would have characterized his work had he been born in the purple. There can be, from the nature of the case, no more alert, untiring, incisive, and exhaustive observer than a parvenu whose success has been in no sense due to wealth. An intuitive swiftness in discerning and reproducing the subtlest shades of sentiment, and the nicest distinctions of speech and of demeanor peculiar to the world in which he is a stranger, is the inexorable condition of his naturalization in it. From this point of view it may be said that no novelist has been so thoroughly qualified to depict English Society as was Benjamin Disraeli, who was born, it may be said, outside of it, and who has conquered it with an almost unexampled splendor and completeness of conquest.

Those self-improving persons, however, who con one of Disraeli's novels as if it were an infallible manual of etiquette and a precious repository of conventional lore, will be in some measure disappointed by " Endymion." The society depicted in this novel is not contemporaneous, but separated from us by more than a generation in point of time, and by a much wider gulf as regards the change in manners, customs and ideas. Regarded as a storehouse of acute observations and shrewd comments, it would prove less useful to the student of existing types and standards than as a *mémoire pour servir* in the estimate of a past epoch. The story begins with the death of Canning, and ends, if we are justified in identifying the mysterious personage variously designated as the " Count of Otranto " and " Col. Albert " with Louis Napoleon, some time after the establishment of the second empire in France. The main action of the story covers the years which intervened between the first reform act, and the disruption of the Tory party after the repeal of the corn laws. The preceding period is but faintly outlined, while the allusions to events subsequent to 1848 are of a relatively casual and fugitive character, and suggest the retouching of a substantially completed but unpublished work. At many points, too, in the main current of the narrative there are signs of revision on the part of the author, as if he wished to adjust statements and opinions to later and more accurate knowledge or to his present point of view. In general it may be said both of "Endymion" and "Lothair" that the writer deports himself with much more self-restraint and circumspection, and is far less ready to occupy the seat of judgment than he was in his earlier books. His strictures are not so sweeping, so trenchant, or so confident. He does not pronounce on legislation and appraise the abilities of statesmen with the glibness of "Vivian Grey;" he does not renovate society and settle the fate of empires with the complacency evinced in "Coningsby" and "Sibyl." In a word, his pen seems to have lost much of its old acridity, not to say gall and venom, since his own public life has been a target to the shafts of irony and satire. He seems to have arrived at the conclusion that a caustic vein is less discreet and sapient, as this world goes, than a relatively genial, tolerant, conciliatory strain. He writes in his last two novels much as well-bred men talk, fluently, tentatively, unpretentiously, unargumentatively. His opinions are hinted rather than expounded, brought out with the wary hesitation of the experienced politician who has learned that he may have at any moment to adopt measures previously rejected, and to accept as friends the enemies of yesterday.

Except in so far as it presents a record of its author's observations and reflections, and helps us to understand some phases of his own remarkable career, we cannot see that this new novel has much to recommend it. Considered as a work of art to be scrutinized and judged in comparison with the approved standards of novel writing, it is neither much better nor much worse than preceding ventures by the same hand in the same direction. Were "Endymion" the work of an utterly unknown writer, it might pique the curiosity of a few survivors of the period it depicts, because they would recognize in its author an habitué of their old world; but we suspect that the mass of readers would pronounce it a dull book. We will risk, indeed, the assertion that few, even among those for whom Lord Beaconsfield himself, and the society he paints, have a powerful fascination, have been able to finish either "Lothair" or "Endymion" at a sitting. Of the specific qualities which accredit a first-rate novel, more than one is wanting in these stories. Of the several ways in which a literary artist may evince skill within this field, in construction, characterization, observation, comment, and that agreeable diction which is the indispensable vehicle of the whole, it is only in the three respects last named that Disraeli's novels have deserved much consideration. Of structure in the sense that a novel of Fielding or Balzac is structural; of the nice inter-relation of parts to one another and to the central motive which unifies them all; of the exquisite adaptation of incidents and situation to the swift, continuous unfolding of the plot; there is scarcely an indication in "Endymion." In the first chapters of the tale we follow the declining fortunes of the hero's family, while the remainder of the book reproduces not so much an epoch as a section of the hero's life; a section hewn off in the rough, like a fragment of biography, not stamped with any dramatic or psychological completeness, unless the fact that Endymion becomes a cabinet minister can be deemed an artistic culmination of a romance. So far as the story of Endymion and his sister is concerned—and these, if any, are the pivotal figures—it might have been told in one quarter of the space occupied; and if we are not repelled by the maladroit profusion of superfluous persons and irrelevant events, it is for reasons quite extrinsic to a candid appreciation of the author's technical proficiency in the task of tale-weaving.

If now the reader looks to see exemplified in "Endymion" the conception and projection of character which we expect from a first-rate novelist, he will be, at first, a little perplexed and baffled by the aspect of realism, coupled with the absence of vitality, exhibited by the persons of the tale. The fact is that most of them give us upon close scrutiny, the impression of wax-work fac-similes of beings once alive, but now, to all intents and purposes, defunct. Our intellect accepts the fact of their historical existence, but our imagination does not recognize them as living, breathing things. We do not share their emotions, kindle with their hopes, thrill with their loves, droop with their sorrows, as we do for those palpitating figures warmed and quickened by the hand of truly creative genius. In a word, the cold, inert, eclectic realism exhibited in "Endymion" is, to the animated, glowing, profund verity of such an artist as George Eliot, what a plaster cast reproducing a man's very lineaments would be to a portrait of the same face by Velasquez. We cannot bring ourselves to care much about the persons encountered in this novel, except so far as one of them is supposed in some respects to personate the author, or as others are indentified with people holding intimate or important relations to Mr. Disraeli, or with men and women of mark in the social and political history of this century.

To say that a novelist is deficient in the power not only of construction but of characterization also, if the latter word be used in a high, creative sense, would in nine cases out of ten effectually dispose of his claims to serious attention. When we add that "Endymion" and its companion narratives are seldom enlivened by the jocund, sly, or cynical humor in which the works of Dickens, Thackeray, and Bret Harte are so rich, it might seem at first sight that the process of elimination had left behind little of substantial value. This, however, would be a grave mistake. Lord Beaconsfield's experience has been so wide, and his natural astuteness of intellect has coöperated with circumstances to generate such a fund of worldly wisdom, that his novels, aside from their autobiographical interest, constitute a vast and incomparable treasury of useful information and sage suggestion. They will prove more helpful to the future student of the later Georgian and Victorian eras than even such books as Greville's memoirs, for the author's opportunities were far greater, and have been turned to very much better account, than Greville's. Indeed, we see no reason why Lord Beaconsfield's social studies, taken collectively, should not be looked upon hereafter as presenting a no less comprehensive and trustworthy tableau of London society in the nineteenth century than Balzac's Comédie Humaine is supposed to offer for the Paris of the Restoration and of the reign of Louis Philippe. On the score of authenticity, indeed, few persons would dream of contesting the superior authority of the English writer, for although the naïve *étudiant* of the *Quartier Latin* deems it pertinent and profitable to explore Paris in the pages of Balzac, there are those who smile at his credulity.

While Lord Beaconsfield has much to tell us, he tells it in a singularly lucid and effective way. He can scarcely be credited with wit, for what might pass for wit in his writings lacks the flash, if not the sting; but he has a gift of fashioning compact and memorable sentences in which the neatness of the phrase lends wings to the apt matter. His descriptive style in "Endymion" and "Lothair" is free, for the most part, from the artificial, euphemistic tinge conspicuous in the earlier novels. It seems, by comparison, spontaneous and impersonal. It has a limpid current of its own, which recalls the fluent, gentle murmur of discourse in a drawing-room. The obvious superiority of the present book in this respect over " Coningsby " attests how rigorous a revision the author must have lately given it, if it be, as we incline to think, a work whose first draught was made at least thirty years ago. When, on the other hand, the flow of description is interrupted by comment or colloquy, the writer's thought perpetually tends to cast itself in laconic, pithy, epigrammatic form, ornamented with fit metaphor and pointed with not too far fetched antithesis: This, of course, was always a distinguishing feature of Disraeli's diction, whether in his literary work or in his spoken utterance. We think, indeed, that more crisp sayings could be culled from " Endymion " than from any of his previous publications. His judgments on men and things are less frequently couched, as we have. said, in tones of sneer and sarcasm, but the irony, perhaps, is not less pungent because it is less palpable.

It is natural enough that the reader should try to identify the characters that figure in this story with this or that personage in real life, since this species of mechanical reproduction has always been Disraeli's forte, and is, indeed, the only kind of realism which we have learned to expect from him. Nor is it often difficult to discern whom the author has in mind in sketching a particular portrait, so far as the physical, mental, and moral traits are concerned, although he almost always seeks to foil and disconcert the inquisitive eye by some glaring incongruity of circumstance. Endymion himself, for instance, from a psychological point of view, presents many obvious points of likeness, if not to what young Disraeli was, yet to what Lord Beaconsfield would have us think he was. Nothing, however, could be more ludicrously irreconcilable with the facts of the author's career than certain events in the life of " Endymion," such as his successively holding the relation of brother-in-law to Lord Palmerston and Louis Napoleon. If we except the irrelevancy of some incidents, the delineation of Palmerston, under the name of Lord Roehampton, seems, on the whole, more faithful and complete than any of the other attempts at photography, although the features of the Whig leader are a good deal refined, and nobody would guess that in real life Lord Roehampton could be popularly known by the sobriquet of " Pam." The supposed recognition of Lord Melbourne behind the mask of Lord Montfort appears to us a manifest blunder. There is scarcely anything in the public or private life of Melbourne which finds a counterpart in the description of Montfort, nor anything in his personal character, except possibly the listlessness which in Melbourne's case was affected, and never, as a matter of fact, hindered him from discharging official business. Neither can Montfort possibly be meant for Lord Normanby, though it is certain that Lady Montfort can be no other than the Marchioness of Normanby, the heroine of the famous *question de jupons*. That so great a dame as Lady Montfort should, at a later point of the story, be confounded with the estimable yet by no means equally distinguished lady whom Mr. Disraeli married, is an incongruity creditable enough to the author's conjugal affection. As for Montfort, while he has almost no points in common with Lord Normanby, there are many signs that the writer meant to reveal in him the veritable features of the Marquess of Hertford, the reader being expected to draw the obvious inference that Thackeray had no acquaintance with that nobleman, and relied exclusively on vulgar rumor, when he undertook to draw him in the person of the Marquis of Steyne. There is, it seems to us, in "Endymion" more than one covert insinuation levelled at the author of "Vanity Fair," and designed to depreciate that artist's esoteric knowledge of the great London world. Nor does the genius of Dickens fare much better at the hand of Lord Beaconsfield, if it be, as we surmise, that novelist who is made the object of occasional allusions under the name of "Gushy." We take for granted that Thackeray sat for St. Barbe, although the likeness seems to have been purposely defaced out of deference to certain critics, with whom Thackeray has become a sort of fetish. In Nigel Penruddock we have a composite figure in whose features those who think it worth while may differentiate what belongs to Wiseman, what to Newman, and what to Manning. As for Roebuck and Cobden, they are limned with sufficient distinctness in "Jorrocks" and "Job Thornberry;" and other politicians, as well as divers men and women of fashion, may be detected without any great display of acumen, by the reader who cares to know—not exactly Lord Beaconsfield's opinion of them, but so much of his opinion as he chooses to put into a novel.

In the effort to illustrate by excerpts the author's worldly knowledge and social philosophy—the scope and minuteness of his scrutiny and the shrewdness of his verdicts—we are embarrassed to an extent not equalled or approached in any recent book by the redundancy of interesting material. There is scarcely a page, much less a chapter, which has not something in it likely to rivet the attention, some conclusion or suggestion not unapt to strike and occupy the historical student, politician, social scientist, or man of the world. Perhaps we cannot do better than begin with the portrait of the ex-Queen Hortense, who is somewhat grotesquely designated as " Agrippina." Inasmuch as the author takes the favorable view of that lady's character lately propounded in Madame De Rémusat's memoirs, it is plain that he disclaims for her the vices, while he surely would not assert for her the virile qualities of Nero's mother. Lord Beaconsfield's impressions, however, of Queen Hortense being derived from personal acquaintance, are well worth citing.

The lady was fair and singularly thin. It seemed that her delicate hand must really be transparent. Her cheek was sunk, but the expression of her large brown eyes was inexpressibly pleasing. She wore her own hair, once the most celebrated in Europe, and still uncovered. Though the prodigal richness of the tresses had disappeared, the arrangement was still striking from its grace.

That rare quality pervaded the being of this lady, and it was impossible not to be struck with her carriage as she advanced to meet her guest; free from all affectation, and yet full of movement and gestures, which might have been the study of painters.

Then follows an intimation that the charges of coarse depravity levelled by Madame de Rémusat at the courts of the Consulate and the Empire are not, in Lord Beaconsfield's opinion, by any means deserved:

"And I read," said the lady, a little indignant, "in some memoirs the other day that our court was a corrupt and dissolute court. It was a court of pleasure, if you like; but of pleasure that animated and refined, and put the world in good humor, which, after all, is good government. The most corrupt and dissolute courts on the Continent of Europe that I have known," said the lady, "have been outwardly the dullest and most decorous."

" My memory of those days," said Mr. Wilton, " is of ceaseless grace and inexhaustible charm."

"Well," said the lady, " if I sinned I have at least suffered. And I hope they were only sins of omission. I wanted to see everybody happy, and tried to make them so."

On the signal change which has come over London society within the last fifty years, as regards comprehensiveness and complexity, Lord Beaconsfield offers some remarks which, trite as the subject is, will repay attention:

The great world then, compared with the huge society of the present period, was limited in its proportions, and composed of elements more refined though far less various. It consisted mainly of the great landed aristocracy, who had quite absorbed the nabobs of India, and had nearly appropriated the huge West Indian fortunes. Occasionally an eminent banker or merchant invested a large portion of his accumulations in land, and in the purchase of Parliamentary influence, and was in time duly admitted into the sanctuary. But those vast and successful invasions of society by new classes which have since occurred, though impending, had not yet commenced. The manufacturers, the railway kings, the colossal contractors, the discoverers of nuggets, had not yet found their place in society and the senate. There were then, perhaps, more great houses open than at the present day, but there were very few little ones. The necessity of providing regular occasions for the assembling of the miscellaneous world of fashion led to the institution of Almack's, which died out in the advent of the new system of society, and in the fierce competition of its inexhaustible private entertainments.

Not only was society a much narrower and more exclusive thing when Endymion came up to the metropolis in the reign of "Sailor Bill," but London life in general was to the stranger, the lounger, to all, in fact, except the privileged habitués of a small patrician circle, decidedly tame and irksome.

At this time London was a very dull city, instead of being, as it is now, a very amusing one. Probably there never was a city in the world with so vast a population which was so melancholy. The aristocracy probably have always found amusements adapted to the manners of the time and the age in which they lived. The middle classes half a century ago had little distraction from their monotonous toil and melancholy anxieties, except, perhaps, what they found in religious and philanthropic societies. Their general life must have been very dull. Some traditionary merriment always lingered among the working classes of England. Both in town and country they had always their games and fairs and junketing parties, which have developed into excursion trains and colossal picnics. But of all classes of the community in the days of our fathers there was none so unfortunate in respect of public amusements as the bachelors about town. There were, one might almost say, only two theatres, and they so huge that it was difficult to see or hear in either. Their monopolies, no longer redeemed by the stately genius of the Kembles, the pathos of Miss O'Neill, or the fiery passion of Kean, were already menaced, and were soon about to fall ; but the crowd of diminutive but sparkling substitutes which have since taken their place had not yet appeared, and half price at Drury Lane or Covent Garden was a dreary distraction after a morning of desk work. There were no Alhambras then, and no Cremornes, no palaces of crystal in terraced gardens, no casinos, no music halls, no aquaria, no promenade concerts. Evans's existed, but not in the fulness of its modern development ; and the most popular place of resort was the barbarous conviviality of the Cider Cellar.

Here is a description of the Anglican Church, as it was just before the outbreak of the Tractarian movement :

The English Church had no competent leaders among the clergy. The spirit that has animated and disturbed our later times seemed quite dead, and no one anticipated its resurrection. The bishops had been selected from college dons, men profoundly ignorant of the condition and the wants of the country. To have edited a Greek play with second-rate success, or to have been the tutor of some considerable patrician, was the qualification then deemed desirable and sufficient for an office which at this day is at least reserved for eloquence and energy. The social influence of the Episcopal bench was nothing. A prelate was rarely seen in the saloons of Zenobia. It is since the depths of religious thought have been probed, and the influence of woman in the spread and sustenance of religious feeling has again been recognized, that fascinating and fashionable prelates have become favored guests in the refined saloons of the mighty, and, while apparently indulging in the vanities of the hour, have re-established the influence which in old days guided a Matilda or the mother of Constantine.

And here is a remarkable passage in which the author makes a foreign diplomatist, talking in 1830, anticipate the profound transformation which has since taken place in the aims of the European revolutionary party. Although the speaker's language is manifestly warped by what we should now call conservative, not to say reactionist tendencies, he yet distinguishes clearly between the Jacobin ideals, based as they were on the root conception of individualism, and the new principles and projects which, under the names of Saint Simonism, Fouricrism, and Socialism, have to a large extent supplanted them.

"You know I am a Liberal, and have always been a Liberal," said the Baron ; "I know the value of civil and religious liberty, for I was born in a country where we had neither, and where we have since enjoyed either very fitfully. Nothing can be much drearier than the present lot of my country, and it is probable that these doings at Paris may help my friends a little, and they may again hold up their heads for a time ; but I have seen too much, and am too old, to indulge in dreams. You are a young man, and will live to see what I can only predict. The world is thinking of something else than civil and religious liberty. Those are phrases of the eighteenth century. The men who have won these 'three glorious days' at Paris want neither civilization nor religion. They will not be content till they have destroyed both. It is possible that they may be parried for a time ; that the adroit wisdom of the house of Orleans, guided by Talleyrand, may give this movement the resemblance, and even the character, of a middle-class revolution. It is no such thing ; the barricades were not erected by the middle class. I know these people ; it is a fraternity, not a nation. Europe is honeycombed with their secret societies. They are spread all over Spain. Italy is entirely mined. I know more of the Southern than the Northern nations, but I have been assured by one who should know that the brotherhood are organized throughout Germany and even in Russia. I have spoken to the Duke about these things. He is not indifferent, or altogether incredulous, but he is so essentially practical that he can only deal with what he sees. I have spoken to the Whig leaders. They tell me that there is only one specific and that a complete one—constitutional government : that with representative institutions secret societies cannot exist. I may be wrong, but it seems to me that with these secret societies representative institutions rather will disappear."

There is a great deal in this book about the Rothschilds, who figure as the "Neuchatels." It was natural, perhaps, that the son of Isaac Disraeli should speak in a highly appreciative, not to say obsequious, tone, of the great Hebrew banking house. Every phase and incident of their striking history, undergoes in his hands a softening process, whose keynote is struck in making their founder issue from a Swiss town instead of the Frankfort Ghetto. Here is the expurgated story of their beginnings :

One of the most remarkable families that have ever flourished in England were the Neuchatels. Their founder was a Swiss, who had established a banking house of high repute in England in the latter part of the eighteenth century, and, irrespective of a powerful domestic connection, had in time pretty well engrossed the largest and best portion of foreign banking business. When the great French revolution occurred, all the emigrants deposited their jewels and their treasure with the Neuchatels. As the disturbances spread, their example was followed by the alarmed proprietors and capitalists of the rest of Europe: and, independently of their own considerable means, the Neuchatels thus had the command for a quarter of a century, more or less, of adventitious millions. They were scrupulous and faithful stewards; but they were doubtless repaid for their vigilance, their anxiety, and often their risk, by the opportunities which these rare resources permitted them to enjoy. One of the Neuchatels was a favorite of Mr. Pitt, and assisted the great statesman in his vast financial arrangements. This Neuchatel was a man of large capacity, and thoroughly understood his period. The Minister wished to introduce him to public life, would have opened Parliament to him, and no doubt have showered on him honors and titles. But Neuchatel declined these overtures. He was one of those strong minds who will concentrate their energies on one object; without personal vanity, but with a deep seated pride in the future. He was always preparing for his posterity. Governed by this passion, although he himself would have been content to live forever in Bishopsgate street, where he was born, he had become possessed of a vast principality, which, strange to say, with every advantage of splendor and natural beauty, was not an hour's drive from Whitechapel.

The Elder "Neuchatel" departed this life, we are told, a little before the second French revolution of 1830, and it is his eldest son and successor, "Adrian," of whom we hear continually in this novel :

Adrian had inherited something more, and something more precious, than his father's treasure—a not inferior capacity, united in his case, with much culture, and with a worldly ambition to which his father was a stranger. * * *

Adrian purchased a very fine mansion in Portland Place, and took up his residence formally at Hainault. He delighted in the place, and to dwell there in a manner becoming the scene had always been one of his dreams. Now he lived there with unbounded expenditure. * * *

Sunday was always a great day at Hainault. The Royal and the Stock Exchanges were both of them always fully represented; and then they often had an opportunity, which they highly appreciated, of seeing and conferring with some public characters, M. P.'s of note or promise, and occasionally a secretary of the treasury or a privy councillor. "Turtle makes all men equal," Adrian would observe. "Our friend Trodgits seemed a little embarrassed at first when I introduced him to the Right Honorable; but when they sat next each other at dinner they soon got on very well."

Endymion's sister, Myra, becomes a governess in the banker's family, and with her we are introduced to the Neuchatel household :

She was much diverted by the gentlemen of the Stock Exchange, so acute, so audacious, and differing so much from the merchants in the style even of their dress, and in the case, perhaps the too great facility, of their bearing. They called each other by their Christian names, and there were allusions to practical jokes which intimated a life something between a public school and a garrison. On more solemn days there were diplomatists and men in public office; sometimes great musical artists, and occasionally a French actor. But the dinners were always the same; dishes worthy of the great days of the Bourbons, and wines of rarity and price, which could not ruin Neuchatel, for in many instances the vineyards belonged to himself.

One of Endymion's friends, Mr. St. Barbe, who is a sour, conceited, heretofore unsuccessful man of letters, dines one evening at the "Neuchatels'," and if any reader doubts that Thackeray was the original of this gentleman, let him ponder the following paragraphs :

St. Barbe was not disappointed in his hopes. It was an evening of glorious success for him. He had even the honor of sitting for a time by the side of Mrs. Neuchatel, and being full of good claret, he, as he phrased it, showed his paces : this is to say, delivered himself of some sarcastic paradoxes duly blended with fulsome flattery. Later in the evening he contrived to be presented both to the Ambassador and the Cabinet Minister, and treated them as if they were demigods ; listened to them as if with an admiration which he vainly endeavored to repress ; never spoke except to enforce and illustrate the views which they had condescended to intimate ; successfully conveyed to his Excellency that he was conversing with an enthusiast for his exalted profession; and to the Minister that he had met an ardent sympathizer with his noble career. * *

"I have done business to-night," said St. Barbe to Endymion toward the close of the evening. "Foreign affairs are all the future, and my views may be as right as anybody else's ; probably more correct, not so conventional. What a fool I was, Ferrars! I was asked to remain here to-night, and refused! The truth is, I could not stand those powdered gentlemen, and I should have been under their care. They seem so haughty and supercilious. And yet I was wrong. I spoke to one of them very rudely just now, when he was handing coffee, to show I was not afraid, and he answered me like a seraph. I felt remorse."

That touch about the flunkies is unmistakable. And here is another patent allusion to the author of the "Yellowplush Papers" in the account of St. Barbe's later years, when that novelist's works had proved successful, and he was going about a good deal among what he called the big wigs. The words put into St. Barbe's mouth could only have been pronounced by Thackeray:

We must not forget our old friend St. Barbe. Whether he had written himself out or had become lazy in the luxurious life in which he now indulged, he rarely appealed to the literary public, which still admired him. He was always intimating that he was engaged in a great work, which, though written in his taking prose, was to be really the epopee of social life in this country. Dining out every day, and ever arriving, however late, at those "small and earlies" which he once despised, he gave to his friends frequent intimations that he was not there for pleasure, but rather following his profession; he was in his studio, observing and reflecting on all the passions and manners of mankind, and gathering materials for the great work which was eventually to enchant and instruct society and immortalize his name.

"The fact is, I wrote too early," he would say. "I blush when I read my own books, though compared with those of the brethren they might still be looked on as classics. They say no artist can draw a camel, and I say no author ever drew a gentleman. How can they, with no opportunity of ever seeing one? And so, with a little caricature of manners, which they catch second-hand, they are obliged to have recourse to outrageous nonsense, as if polished life consisted only of bigamists, and ladies of fashion were in the habit of paying blackmail to returned convicts. However, I shall put an end to all this. I have now got the materials, or am accumulating them daily. You hint that I give myself up too much to society. You are talking of things you do not understand. A dinner-party is a chapter. I catch the Cynthia of the minute, sir, at a soirée. If I only served a grateful country, I should be in the proudest position of any of its sons; if I had been born in any country but this, I should have been decorated, and perhaps made Secretary of State like Addison, who did not write as well as I do, though his style somewhat resembles mine."

During the greater part of the story Lord Palmerston is constantly in the foreground under the name of the Earl of Roehampton, who by an extraordinary divergence from biographical fact, is made to marry a sister of Endymion (Disraeli). Here is one of the author' comments on the great Whig minister :

The Earl of Roehampton was the strongest member of the Government, except, of course, the premier himself. He was the man from whose combined force and flexibility of character the country had confidence that in all their councils there would be no lack of courage, yet tempered with adroit discretion. Lord Roehampton, though an Englishman, was an Irish peer, and was resolved to remain so, for he fully appreciated the position which united social distinction with the power of a seat in the House of Commons. He was a very ambitious, and, as it was thought, worldly man, deemed even by many to be unscrupulous, and yet he was romantic. A great favorite in society, and especially with the softer sex, somewhat late in life he had married suddenly a beautiful woman, who was without fortune, and not a member of the enchanted circle in which he flourished.

And this is what the banker Neuchatel (Rothschild) said of him :

I like Lord Roehampton, and, between ourselves, I wish he were First Minister. He understands the Continent, and would keep things quiet. But, do you know, Miss Ferrars, with all his playful, good-tempered manner, as if he could not say a cross word or do an unkind act, he is a very severe man in business. Speak to him on business, and he is completely changed. His brows knit, he penetrates you with the terrible scrutiny of that deep-set eye: he is more than stately, he is austere. I have been up to him with deputations—the governor of the bank, and all the first men in the city, half of them M. P.'s, and they trembled before him like aspens.

After the death of Lord Roehampton, his widow is invited to share the throne of a sovereign (Louis Napoleon), of whom, under the titles of Count of Otranto and Prince Floristan, and the pseudonym of Col. Albert we hear a good deal in this novel. He was much at Hainault House, having some secret business with Mr. Neuchatel, and he was liked, we are told, by the female members of the banker's family.

And yet it cannot be said that he was entertaining, but there are some silent people who are more interesting than the best talkers. And when he did speak he always said the right thing. His manners were tender and gentle ; he had an unobtrusive sympathy with all they said or did, except, indeed, and that was not rarely, when he was lost in profound abstraction.

Endymion's sister, who before her first marriage, was domiciled at Hainault, used to insist that "Colonel Albert" had a "good heart :"

"They say he is the most unscrupulous of living men," said Mr. Neuchatel, with his peculiar smile.

"Perhaps he is the most determined," said Myra. "Moral courage is the rarest of qualities, and often maligned."

From a Baron Sergius, the chief confidant and adviser of Colonel Albert during his exile, Endymion received the following impression of the French adventurer's character :

"The Prince rarely gives an opinion," said the Baron. "Indeed, as you well know, he rarely speaks, he thinks and he acts."

"But if he acts on wrong information," continued Endymion, "there will probably be only one consequence."

"The Prince is very wise," said the Baron, "and, trust me, knows as much about mankind and the varieties of mankind as any one. He may not believe in the Latin race, but he may choose to use those who do believe in it. The weakness of the Prince, if he have one, is not want of knowledge or want of judgment, but an over confidence in his star, which sometimes seduces him into enterprises which he himself feels at the time are not perfectly sound."

Apropos of Louis Napoleon, it is interesting to note what his counterpart in this novel is made to say about us after his return from a compulsory visit to the United States :

"I suppose their society is like the best society in Manchester?" said Lord Roehampton.

"It varies in different cities," said Colonel Albert. "In some there is considerable culture, and then refinement of life always follows.

"Yes, but whatever they may be, they will always be colonial. What is colonial necessarily lacks originality. A country that borrows its language, its laws, and its religion, cannot have its inventive powers much developed. They got civilized very soon, but their civilization was second-hand."

"Perhaps their inventive powers may develop themselves in other ways," said the Prince. "A nation has a fixed quantity of invention, and it will make itself felt."

Another impressive personage stalks now and then across the stage ; this is the Count of Ferroll, in whom the most careless reader cannot help recognizing Bismarck. When this book is perused upon the Continent no passage, probably, will be scanned with more curiosity than Lord Beaconsfield's description of the prospective Chancellor :

The Count of Ferroll was a young man, and yet inclined to be bald. He was chief of a not inconsiderable mission at our court. Though not to be described as a handsome man, his countenance was striking ; a brow of much intellectual development, and a massive jaw. He was tall, broad-shouldered, with a slender waist. He greeted Endymion with a penetrating glance, and then with a winning smile.

The Count of Ferroll was the representative of a kingdom which, if not exactly created, had been moulded into a certain form of apparent strength and importance by the Congress of Vienna. He was a noble of considerable estate in a country where possessions were not extensive or fortunes large, though it was ruled by an ancient and haughty and warlike aristocracy. Like his class, the Count of Ferroll had received a military education ; but when that education was completed, he found but a feeble prospect of his acquirements being called into action. It was believed that the age of great wars had ceased, and that even revolutions were for the future to be controlled by diplomacy. As he was a man of an original, not to say eccentric, turn of mind, the Count of Ferroll was not contented with the resources and distraction of his second-rate capital. He was an eminent sportsman, and for some time took refuge and found excitement in the breadth of his dark forests, and in the formation of a stud, which had already become celebrated. But at this time, even in the excitement of the chase, and in the raising of his rare-bred steeds, the Count of Ferroll might be said to have been brooding over the position of what he could scarcely call his country, but rather an aggregation of lands baptized by protocols, and christened and consolidated by treaties, which he looked upon as eminently untrustworthy. One day he surprised his sovereign, with whom he was a favorite, by requesting to be appointed to the legation at London, which was vacant.

The Count of Ferroll now and then bestows some suggestions on Endymion.   Here is one of them :

"You will find it of the first importance in public life," said the Count of Ferroll, "to know personally those who are carrying on the business of the world, so much depends on the character of an individual, his habits of thought, his prejudices, his superstitions, his social weaknesses, his health.   Conducting affairs without this advantage is, in effect, an affair of stationery ; it is pens and paper who are in communication, not human beings."

In the next excerpt the Count of Ferroll is made to review the state of Europe not long before the outbreak of the revolution of 1848.   He is speaking to Lady Montfort :

"Everything is quite rotten throughout the Continent.   This year is tranquillity to what the next will be.   There is not a throne in Europe worth a year's purchase.   My worthy master wants me to return home and be Minister.   I am to fashion for him a new constitution.   I will never have anything to do with new constitutions ; their inventors are always the first victims.   Instead of making a constitution, he should make a country, and convert his heterogeneous domains into a patriotic dominion."
"But how is that to be done ?"
"There is only one way ; by blood and iron."

"My dear Count, you shock me!"

"I shall have to shock you a great deal more before the inevitable is brought about."

The portrait of Poole, the tailor, as he was at the apogee of his career, will be promptly recognized by those who had the pleasure of that distinguished man's acquaintance in the later years of his useful life. It was Endymion's good fortune, as it has been, we believe, that of other promising youth, to be sumptuously clothed for some years by Mr. Poole on the credit of their future.

That friend was no common person; he was Mr. Vigo, by birth a Yorkshireman, and gifted with all the attributes, physical and intellectual, of that celebrated race. At present he was the most fashionable tailor in London, and one whom many persons consulted. Besides being consummate in his art, Mr. Vigo had the reputation of being a man of singularly good judgment. He was one who obtained influence over all with whom he came in contact, and as his business placed him in contact with various classes, but especially with the class socially most distinguished, his influence was great. The golden youth who repaired to his counters came there not merely to obtain raiment of the best material and the most perfect cut, but to see and talk with Mr. Vigo, and to ask his opinion on various points. There was a spacious room where, if they liked, they might smoke a cigar, and "Vigo's cigars" were something which no one could rival. If they liked to take a glass of hock with their tobacco, there was a bottle ready from the cellars of Johannisberg. Mr. Vigo's stable was almost as famous as its master; he drove the finest horses in London, and rode the best hunters in the Vale of Aylesbury. Without this, his manners were exactly what they should be. He was neither pretentious nor servile, but simple, and with becoming respect for others and for himself. He never took a liberty with any one, and such treatment, as is generally the case, was reciprocal.

As we have said, the somewhat carefully drawn figure of Lord Montfort suggests the ironical design of contrasting the veritable lineaments of Lord Hertford with the apocryphal traits assigned by Thackeray to the Marquis of Steyne. It was, perhaps, with the same purpose of raillery that in this book "St. Barbe," in whom Thackeray is but thinly veiled, is introduced for the first time to Lord Montfort, after his novel, "Topsy Turvy" ("Vanity Fair") had been given to the world. Humorously, too, Lord Montfort is represented as reading "Topsy Turvy" with uncommon pleasure. Of the same nobleman we are told that he suddenly left his country without giving any one notice of his intentions, and entered into and fulfilled a vast scheme of adventurous travel—an incident in the actual career of the Marquess of Hertford. "His flag had floated in the Indian Ocean, and he had penetrated the dazzling mysteries of Brazilian forests." He was "heard of in every capital except his own—wonderful exploits at St. Petersburg and Paris and Madrid, deeds of mark at Vienna, and eccentric adventures at Rome." At last it would appear that the restless Lord Montfort—again like the nobleman whom Balzac drew in "Lord Seymour," and in whom Thackeray thought he discerned "Lord Steyne"—had found his true place, and that place was Paris. There he "dwelt for years in Sybaritic seclusion. He built himself a palace, which he called a villa, and which was the most fanciful of structures, and full of every beautiful object which rare taste and boundless wealth could procure, from undoubted Raphaels to jeweled toys." It was said that Lord Montfort saw no one; he certainly did not "court, or receive his countrymen, and this, perhaps, gave rise to, or at least caused to be exaggerated, the tales that were rife of his profusion, and even his profligacy." But according to Lord Beaconsfield he was not entirely isolated :

He lived much with the old families of France in their haughty faubourg, and was highly considered by them. It was truly a circle for which he was adapted. Lord Montfort was the only living Englishman who gave one an idea of the nobleman of the eighteenth century. He was totally devoid of the sense of responsibility, and he looked what he resembled. His manner, though simple and natural, was finished and refined, and free from forbidding reserve, was yet characterized by an air of serious grace.

*   *   *   *   *   *   *   *   *

There was no subject, divine or human, in which he took the slightest interest. He entertained for human nature generally, and without any exception, the most cynical appreciation. He had a sincere and profound conviction that no man or woman ever acted except from selfish or interested motives. Society was intolerable to him—that of his own sex and station wearisome beyond expression.; their conversation consisted only of two subjects, horses and women, and he had long exhausted both. As for female society, if they were ladies, it was expected that, in some form or other, he should make love to them, and he had no sentiment. If he took refuge in the *demi-monde*, he encountered vulgarity, and that to Lord Montfort was insufferable. He had tried them in every capital, and vulgarity was the badge of all their tribe. He had attempted to read ; a woman had told him to read French novels, but he found them only a clumsy representation of the life which for years he had practically been leading. * * *

No one could say Lord Montfort was a bad-hearted man, for he had no heart. He was good-natured, provided it brought him no inconvenience ; and as for temper, his was never disturbed, but this not from sweetness of disposition, rather from a contemptuous fine taste, which assured him that a gentleman should never be deprived of tranquillity in a world where nothing was of the slightest consequence.

It must be owned, we think, that Balzac's sketch is dim, and Thackeray's coarse, beside this picture, which has the fine lines and the subtle half shades of life.

We have room for one more citation. In this paragraph Lord Beaconsfield touches on a theme with which he should be preëminently conversant—the influence of the Semitic race :

The Semites are unquestionably a great race, for among the few things in this world which appear to be certain, nothing is more sure than that they invented our alphabet. But the Semites now exercise a vast influence over affairs by their smallest though most peculiar family, the Jews. There is no race gifted with so much tenacity and such skill in organization. These qualities have given them an unprecedented hold over property and illimitable credit. As you advance in life, and get experience in affairs, the Jews will cross you everywhere. They have long been stealing into our secret diplomacy, which they have almost appropriated ; in another quarter of a century they will claim their share of open government. Well, there are races, men and bodies of men influenced in their conduct by their particular organization, and which must enter into all the calculations of a statesman. But what do they mean by the Latin race ? Language and religion do not make a race. There is only one thing which makes a race and that is blood.

Most persons will find it hard to accept, or even to understand, the definition propounded in the last sentence. So far as the term race means anything deserving the attention of the thinker or the statesman, it denotes something more than mere congenial proclivities, which may be checked, warped, and ultimately effaced by a change of circumstances. It seems to postulate cohesion, coöperation, community of sentiments, identity of interests. These attributes of a people are generated by the pressure of a common language, a common religion, and common geographical boundaries rather than by any evanescent affinities of blood. What is it but language and religion which has hindered the Poles from coalescing with their fellow Slavs of Muscovy ? What weighty agency now exists, except a difference of language, to hold back Portugal from fusion with the main body of the Iberian peninsula ? What is it but a difference of religion which has kept the Catholic Celts of Ireland radically separate from the kindred Celts who, having once migrated from Ireland to Scotland, came back again to occupy the province of Ulster ? And what has developed in the Jews themselves the tenacity of purpose and capacity of organization to which Lord Beaconsfield adverts, but the maintenance of their national

faith, and, so far as Hebrew is retained in their religious services, of their national language ?

As we lay down this book we feel that the choice of
title, which at first struck us as fantastic, is sufficiently
apposite. With all the author's worldly wisdom and
political sagacity, he has given us in "Endymion" a
very sentimental book. Has he ever given us anything
else, and is not this tender, sympathetic accent, which
is scarcely drowned even in his cynical affectations, the
keynote of his character, and the secret of his conquest
of society ? From one point of view this latest novel
might be termed the apotheosis of woman, considered as
a social and political force. It is not one goddess only
who deigns to look on this Endymion, but three god-
desses who vie with one another in assuring to the lucky
youth a place among the immortals. "Women," his
sister tells him in the days of his obscurity, "will be
your best friends in life ; " and really it seems that to
this sister, or to Lady Montfort, or to Adriana Neuchatel, or to Lady Beaumaris every step of his advancement
must be credited. If this story can be regarded as in
any sense autobiographical, it must be owned that the
author's acknowledgment of his profound indebtedness
to women presents a curious psychological phenomenon.
We should scarcely look for it from a proud man, though
we might expect it from a vain man. Those, however,
who are familiar with the prejudice against men of Is-
raelite origin, which not long ago was rampant and is
still rife in English society, will appreciate the self-com-

placency which recalls how a Hebrew youth found favor
with the daughters of the Philistines. After all, the
main thing which concerns us in this matter of the alleged influence of women is not the good taste but the
truth of Lord Beaconsfield's assertion. Are women such
potent factors in the shaping not only of man's social
but of his political career ? Balzac said they were ; indeed, the paradox is unceasingly developed in the Comédie Humaine. And now a far higher authority than the
French novelist comes forward in a narrative wherein
readers are invited, or at least not forbidden, to trace
the story of his life, and lends the weight of his observation and striking personal experience to the unmeas-
ured exaltation of woman's importance in the world.

We do not think that Mr. Henry James, jr., has increased his reputation by his life of Hawthorne, which forms a volume in the series of "English Men of Letters." Neither as a biography nor as a critical estimate is this book satisfactory. It tells us nothing about Hawthorne's private circumstances with which we were previously unacquainted, although there is much we need to know in order to comprehend the peculiar character of the man. It supplies us with no definite and exhaustive conception of his intellectual acquirements and capacities; indeed, we derive from its perusal an impression much more meagre, fractional, and nebulous than we gained from Mr. Lathrop's memoir. When we consider the responsibilities imposed on a new biographer of Hawthorne, and the opportunities offered for fresh, trenchant, and candid criticism, the shortcomings of this performance are not easily explicable on grounds creditable to the writer. We cannot well escape the inference that the aim of this undertaking was not so much a patient, unflinching exposition of the subject as an elaborate display of the literary faculty on the part of the biographer. There is ample proof in every chapter, and, for that matter, in every page, of a fact with which we were conversant, namely, that the writer is an expert in the art of verbal expression, that he understands better than most of his American contemporaries the use of the file, and that his work, however wanting in breadth and solidity, will always be deftly joined and laboriously polished. But of new facts there is a total dearth, and of new ideas there is an almost equal scarcity. If robust, teemful thought and uncompromising utterance formed the core of his achievement, there would be something fine in the punctilious precision and finish of his style; as it is, there is something finical.

We imagine the disappointment encountered in this volume may be traced to the fundamental principle which governs Mr. James's literary methods, and to the models which he obviously keeps in view. Were it possible, without injustice, to characterize him in a word, we might call him a victim of Sainte-Beuve. The blended social and artistic importance of the French critic seems to have suggested a studious reproduction of his processes with the somewhat credulous hope of compassing an analogous success. Had he appealed, however, to an English or an American audience, Sainte-Beuve himself would probably have invented a different system ; or, failing to adjust his tone and posture to his environment, he must have contented himself with the circumscribed and superficial influence exercised by Matthew Arnold. There is something repugnant to the Anglo-Saxon temper in the cautious, sly, evasive, equivocal attitude of Sainte-Beuve. We incline to withhold confidence from those who deal exclusively in circumlocutions, approximations, insinuations, who nibble at the edges or flutter round the surface of an idea, who prefer skirmish to close fighting, who are too nervous for straight thrusts, too dainty for hard blows. Americans do not appreciate critics who seem to keep one eye on the truth and another on their social status. We have no time to waste in detecting between the lines what a writer has scrupled to avow lest it might affect his standing in somebody's drawing room. For us, the worth of Sainte-Beuve's sentences is measured by their obvious purport, by their positive illuminating value, and we cannot be expected to heed the dexterity with which he could infuse a hint of censure or imbed a sting of calumny without imperilling for a moment his prospect of a seat in the Academy, or his hold on certain salons of the Faubourg St. Honoré. We do not care to see autopsies performed with white kid gloves, or to watch the objects of a just severity or a secret spite done to death with drops of venom through a process of subcutaneous injection. The truth about Sainte-Beuve is that he was an unconscionable, but extremely astute, egoist, with a strong dash of poltroonery in his composition, who wrote criticism because he had the good sense to recognize, after experiment, that he could write nothing else, and who learned to manipulate the pen so as to make it at once a means of livelihood, a lever of social advancement, and an instrument of private vengeance. Voltaire, before him, had managed to elicit all this from literature; but the striking and original feature of Sainte-Beuve's process was his habitual employment of periphrasis and innuendo—the inimitable skill with which, behind the affectation of exaggerated equity and exquisite breeding, he contrived to slake his private pique and depreciate his rivals with impunity. In the hands of other men the pen had been made a sword, but Sainte-Beuve was the first to make it at once an air gun and a rampart. When he meant to say a sharp or ungenerous thing, he was always careful to so arrange things that, in case his adversary showed fight, he could plead *non vult*, or set up an alibi.

The reproduction of Sainte-Beuve's attitude and tactics by American critics would be, we should say, a blunder, even from an egoistic point of view. There is among us no august fraternity like the Immortal Forty, whose suffrages a prudent writer might hesitate to estrange by a too aggressive or cynical demeanor, nor are there any drawing-rooms exile from which would wear the paralyzing terrors of social annihilation. There is, indeed, a grotesque, a ludicrous incongruity in the application of Sainte-Beuvian methods to a raw and chaotic society, to a puny, callow, and amorphous literature. To be in the least appropriate or helpful our American criticism must borrow the manner of the pedagogue, and not that of the courtier ; we need plain speech, not pretty speech ; the truth must be hammered and not filtered into us. It might do us good, for instance, to have Edgar Poe once more in the chair of judgment, although Mr. James pronounces his opinions vulgar and provincial. We are all provincial, perhaps vulgar, and why should we be scared by words which Mr. Matthew Arnold hints are also applicable to contemporary England? If to be a blunt, downright truth seeker and truth teller, if to follow methods the precise converse of those practised by Sainte-Beuve and his disciples, be a sign of vulgarity, then we can only wish that Carlyle, Ruskin, Christopher North, and Edgar Poe may find a horde of equally barbarous successors to save us from the incubus of cosmopolitan hyper-elegance.

The Sainte-Beuvian treatment applied to the career and character of Hawthorne could hardly fail to be particularly sterile. The key to Hawthorne's intellectual and æsthetic shortcomings is probably to be found in his defective education, and the cramped and arid aspect of the social world in which he lived. These drawbacks, there is reason to believe, were aggravated by poverty. Now, why should not Mr. James have searched out, and spoken out, the truth on all these matters? Instead of talking about the petty colonial offices held by some of Hawthorne's progenitors a century and a half before his birth, and aiming to trace the moral cast and drift of the novelist's mind to such remote and legendary sources, he might have given us more pertinent and trustworthy material by setting forth the humble lives of his subject's parents and grandparents. Inasmuch, too, as we see Hawthorne in pecuniary straits after his books began to earn something, we should have liked to know how he managed to keep the wolf from the door during the thirty-five or forty years preceding. How did he subsist, for instance, at Bowdoin College? Was it by keeping school in the vacations, or was it by incurring debts? Who paid for his breakfasts and dinners during the dozen years which he is represented as spending in his Salem bedroom, immersed in lonely meditation, and where, according to his own statement, "fame was born?" What did the newspapers and magazines of the time pay for his stories, and what did his publisher give him for "The Scarlet Letter?" Why is he portrayed by his biographer as being constrained to write for a livelihood in the last years of his life, after his return from Europe, where he had held the most lucrative consulate in the gift of the government? What were his habits as the steward of a family and the master of a household? Did he shoulder a man's responsibilities like a man, or did he shirk them—let us say, like a novelist? What cause associated with his private circumstances or his personal experience is chargeable with the extraordinary diffidence which Hawthorne exhibited up to his last sojourn in England in the company of ladies and in general society? Is there any record in his life of acts of remarkable generosity or self-sacrifice on behalf of his sisters or his friends? Did he leave a profound impression of ability in conversation and chance intercourse? These are questions which must be answered, if we would know something of the man as distinguished from the literary artist; and the putting of such queries is not reckoned either

12

vulgar or provincial in the case of Keats and Shelley, of Goldsmith and Dr. Johnson.

We note a like curious reluctance on the part of Mr. James to recognize or to disclose the extremely slender outfit of mental furniture with which Hawthorne undertook the literary vocation. We are told, for example, that he graduated at Bowdoin College, a statement not unlikely to mislead an English reader. Nevertheless the biographer does not mark, except in a vague and cursory way, the small significance of that performance. In the year 1825 a degree of Bachelor of Arts at Bowdoin, or for that matter at any other New England college, represented a more meagre scholastic equipment than is now demanded of applicants for admission to the Freshman Class at Harvard, or than would have been tolerated at the earlier date in the fourth form of an English public school. Hawthorne's attainments, however, at this stage of his career, were probably quite equal to those of Emerson or of Longfellow, and it was the duty of the biographer to inquire whether, in this case, the work of self-education had been pushed as strenuously and fruitfully as in theirs. If the subject of this memoir, during the dozen years of retirement that followed graduation, had compassed large acquisitions in history, in science, in philosophy, we have a right to expect that Mr. James should trace the direction and results of this self-culture. If Hawthorne, on the other hand, remained content with a thin tincture of information touching some of the most important fields of intellectual energy, these deficiencies should have been resolutely probed and boldly avowed. So, too, if the author of " The Marble Faun " really knew nothing, and cared nothing, for any art save that which finds expression through the medium of written words, this was a strange anomaly which needed to be brought out with peculiar emphasis, and would have well repaid the most studious analysis. The writer's failure, however, to enlighten us on these heads is far less disappointing than his reticence on another topic. No reader of the novelist needs to be told that the common theme of all Hawthorne's stories is the deeper psychology—that they deal, one and all, with what homely folk are disposed to call the mysteries of man's soul and conscience. We say homely folk, because it is plain that the sphere of so-called mysteries is likely to be narrowed in proportion to the widening of man's metaphysical and physiological knowledge. In the case of works like Hawthorne's, it is surely of prime importance to learn precisely what the author's philosophy was ; what was his view of the relation of man to the universe, of human character to circumstances and congenital tendency ; of the relation of the intellect, the will, and the emotions to the cerebral substance in which they find their seat. How can we interpret such books as " The Scarlet Letter " or " The House of the Seven Gables," unless we have some such master key ? It was, we submit, the business of the biographer to seek the key, to expound Hawthorne's philosophy, if he had any, while, if after patient search no trace of a reasoned, symmetrical, coherent system could be found; if, in other words, Hawthorne, whose novels are popularly supposed to be nothing if not psychological, had no clear conceptions of psychology; if he affected all the airs of a philosopher without possessing the rudiments of a philosophy; then it was incumbent on Mr. James, as a paramount obligation, to announce and elucidate this paradox. Certainly Hawthorne's performance would not have seemed to us less extraordinary or less creditable because the appliances should turn out to have been so rude and the materials so scanty.

It is true that Mr. James does manage to leave the impression that Hawthorne had no science, no religion, no philosophy, and no art beyond his marvellous dexterity in conjuring from words the effects of form and color. But there is nowhere any definite statement to that effect, not a sentence which enables the reader to indubitably fix the responsibility of his impression. We are sometimes prompted to surmise that Mr. James is un-. willing to hurt the feelings of this or that relative of Hawthorne's by bringing out distinctly the humble origin and circumstances of the novelist, or by sounding the deficiencies of his intellectual outfit. Such a motive, we need not say, might very properly have led him to decline at the outset the task of writing a biography, but cannot be invoked to excuse a superficial execution of the work. Now and then, on the other hand, the turn of a sentence or the choice of an adjective suggests that Mr. James may incline to disguise from an English audience the very modest, not to say shabby, surroundings in which much of Hawthorne's life was passed, and the somewhat meagre acquirements of one whom we must acknowledge has left behind him a great name, although not the greatest, in our nascent literature. We discern in these pages, here and there, a disposition to force the note, to make things look a little brighter, a little bigger than they actually were. John Winthrop, for instance, is spoken of as a "Royal" Governor, whereas there was no such thing in Massachusetts Bay until after the Restoration. John Winthrop came out as the appointee and local delegate of a London company of merchants and capitalists, and held office for about a year in that capacity, being subsequently re-elected by his fellow colonists. Again, we are told of a classmate of Hawthorne's, who is described as residing on his father's property in Maine, from which the artless English reader would scarcely infer that the young man in question was living on his father's farm.

Though he nowhere distinctly says as much, apparently preferring, after the manner of Sainte-Beuve, to let others bear the burden of iconoclastic speech, Mr. James hints that Hawthorne was in no sense a thinker; that the single active and admirable element in his composition was his imagination; that he was purely and simply a maker, and that his makings took most frequently the unsubstantial form of frostwork and fili-gree. Indeed, the whole of Mr. James's book, so far as

it deals with criticism at all, is devoted to a series of
prolonged and intricate variations on the constant theme
of Hawthorne's "fancy."　On this score the biographer
is not disposed to stint his eulogy, and is at great pains
to frame it in neat and corruscating sentences.　The
labor which Mr. James has here bestowed upon his
diction is not unwise when we consider that the frequent citations from Hawthorne would naturally suggest
a comparison of styles.　It may be well for the biographer if the comparison goes no further.　Meanwhile we
would point out one or two blemishes in the technical
execution of this carefully chiselled work.　Why will
Mr. James insist on enriching the English language
with the Gallicism, "one would say," "one would
think,"'and so forth ?　Is the phrase essential to a perfect simulation of Sainte-Beuve's manner, or does the
writer think the prose of Addison, Sterne, and Goldsmith suffered for the want of it ?　Why, again, must Mr.
James repeat an adjective twenty times because it struck
his ear as fresh and pictorial on its first application ?　In
some men such a repetition would be construed to mean
sterility, and when Hawthorne is guilty of a like trans-
gression Mr. James is quite severe, almost peremptory,
with him.　He animadverts on his subject's "·extreme
predilection for a small number of vague ideas, which
are represented by such terms as 'sphere' and 'sympathies';" and he calls the too liberal use of these two
substantives the "solitary defect of his style."　No sin of
Hawthorne's in this way is at all comparable, however,

with the rank torture of the word "dusky" perpetrated in this volume. We first come upon it in a citation from Hawthorne himself, who speaks of a certain tradition being invested with a dim and "dusky" grandeur. To Mr. James the epithet seems to have the charm of a new discovery, and he goes on fingering and mouthing it till it becomes the stalest and emptiest adjective in his vocabulary. First we hear something of "dusky hours," not long afterward of "dusky flowers," presently of a "dusky conscience," on another page of the "dusky blight," anon of "rich duskiness of color;" then we come on a "dusky preoccupation," followed by a "dusky gaze," to which is subsequently appended a "dusky envelope," and then the same adjective in the superlative, "duskiest flowers." Of this epithet we might say what Mr. James affirms of Hawthorne, that it is vague, unanalytic, indefinable, ineffable. In this case, as in some instances noted by the biographer, vagueness is no doubt a drawback, for it is difficult to point to ethereal beauties; and if the reader shall inform us, after looking a while at the word "dusky," that he perceives nothing in particular, we can only reply, in the words of Mr. James, that in effect the object is a crepuscular one.

THE school of poetry which budded a quarter of a century ago in a little London magazine called *The Germ*, and which, in the hands of Swinburne, Morris, and the Rossettis, has gained not a little reputation, seems to have culminated in the new epic poem by the author of "Jason," and "The Earthly Paradise." We would direct careful attention to this work, the Story of Sigurd the Völsung and the Fall of the Niblungs, both because the sensuous, Pre-Raphaelitic treatment with which readers of recent poetry are familiar, has here found admirable expression, and because the theme is one of the fullest and highest with which a poet of our race could deal.

What is this story, which now for the first time is fittingly told in the English tongue? The tale of Sigurd, as Morris reminded us in a preliminary essay published some six years ago—a translation of the "Völsunga Saga"—is the great story of the North, which should be to all our race what the tale of Troy was to the Greeks—to all our race first, and afterward, when the change of the world has made our race nothing more than a name of what has been—a story too—then should it be to those that come after us no less than the tale of Troy has been to us. We cannot but think it a notable coincidence that this legend, or rather cycle of heroic myths, after having well nigh faded from the memory of the Teutonic folk since the idiom of the Nibelungen Lied ceased to be readily intelligible, should all at once, and almost in the same year, have found two such interpreters as Richard Wagner and William Morris.

The reader may find it interesting to contrast the various treatment which the tale of Sigurd, the Völsung, has received from the Minnesinger who composed the core of that retouched and recast work which is known to us as the Nibelungen Lied—in the dramatic form of Wagner's tetralogy, and finally in this English epic. For that purpose it may be well to condense from the Völsunga Saga and the prose Edda the cardinal features of the original story.

The three gods, Odin, Loki, and Hönir, in their wandering through the world come to a waterfall, whereby sits an otter devouring a fish which he has caught. Loki kills him with a stone and strips off his hide. At nightfall they seek shelter with a farmer, Hreidmar by name, and show him the otter's skin. Hreidmar calls his sons, Fafnir and Regin, and tells them that their brother Otter has been slain, whereupon they seize the gods and bind them. For blood-money the father requires them to fill the skin with gold and cover it with the same metal. Loki is dispatched to seek the ransom, and captures in the water the dwarf Andvari (wearing the form of a fish) whom he compels to buy his freedom with his treasures. One ring, which would

12*

have enabled him to duplicate the gold (Wagner's "Ring of the Nibelungen"), the dwarf would fain keep back; and when Loki takes this also, pronounces a curse upon the hoard. Loki returns and ransoms the gods, but Hreidmar remarks that one hair of the otter's skin remains uncovered, and, at his demand, the ring is added, and with it passes the curse which rests upon the possessor of the treasure. The surviving brothers claim a share of the gold, and when their father refuses to give it them they kill him. Fafnir, however, seizes the whole, and taking the form of a serpent, guards the hoard. Regin, become a fugitive, tempts Sigurd, the son of Sigmund, to avenge him, and forges for him, from the fragments of his father's weapon, a sword so well tempered and sharp that it cleaves an anvil to the ground, and held in a running stream sunders a flock of wool which floats against it. Sigurd goes to Fafnir's abode, digs a pit in the snake's path, and from this ambush thrusts his sword through the reptile. Regin cuts out his brother's heart, and bids Sigurd cook it for him. The latter, wishing to see if the heart is roasted, thrusts his finger in the fat, and then puts it in his mouth, whereupon he understands the language of the birds, and learns that Regin is plotting treachery against him. The young man slays Regin, and becoming the owner of the fatal hoard, carries it away on his horse Grani. He comes presently to a house on a mountain, and finds there a sleeping warrior clad in complete armor, whom, after taking off the helm, he discovers to be a woman.

This is Brynhild, one of Odin's victory-messengers, whom the god had plunged in sleep because in a certain contest she had apportioned victory against his will. The two plight troth to one another, and Brynhild teaches Sigurd runes. Afterward the latter comes to the home of Giuki, a king dwelling by the Rhine, with whose sons, Gunnar, Högni, and Guthorm, he strikes a league of friendship and takes part in their wars. The daughter of Giuki, Gudrun, to whom dreams have foretold misfortune, by the advice of her mother offers Sigurd a love potion, which causes him to forget Brynhild and to wed Gudrun. Gunnar meanwhile is minded to marry Brynhild, the sister of Atli, Budli's son, and Sigurd attends him in his wooing. But Brynhild's castle is encircled by a wall of flames, and only he who forces a passage through them may have her to wife. Gunnar essays it, but his horse starts aside ; and only when Sigurd, who has changed form with his friend, mounts his own horse, Grani, will the latter consent to cross the fire. Sigurd passes the night with Brynhild, but his sword lies between them on the couch. In the morning they exchange rings, Sigurd giving her that of the dwarf, Andvari. Thereupon he leaves the castle, resumes his own form, and Gunnar carries Brynhild home as his wife.

By and by it happens that Brynhild and Gudrun are washing their hair in the Rhine, and the former goes up stream that the water running from Gudrun's locks may not touch her head, seeing she has wedded the better man. They fall to wrangling about the comparative worth of their husbands, and Gudrun discloses how Sigurd had ridden through the flames on behalf of Gunnar, and exchanged rings with the latter's bride. Brynhild goes home in silence, and for seven days lies without sleep or food, brooding upon her wrong. She urges Gudrun's brothers to slay Sigurd, and they stir up Guthorm to the deed. The latter steals to the guest's chamber, but when Sigurd turns on him his gleaming eyes he flies. A second attempt is alike fruitless, but the third time Sigurd is asleep, and his assailant runs him through. Sigurd, springing up, flings his sword after his flying enemy and cuts him in twain. When Gudrun wakes she finds her husband swimming in blood, and Brynhild laughs to hear her rival's outcry. Gudrun sits tearless by Sigurd's body until, one of her sisters drawing the face-cloth from the face, she kisses him and weeps. Meanwhile Brynhild stabs herself and is burned on the same pile with Sigurd. Gunnar and Högni share the treasure, and Gudrun is subsequently married to Atli, King of Hunland, Brynhild's brother. The latter bids Gunnar and Högni to a feast, but before leaving home they bury the so-called hoard of the Nibelungen in the Rhine, whence it was destined never to be recovered. Gudrun attempts to warn her brothers by a message written in runes, but neither this nor the ominous dreams of their own wives avail to deter them. Landing from their ships they ride to Atli's castle, where they are met by an army and the demand for Sigurd's treasure, which is claimed for Gudrun. They refuse, and a fierce battle follows. All the men on their side having fallen, the two brothers are taken and bound, but Atli offers Gunnar his life if he will reveal where the treasure lies. But Gunnar will tell nothing before they show him his brother Högni's heart. To deceive him, they cut the heart out of a slave and bring it him; but, by its quivering, Gunnar recognizes that it is not the heart of Högni. At last Atli bids them cut out Högni's heart; and when Gunnar sees this, he says that now no man save he alone knows where the treasure is, and none shall find it. Thereat Atli orders him to be flung into a pit filled with serpents; but a harp is given him, which he plays with his toes (since his hands are tied), and so tunefully that all the snakes are lulled, except an adder, which stings him to death. The King of Hunland commands a funeral feast to be made for Gudrun's brothers; but the Queen kills her children by Atli, and of their skulls fashions drinking cups, in which she serves the King mead mixed with blood. The same night she kills him, sets fire to the castle, and leaps into the sea. On Gudrun's after fate we need not dwell, since both the lay of the Nibelungen and Morris's poem find here a common acme.

Such are the outlines of this famous legend, reflecting in a dim, uncertain fashion the religion, ethics, arts, and history of the primitive Teutonic stock. It seems to us not a little remarkable that of the three attempts to present this story in epic or dramatic form, the oldest should have diverged most widely from the frame and spirit of the early myth. The mediæval version, whose origin is placed not later than the first . half of the twelfth century, but which received a remodelling of rhythm and the addition of rhyme in the time of the Hohenstaufens, is loaded with anachronisms, the incidents, sentiments and persons of the tale being portrayed from the standpoint of a Christian and feudal knight. The result is that the Lay of the Nibelungen, in spite of the beauty of detached passages and the singular vehemence of the narrative in the latter portion, is utterly wanting in congruity, correlation, and univocal tone, and portrays a world that never was, or could be, on sea or land ; in a word, the poem could neither have been understood in Iceland before the introduction of Christianity, nor at the Court of Barbarossa by those unacquainted with the Norse sagas. For example, the relations of "Brunhilde" and "Siegfried," as exhibited in the "Lay," would be quite unintelligible without some knowledge of the prose Edda, and the fateful significance of the treasure, the coveted "hoard of the Nibelungen " is nowhere plainly indicated. In general, the characters of the story, which in the genuine myth are massive, raw, halfdemoniac figures, are softened and embellished almost beyond recognition. The reader of the Nibelungen Lied is continually reminded that the twelfth century, which in the north of France and England was undoubtedly a bleak, dark epoch, had its oases of civilization, and that Southern Germany, particularly the banks of the upper

Danube, shared in no small degree the refinement of Provence and Northern Italy. Yet although the audience which the Minnesinger addressed was very far removed in feeling from that which called forth the Völsunga Saga, it was perhaps equally distant from that nice perception of artistic aims and methods which belongs to the most enlightened eras. It was reserved for poets of our own day to divest their versions of anything like patent anachronism or incongruity, and to reproduce with creditable fidelity in its native hues and distinctive atmosphere the great story of the North.

With the merits of Wagner, as a composer of operas, we have at present, of course, no concern ; but it seems to us that the purely literary worth of the dramatic poems which he has grouped together, under the general title of the " Ring of the Nibelungen," has not in this country and England, at least, been rightfully appreciated. His tetralogy is in no sense a recasting of the Nibelungen Lied. Aside from the distinction of artistic form, the latter poem differs in respect of theme, spending its best force on the events which, in the old myth, followed the murder of Sigurd, in other words, on the Fall of the Niblungs, whereas Wagner confines himself to the earlier incidents, and ends with the self-slaying of Brynhild. Neither is comparison between the versions possible as regards scrupulous adherence to the texture, feeling, and purpose of the original. It is true that in the second of his dramas, " Die Walküre," Wagner departs somewhat from the letter of the legend, making "Siegfried" the son of "Siegmund" and "Sieglinde," whereas, in the Saga, Sigurd is the son of Hjordis, while Sinfjotli, who has a story of his own, is the son of Sigmund and Signy. Yet, here he follows the Lay of the Nibelungen, and it was perhaps inseparable from the aim of a dramatist to compress the whole life of Sigmund, which claims much space in the Saga, within the scope of a single tragedy. It is certain that the characters of the ill-fated Völsunga pair are projected with wonderful distinctness, yet closely within the outlines of the ancient myth, and that the scenes between "Siegmund" and "Sieglinde" are among the most winning and effective in the whole work. Be that as it may, in the figures of Sigurd and Brynhild and the record of their fortunes as shown to us in the last two dramas, "Siegfried" and "Gotterdämmerung," we catch the very spirit of the Edda, while notwithstanding the limitations entailed by a dramatic form, not a single feature of prime importance seems to be overlooked on Wagner's canvas. In respect, moreover, of essential beauty, apart from their fidelity and dexterity in interpretation, these dramas are singularly affluent, and we should find it hard, for instance, to parallel in the work of any recent poet the exquisite tenderness and profound passion which gleam and throb through the dialogue allotted to "Siegfried" and "Brünhilde" at the close of the third play, or the remorseful agony which shivers through the death-song of "Brünhilde" in the last scene of the concluding drama. There is another point worth notice, and that is the moral atmosphere which bathes these poems, and which to those unfamiliar with old Norse literature may appear inappropriate, but it will be convenient to glance at this in connection with Morris's treatment of the same theme.

It was inevitable that the Pre-Raphaelitic poets would turn at last from Greek myths to the Norse Sagas, and it will probably be conceded that Morris had given fullest proof of the sustained power requisite for handling such large materials. Whether, however, the characteristic standpoint and manner of the school was calculated to insure a faithful transcript of the Icelandic epic might have been held open to question. For what is the burden of their song ? That the absence of pleasure and of poetry in the routine of our daily work, the spreading of the hideous town, the prosaic outward furniture of modern life are become a grievance and a reproach. Yet if something more sightly is no longer to be found in the actual world without, we have still the power of creating some shadow of it with the aid of imagination. The world must have had a childhood once and the endeavor of the Pre-Raphaelites is to bring back again the golden age—the days of the infancy of the race. They seem to embody most distinctly the ideal of childhood in its two main features, vivid enjoyment of the pleasures of sense, and freedom from moral responsibility. A state of enjoyment where the outward delights of mere sensation are felt with a keenness which is unknown to us now, but yet—and here rises the doubt as to the entire fitness of such writers to treat such themes as the Edda—coupled with a certain esoteric refinement of artistic sentiment is the picture they are constantly drawing of the past. Whether Morris describes the course of the ship "Argo," or follows Norwegian mariners into the unknown West, or recites the tales which charmed the dwellers in an " Earthly Paradise," wherever the scenes of his ideal life are cast, they all belong to the world's childhood, but a childhood which cannot wholly free itself from the memories of age, to a dreamland which is haunted with a consciousness that it is but a dream. Now the tone of feeling which this sort of work engenders, and which may be called a self-contemplative sensuousness, is a quite different thing from sensuality, yet it is likewise wholly distinct from a sensuousness which is not introspective, from the power of enjoyment which belongs to childhood, to the infancy of mankind more than its maturer age, to some races and some nations more than others, and which seems to have been the peculiar birthright of those Norse heroes who held themselves to be sons of Odin. It might therefore have been expected that the trace of self-consciousness which flickers across the open-eyed delight of Jason's Hellenic comrades would appear even more incongruous in the persons of Icelandic story, yet we are bound to say, that, as a matter of fact, the blemish—if blemish it be—is less noticeable in the present work. This is partly due, we imagine, to the closeness, almost literalness, with which Morris has followed the metrical fragments which are left to us of the poetic Edda as well as the text of the prose versions. In the circumstances it is not likely that any will cavil at such direct reproduction, seeing that the numerous gaps and slurs in the primitive record leave ample room for expansion and elaboration. These acknowledgments made, it is still true that the new epic is not wholly free from that tinge of introversion and self-pity which hovers like a faint cloud over the horizon of all Morris's work, and in this respect we think that Wagner has compassed more nearly the right atmosphere, the figures of his Völsungs standing forth crisp and bold in a clear, cool radiance like that of their own northern summer night.

One word as to the metrical form which Morris has adopted, and then we will try to offer the reader a glimpse of Sigurd's story in the new version. The "Lay of the Nibelungen," as we now have it, is written in rhymed iambic quatrains, each line having six or six and a half feet with a strongly marked, invariable cæsura in the middle of each verse. Morris's epic is not unlike this in effect, for although the scheme of the verse is anapæstic the number of feet in a line is the same, and the cæsura occupies a corresponding place. The similarity will be plain enough upon comparison of a distich from each poem :

Dô wuohs in Niderlanden—eins edlen küneges kint
Des vater der hiez Siegemunt—sin muoter Sigelint,

But Sigmund laughed and answered—and he spake a scornful word
"And if I take twice that treasure—will it buy me Odin's sword ? "

From the extracts which we may make the reader will probably infer that the measure which Morris has here chosen is capable of great variety and melody.

The poem opens with a description of King Völsung's dwelling and the wedding of his daughter Signy—we repeat that Morris covers the whole ground divided between the mediæval "Lay" and Wagner's tetralogy. We quote half a dozen of the initial couplets in order to illustrate the rhythm and music of the verse, and we might also point out the characteristic touch in the last lines :

There was a dwelling of kings ere the world was waxen old ;
Dukes were the door-wards there, and the roofs were thatched with
    gold ;
Earls were the wrights that wrought it, and silver nailed its doors ;
Earls' wives were the weaving women, queens' daughters strewed
    its floors,
And the masters of its song-craft were the mightiest men that cast
The sails of the storm of battle adown the bickering blast.
There dwelt men merry-hearted, and in hope exceeding great
Met the good days and the evil as they went the way of fate ;
There the gods were unforgotten, yea whiles they walked with men
Though e'en in that world's beginning rose a murmur now and
    again
Of the midward time and the fading and the last of the latter days,
And the entering in of the terror and the death of the People's
    Praise.

That the reader may judge how carefully the text of

the old myth is reproduced, we set beside the words ascribed to Signy in the crisis of what may be called the first catastrophe, the corresponding passage of the " Völsunga Saga."

And she said, "My youth was happy, but this hour belike is best
Of all the days of my life-tide that soon shall have an end,
I have come to greet thee, Sigmund, then back again must I wend,
For his bed the Goth-king dighteth ; I have lain therein, time was,
And loathed the sleep I won there : but lo, how all things pass,
And hearts are changed and softened, for lovely now it seems.
Yet fear not my forgetting ; I shall see thee in my dreams
A mighty king of the world 'neath the boughs of the Branstock
    green,
With thine earls and thy lords about thee, as the Völsung fashion
    hath been ;
And then shall all ye remember how I loved the Völsung name,
Nor spared, to spend for its blooming, my joy and my life and my
    fame.
For hear thou, that Sinfiotli, who hath wrought out our desire,
Who hath compassed about King Siggeir with his sea of a deadly
    fire,
Who brake thy grave asunder—my child and thine he is,
Begot in that house of the Dwarf-kind for no other end than this.
The son of Völsung's daughter, the son of Völsung's son,
Look, look ! Might another helper this deed with thee have done ?

The Icelandic prose paraphrase runs as follows :

But she answered, "Take heed now and consider if I have kept King Siggeir in memory and his slaying of Völsung the king. I let slay both my children whom I deemed worthless for the revenging of our father, and I went into the wood to thee in a witch-wife's shape; and now behold Sinfiotli is the son of thee and of me both ! and therefore has he this so great hardihood and fierceness in that he is the son both of Völsung's and Völsung's daughter ; and for this and for naught else have I so wrought that King Siggeir might get his bane at last ; and all these things have I done that vengeance might fall on him, and that I too might not live long, and merrily now will I die with King Siggeir though I was naught merry to wed him.

We would gladly quote at greater length (although an epic poem cannot of course be judged from citations), and especially should we like to reproduce the forging of the sword, Fafnir's bane, the slaying of Fafnir, the awakening of Brynhild, and all those scenes and incidents which are handled in Wagner's dramas. It would be interesting, too, to trace in the fourth book of the English poem a parallel with the latter and stronger half of the Nibelungen Lied. That, however, would carry us too far, and the reader has perhaps already seen reason to believe that the appearance of this latest, ripest, and most ambitious of Morris's works is indeed no ordinary event, and that this new version of the great legend of the North is one of the most signal contributions to English poetry since the writing of Childe Harold.

IT used to be noted thirty years ago by those who knew Europe well that the only American author whose works had been transplanted into all the literary languages, and whose name had struck firm root in foreign soils, was James Fenimore Cooper. You found his novels everywhere, as you found Scott's—in Lisbon, Seville, and Palermo, and Prague and Moscow, Stockholm and Copenhagen—not only crowned with popular favor, but studied and discussed by accomplished and inquisitive intellects, who apparently had never heard of those transatlantic coteries which affected to make light of the Leatherstocking Tales. Marking this phenomenon, the young Bostonian of that day was led to reconsider some of his second-hand opinions, and to query whether such cosmopolitan esteem could be gained without substantial merit. Here, at all events, was a great fact, and he was not unlikely to infer from it that the judgment of other countries anticipates the verdict of the future : that foreign nations are banks of discount competent to cash the drafts which an artist draws upon posterity.

Cooper's is no longer the only American name familiar to cultivated men and women throughout Europe. During recent years the reputation of Bret Harte has grown with signal rapidity, not only in France and Germany, but in the Latin countries of the South, less prompt to gauge aright the worth of an English book, and even in those capitals of the North, centres of Slavic and Scandinavian activity, which seem to have least in common with the American novelist. Of this fact periodical literature and the book lists of foreign publishers afford sufficient proof. Reviews or translations of Mr. Harte's tales have appeared in critical journals and magazines printed at Lisbon and Madrid; the specific qualities of his work have been more than once examined by that arbiter of Italian opinion, the "Rivista Europea" Sacher-Masoch, the Galician novelist, who delights to be called an imitator of Bret Harte, has filled the Vienna press with praises of his model, while the name and many of the stories of the American artist are familiar to the readers of the "Moscow Gazette," who, it is safe to say, include all cultivated Russians. Other facts not less pertinent, but more notorious, might be cited, such as the large amount of space given to translations from Bret Harte in the pages of the "Revue des deux Mondes," whose *clientèle*, we need not remind the reader, embraces the *élite* of Continental society. We might point also to the circumstance that one of the author's tales was secured for simultaneous publication by the "Deutsche Rundschau," which aims to maintain at Berlin a position analogous to that of M. Buloz's famous Parisian periodical. Now, these are facts whose large significance requires no interpreter; they attest a breadth and solidity of reputation which it would be absurd to claim for any other contemporary American ; they prove that this man's genius needs the stamp of no clique or coterie to pass current everywhere ; they certify that his draft upon posterity has been honored ; that his achievement has passed into history.

We are reminded of these things by the appearance of a new volume, "The Story of a Mine." Such considerations as we have above referred to greatly simplify the work of a reviewer, for he knows that in this instance the world has made up its mind, and that nothing he can say is likely to affect its verdict. They are apt, moreover, to modify his attitude, smoothing the rugged independence of anonymous criticism to a deference which is but due to a bright and established name. Good wine, of course, needs no bush, and all that the reading public seeks to learn of its book in such cases is whether the particular flask is of the proprietor's best vintage. It is certain that this "Story of a Mine" exhibits some of the most careful and delicate work that has come from the author's hand. Few men have a happier faculty of drawing lifelike and charming women, yet there is in this volume a study of a Spanish-Californian young lady, Miss Carmen De Haro, which is singularly captivating. All the masculine figures—and a much larger number than is usual with the writer are grouped upon the canvas—have the crisp, sharp outlines and the semblance of vitality which lead the uninitiated, who overlook the toil and insight applied in selection and projection, to mistake Bret Hart's por-

13

traits for photographs from real life. But no one ever saw, or if he saw, understood, the originals of these characters. It was reserved for the artist to divine and reveal in a stroke or two the shape and color of a mind and life; and these are powers, we need not say, which transcend the capabilities of the ordinary observer. The power of portraiture, exercised under the right dramatic conditions of self-betrayal through colloquy and incident, is not, as some simple-minded students of Bret Harte imagine, to be confounded with a lively faculty of reminiscence which enables an eye-witness to reproduce a scene. It would be ludicrous, if it did not bring home to us an inveterate vice of human nature, the detraction which inevitably dogs the footsteps of success, to see Bret Harte's reputation explained, as we sometimes do see it on the part of petulant or discontented persons, by a happy accident, a lucky hit, as if any magazine writer or newspaper reporter who had chanced to see a Chinaman playing cards, or had spent a week in a mining camp could have worked up the novel materials to the same large results. We will not ask those gentlemen who conceive that Bret Harte's success should be credited to his opportunity to compute how many Agamemnons may have existed before Homer, but we will merely remind them that some three and a half centuries had elapsed since the afflux of adventurers to the mines of Peru and Mexico created conditions substantially identical with those of " Roaring Camp " and " Poker Flat," while the mining life of

California was, at a later period, duplicated in Australia; yet neither before nor since, nor by any other writer in any language, have the characteristic stamp and flavor of a gold hunter's existence, and the strange traits of a community smitten through and through with the gold fever, been truthfully, effectively, and delightfully reproduced.

After all deductions have been made on the score of a peculiarly fresh and fruitful theme, it is plain that the author of the " Condensed Novels " would have made his opportunity, if he had not found it. Neither is it in accordance with the facts to speak of this man's talent as limited by local conditions—as the specific product of a particular soil. It may no doubt be satisfactory to certain minds to thus identify an artist's performance with his circumstances, for the theory seems to carry the implication that they, too, might have done something creditable in a like stimulating environment. But the truth is that genius is a hardy and hungry plant, tolerably certain to find sustenance anywhere. Those who are thoroughly acquainted with the writings of this novelist know how broad and diverse is the field covered by his scrutiny. Even in that feverish world which lies between the Sierras and the Golden Gate, there is a multitude of types, there are innumerable phases of social life, all the elements of a microcosm, indeed, whose study might well qualify an interpreter of the human comedy. We expect to find, and we do find, the same penetration and the same faculty of artistic exposition when the author passes from a sketch of "Mrs. Skagg's husbands," to a transcript of contemporary society in some relatively old Atlantic city, or to an historical picture of village and army life in the Jerseys at the epoch of the Revolution. Thus in one of Bret Harte's tales we are transported from a decayed mining town, which we take to be Placerville, to Newport, and assuredly there is a considerable difference between the social atmosphere of those pleasant and somewhat stately houses which fringe the Cliff, and the manners of Poker Flat: yet the author's page is as faithful and suggestive, if not as startling, in the one case as the other. So, too, in the book before us the scenes and the persons proper to a Mexican village on the Californian coast in the early years of American occupation, are not a whit more truthfully and skilfully described than is the city of Washington as we know it to-day. By way of demonstration we need only place a couple of paragraphs side by side. Let us take, for instance, a few lines which paint a cañon in the Coast Range, where a deposit of cinnabar is discovered :

The scene was weird enough without Wiles's eye to add to its wild picturesqueness. The mountain towered above—a heavy Rembrandtish mass of black shadow—sharply cut here and there against a sky so inconceivably remote that the world-sick soul must have despaired of ever reaching so far or of climbing its steel-blue walls. The stars were large, keen, and brilliant, but cold and steadfast. They did not dance nor twinkle in their adamantine setting. The furnace fire painted the faces of the men an Indian red, glanced on brightly-colored blanket and *serapé*, but was eventually caught and absorbed in the waiting shadows of the black mountain, scarcely twenty feet from the furnace door. The low, half-sung, half-whispered foreign speech of the group, the roaring of the furnace, and the quick, sharp yelp of a coyote on the plain below were the only sounds that broke the awful silence of the hills.

Now we may turn to the record of the impression left upon the mind by an August day in the national capital.

It was a midsummer's day in Washington. Even at early morning, while the sun was yet level with the faces of pedestrians in its broad, shadeless avenues, it was insufferably hot. Later, the avenues themselves shone like the diverging rays of another sun—the Capitol—a thing to be feared by the naked eye. Later yet it grew hotter, and then a mist arose from the Potomac, and blotted out the blazing arch above, and presently piled up along the horizon delusive thunder clouds that spent their strength and substance elsewhere, and left it hotter than before. Towards evening the sun came out invigorated, having cleared the heavenly brow of perspiration, but leaving its fever unabated.

And here is a type which will be easily recognized—the average American legislator:

In this capital, on this languid midsummer day, in an upper room of one of its second-rate hotels, the Hon. Pratt C. Gashwiler sat at his writing-table. There are certain large, fleshy men with whom the omission of even a necktie or collar has all the effect of an indecent exposure. The Hon. Mr. Gashwiler, in his trousers and shirt was a sight to be avoided by the modest eye. There were such palpable suggestions of vast extents of unctuous flesh in the slight glimpse offered by his open throat, that his dishabille should have been as private as his business. Nevertheless, when there was a knock at his door, he unhesitatingly said, "Come in !"

pushing away a goblet crowned with a certain aromatic herb with his right hand, while he drew towards him with his left a few proof slips of his forthcoming speech. The Gashwiler brow became, as it were, intelligently abstracted.

"You are at work, I see," the intruder said, apologetically.

"Yes," replied the Congressman, with an air of perfunctory weariness—"one of my speeches. Those d——d printers make such a mess of it. I suppose I don't write a very fine hand."

If the gifted Gashwiler had added that he did not write a very intelligent hand, or a very grammatical hand, and that his spelling was faulty, he would have been truthful, although the copy and proof before him might not have borne him out. The near fact was that the speech was composed and written by one Expectant Dobbs, a poor retainer of Gashwiler, and the honorable member's labor as a proof-reader was confined to the introduction of such words as "anarchy," "oligarchy," "satrap," "palladium," and "Argus-eyed" in the proof, with little relevancy as to position or place, and no perceptible effect as to argument.

Now this etching is obviously more faithful, while it is not less biting, than Dickens's sketch of our indigenous politician in "American Notes." Nor could we better signalize the thoroughly impartial, and, so to speak, impersonal attitude which distinguishes the artist from the satirist, than by contrasting with the Hon. Mr. Gashwiler a very different type of statesman, whose solid worth is clearly marked, although at the same time his foibles are touched with delicate irony. The reader will of course recognize the portrait of Senator Sumner, for in this instance—unique, so far as we know—the author has allowed himself to transfer, without adjustment or sublimation, the lineaments of life :

There was at this time in the Senate of the United States an eminent and respected gentleman, scholarly, orderly, honorable, and radical—the fit representative of a scholarly, orderly, honorable, and radical commonwealth. For many years he had held his trust with conscious rectitude and a slight depreciation of other forms of merit ; and for as many years had been as regularly returned to his seat by his constituency with equal consciousness of rectitude in themselves and an equal scepticism regarding others. Removed by his nature beyond the reach of certain temptations, and by circumstances beyond even the knowledge of others, his social and political integrity was spotless. An orator and practical debater, his refined tastes kept him from personality, and the public recognition of the complete unselfishness of his motives, and the magnitude of his dogmas, protected him from scurrility. His principles had never been appealed to by a bribe ; he had rarely been approached by an emotion.

We must find space for one more extract, namely, the inimitable interview between the New England Senator and an impulsive Mexican young lady, whose knowledge of our idioms is traceable to Californian sources :

" Ah," said Carmen, sadly, " it is true, then, all this that I have heard ? It is true—that what they have told me—that you have given up the great party—that your voice is not longer heard in the old—what you call this—eh—the old *issues?* "

"If any one has told you that, Miss De Haro," responded the Senator, sharply, "he has spoken foolishly. You have been misinformed. May I ask who——"

" Ah," said Carmen, "I know not ! It is in the air ! I am a stranger. Perhaps I am de-ceived. But it is of all. I say to them when shall I hear him speak ? I go day after day to the Capitol. I watch him, the great Emancipator, but it is of business, eh ?—it is the claim of that one, it is the tax, eh ?—it is the impost, it is the Post Office, but it is the great speech of human rights—*never,* NEVER, I say. 'How arrives all this ?' And some say and shake their heads, 'Never again he speaks.' He is what you call 'played' —yes, it is so, eh ?—'played out.' I know it not ; it is a word from Bos-ton, perhaps ? They say he has—eh, I speak not the English well—the party he has shaken, 'shook'—yes—he has the party 'shaken,' eh ? It is right—it is the language of Boston, eh ? "

"Permit me to say, Miss De Haro," returned the Senator, rising with some asperity, "that you seem to have been unfortunate in your selection of acquaintances, and still more so in your ideas of the derivations of the English tongue. The-er-the-er-express. ions you have quoted are not common to Boston, but emanate, I believe, from the West."

Carmen De Haro contritely buried everything but her black eyes in her shawl.

It would be superfluous to enlarge at this late day on the intense sympathy with nature, and the luminous, unerring rendition of all her moods and aspects, which, except in the pages of William Black, Thomas Hardy, and of this writer, are so seldom found among living English novelists, coupled with any very profound or comprehensive knowledge of men. The author of " Gabriel Conroy " has the power of placing a land-scape before the eye, not only in its native tinge and outline, but bathed in congenial feeling ; and he is wont to suggest the dominant tone of the composition by deftly striking the key-note in one or two apt adjectives. It is perhaps reasonable to say, that as a prose painter of nature—were that his sole conspicuous merit—our

American novelist would deserve to rank with Hardy and Black, who have in other respects much less considerable claims to special recognition.

It is a significant fact, and one well calculated to impress the observer with the breadth and diversity of Bret Harte's performances, that we hear very little about his landscape drawing from his foreign reviewers. They insist most, as is fitting, on the prime function of the novelist, the keen, exhaustive scrutiny of his fellow men, and the graduated, consistent, yet brisk and scintillant evolution of character under the impact of incident and the swift pulse of dialogue. They note, as we all do, that Bret Harte is not over circumspect or happy in the concatenation of plot ; but that is a matter about which English readers have not learned to be particularly sedulous, since, if we except Fielding, and, in some of her books, George Eliot, no English novelist of the first rank has paid much attention to the skeleton of his composition. And after all, the superlative achievement of narrative art is the creation of human beings challenging, by the right of a glowing personality, a place among those denizens of the world of fiction who are the immortal friends and comrades of our dreams.

To communicate to his figures that infectious vitality toward which we warm with an instinctive sympathy and an intuitive apprehension of motive and temper is, of course, only given to an author whose mind vibrates to every semi-tone of human emotion, who is blessed, or afflicted, with that exquisite sensibility, which,

> "Like the needle true,
> Turns at the touch of joy or woe,
> And turning, trembles too."

It is when to the artist's organization is added the power of translating and propagating the finer and more evanescent shades of feeling through the stiff medium of speech, that we have the final product of genius—those consummate instruments of spiritual empire which we call humor and pathos. Now the sway which a given author exerts over the feelings is something to be certified by experience, not tested by analysis ; and it is but justice to point out that by the consensus of qualified opinion, both at home and abroad, very few prose writers of our own, or of any recent generation, can vie with Bret Harte in the mastery of our smiles and tears. And certainly it is unreasonable to compare any American novelist on the score of daintiness or hyper-refinement of diction, or anomalous capacity of morbid self-introspection, or nice exploration of some shallow phase . of high society, with this spacious, teeming, fervid, laughter-rousing and sob-compelling intellect. Such a man, we may be sure, owes very little to accident. It was by virtue of their sovereign veracity in the broad lines of human nature, and by the electric quality which defies the barriers of speech and race, that his works passed the sea and found a domicile in so many European households. Now and then, in some Paris or Berlin coterie, you may meet with an eclectic, inquisitive person who has learned something about other American writers of prose fictions, but it the simple truth that Bret Harte is known to every cultivated man in Europe, and not seldom his travelling countrymen have found in the delightful impression produced by our chief novelist a standing letter of credit and a sure passport to good will.

ONLY recently has an account, at once authentic, adequate and popular, of Gautama, the teacher of a lofty and benignant gospel, which, at this day, counts among its votaries more than a third of the earth's denizens, been accessible to English readers. Five years ago, Dr. Samuel Beal, Professor of Chinese in London University, published a succinct narrative of the Hindu evangelist's life, under the title of " The Romantic History of Buddha." About the same time he was charged with the editing of the Buddhist canonical scriptures, which, embodied in a series of two thousand volumes, had been presented to England by the Japanese Government. He is said to be now preparing a compendious report upon the so-called Tripitaka, or triple basket of ethics, ritual, and philosophy. Happily we shall not need to await the fruit of his labors in order to dispel the incongruity exhibited in the eagerness of English-speaking peoples to convert the heathen while they remained profoundly ignorant of all religions except their own, and especially of that great Aryan faith which presents so many close and curious parallels to Christianity. The function of eloquent, sympathetic interpretation, which scholars had too long neglected, has been undertaken by a poet, and the story of Buddha will at last be read by thousands, by

whom a critical exposition might have been passed un-
heeded. We refer, of course, to the remarkable epic
poem called "The Light of Asia," written by Mr. Edwin
Arnold, from the point of view of an Indian Buddhist.

Why Mr. Arnold's earlier studies should have taken
the direction of the Hindu philosophies, and of their
consummate blossom in the Buddhist faith, is intelligible enough when we are told that he spent some seven
years in India as the president of a college at Poona.
But it is surprising that a journalist, plunged in the
most exacting and exhaustive of vocations, should have
found time or will to continue his researches ; and our
astonishment is heightened when we find the acquisitions
of learning and industry not only fused and organized
in lucid narrative, but that narrative embroidered with
an artist's felicity, illumined with a poet's fancy, and
cast in the rhythmic flow of delightful verse. A design
of such scope and difficulty would tax the unexpended
energies of an unburdened life, and grave shortcomings
in execution might have been pardoned in a work to
which an unleisured author gave, not all the strength it
asked, but all he could command. There is no occasion,
however, for such extrinsic considerations, or for apology
of any kind in "The Light of Asia." · Mr. Arnold has
made an epic poem whose beauty is its own voucher, and
whose lessons are commended with a sweetness such as
Sidney contemplated when he likened a poet's winning
ministrations to a medicine of cherries. How patiently
and happily the large scheme has been compassed we

shall leave the reader to judge from a series of citations which, at the same time, illustrate the author's various powers, and exhibit in outline the capital stages of Gautama's life and ministry. We will merely premise that while the eighth and concluding book is essentially didactic, aiming to formulate the philosophic and ethical doctrines of the Buddhist system, the first seven books are primarily and mainly narratives reciting with admirable freshness and simplicity the story of the hero prince who has given light and consolation to one-half of Asia. In all this part of his work the author means to discharge the function of the tale-weaver in the most straightforward and effective fashion, and therefore, although glimpses of fair, strange landscapes, transcripts of quaint, long-vanished manners, bursts of lyric joy or tenderness, and even august musings or gentle homilies, are not wanting, these are only the episodes or accessories subordinate to the artistic conditions of a central epic purpose. We should find it hard to name another among contemporary singers who can at once acquit himself so deftly in short flights and yet remain so long upon the wing. It is very seldom that the power of facile self-surrender to transitory moods has been conjoined with an equal capacity of evolving a coherent, symmetrical, majestic performance.

Mr. Arnold tells us in his preface that he has modified more than one passage in the received narratives, but he does not mention whether he prefers the authority of the Cingalese canon, fixed by the great council held under King Asoka about 246 B.C., and which occupies to

Buddhism much such a relation as the Council of Nice
to Christianity, or the somewhat fuller scriptures embraced in the Thibetan or Chinese canon, determined in
a council held in Cashmere about the beginning of the
Christian era. Both of these collections, however, are
said to substantially agree in the legends regarding the
birth of Buddha, with which the poem opens. The
parity of the extraordinary and miraculous circumstances
which attended this event with those which preceded or
followed Christ's nativity has often been remarked.
Thus, Gautama was said to have already attained the
perfection of being in the highest of the heavens; nevertheless, he was so moved by the wretched condition both
of mankind and of all sentient creatures, that by the
force of his exceeding love he once more took upon him
the form of man, in order that he might save the world.
He chose, too, as his earthly mother the wife of the King
of Kapilavastu, named Mâyâ, who was henceforth
known as the "Holy Mother Mâyâ." He was her first
and only son, and he was immaculately conceived. In
the Chinese account of his incarnation the description of
the event is thus literally translated : "The Holy Ghost
descended into the womb." We are told further that on
the day of the child's birth the heavens shone with divine light, and the earth quivered while angelic hosts
sang : " To-day Buddha is born on earth to give joy and
peace, to give light to those in darkness, and sight to the
eyes of the blind." Again, merchants from far countries bring gifts to the newly born, and the incident re-

lated of Simeon by Luke coincides with a tradition of an aged hermit of the Himalayas, who, being divinely guided to the spot where the young child lay in the arms of Máyá, his mother, placed his venerable head under the tiny feet of the infant, and spoke of him as the "Deliverer from sin, and sorrow, and death."

Even the jealous apprehensions of Herod find an analogy in the reference to a neighboring king of Maghadha, who was advised to send an army to destroy the child that would become a universal monarch. Finally, we learn that the child (called Gautama, from his foster mother) astonished his teachers when he entered the schools of letters and of arms, so that they said, "Surely, this is the instructor of gods and men who condescends to seek for a master." As regards the date of these legends, it is impossible to say just when this or that myth originated. We only know that all must have arisen during the five centuries which elapsed between Buddha's death, fixed by the most trustworthy data at about 543 B.C., and the formation of the Northern canon at the beginning of our era. It is certain that they never circulated in the lifetime of the teacher, who would have rejected all such appeals to the miraculous. Buddha himself never refers to them, and it is equally noteworthy that Jesus Christ does not allude to the supernatural occurrences connected with his nativity which are recounted in the first and second chapters of Matthew's and Luke's Gospels.

Let us see now how these mythical accretions, which

gradually encrusted the true biography of the holy man of India, are treated by Mr. Arnold. Here, for example, is his version of Buddha's incarnation, when watching from the sky the tangle of earth's miseries he willed to go again to help the world :

> That night the wife of King Suddhôdana
> Mâyâ the queen, asleep beside her lord.
> Dreamed a strange dream —
>
>   *   *   *   *   *   *
>
>   Awaked,
> Bliss beyond mortal mother's filled her breast,
> And over half the earth a lovely light
> Forewent the morn.   The strong hills shook ; the waves
> Sank lulled ; all flowers that blow by day came forth
> As 'twere high noon ; down to the farthest hells
> Passed the queen's joy, as when warm sunshine thrills
> Wood-glooms to gold, and into all the deeps
> A tender whisper pierced.   "Oh ye," it said,
> " The dead that are to live, the live who die,
> Up rise, and hear, and hope !   Buddha is come ! "
> Whereat in limbos numberless much peace
> Spread, and the world's heart throbbed, and a wind blew
> With unknown freshness over lands and seas.

When in due time the boy thus harbingered and thus conceived was born to Mâyâ, there came, as we have said, "merchantmen from afar bringing, on tidings of this birth, rich gifts on golden trays ; " and it seemed fit to call this child of the people's hope the Prince Savarthasiddh—" All Prospering "—which we find in the poem abbreviated to Siddârtha.   After eight years have passed, the king bethinks him to have Siddârtha taught the Braminic lore, together with the accomplishments of the warrior caste, and seeks out for that purpose a certain sage, accounted "the wisest one, the furthest seen in scriptures, and the best in learning, and the manual arts, and all." We pass over some interesting scenes, in which the poet exhibits a curious acquaintance with Hindu science, including the elaborate methods of enumeration and measurement, and in which the Prince approves himself the "teacher of his teachers." We come to an occurrence that first disclosed the breadth of Buddha's benignant mission, which comprehended, as we know, not merely men, like those of other evangelists, but the lower animals, and all beings that have conscious life. It befell, we are told, in the royal garden, on a day of spring :

> A flock of wild swans passed voyaging north
> To their nest-places on Himâla's breast.
>
>   *   *   *   *   *   *
>
> And Devadatta, cousin of the prince,
> Pointed his bow, and loosed a wilful shaft
> Which found the wide wing of the foremost swan
> Broad-spread to glide upon the free blue road,
> So that it fell, the bitter arrow fixed,
> Bright scarlet blood-gouts staining the pure plumes.
> Which seeing, Prince Siddârtha took the bird
> Tenderly up, rested it in his lap—
> Sitting with knees crossed, as Lord Buddha sits—
> And, soothing with a touch the wild thing's fright,
> Composed its ruffled vans, calmed its quick heart,

Caressed it into peace with light kind palms
As soft as plantain leaves an hour unrolled.

But while the boy's hand draws the steel point from the wound, and seeks with honey and cool leaves to heal the smart, his cousin claims the bird as being the lawful prize of him who fetched it down. The young Gautama's demurrer is set forth in a passage of so much tenderness and beauty that we must be permitted to cite it at length :

> Then our Lord
> Laid the swan's neck beside his own smooth cheek
> And gravely spake, " Say no ! the bird is mine,
> The first of myriad things which shall be mine
> By right of mercy and love's lordliness.
> For now I know, by what within me stirs,
> That I shall teach compassion unto men
> And be a speechless world's interpreter,
> Abating this accursed flood of woe,
> Not man's alone ; but, if the prince disputes,
> Let him submit this matter to the wise
> And we will wait their word." So was it done ;
> In full divan the business had debate,
> And many thought this thing and many that,
> Till there arose an unknown priest who said :
> " If life be aught, the saviour of a life
> Owns more the living thing than he can own
> Who sought to slay—the slayer spoils and wastes,
> The cherisher sustains ; give him the bird :"
> Which judgment all found just ; but when the king
> Sought out the sage for honor, he was gone ;
> And some one saw a hooded snake glide forth—

> The gods come ofttimes thus !   So our Lord Buddha
> Began his works of mercy.

As the son of a king, Siddârtha is brought up in all the luxury of an Oriental court, but his wistful and meditative ways alarm his warlike father, who has no mind that any son of his shall tread the path of self-denial, wherefore he craves council of his ministers how the boy's pensive moods may be dispelled, and his feet turned into some road befitting his years and station. The eldest of them suggests what he assures the king will cure these thin distempers, and that is to weave the spell of woman's wiles about the young man's heart :

> Find him soft wives and pretty playfellows ;
> The thoughts ye cannot stay with brazen chains
> A girl's hair lightly binds.

So they devise a plan by which, unconsciously, the prince shall choose a bride and cheat himself into happiness. A festival is arranged, at which the loveliest maidens of the realm are made competitors in youth and grace, and as the victors pass the king's son to receive their prizes from his hands, certain of the councillors are charged to mark " if one or two change the fixed sadness of his tender cheek." Yet we are told that the beauteous march was ending and the prizes spent, while still the Prince sat passionless, when last

> Came young Yasôdhara, and they that stood
> Nearest Siddârtha saw the princely boy
> Start, as the radiant girl approached.   A form

Of heavenly mould ; a gait like Parvati's ;
Eyes like a hind's in lovetime, face so fair
Words cannot paint its spell ; and she alone
Gazed full—folding her palms across her breast—
On the boy's gaze, her stately neck unbent.
" Is there a gift for me ?" she asked and smiled.
" The gifts are gone," the prince replied ; " yet take
This for amends, dear sister, of whose grace
Our happy city boasts ; " therewith he loosed
The emerald necklet from his throat, and clasped
Its green beads round her dark and silk-soft waist;
And their eyes mixed, and from the look sprang love.

Yasôdhara is given to the prince, and it is worth noting that Gautama has but this one wife, thus lending to monogamy the sanction of his example, though polygamy was afterward tolerated by Buddhism in countries where the practice was firmly rooted. Meanwhile, however, the boy's father does not trust to love alone, but creates a species of walled pleasure-place, like the Happy Valley of Rasselas, from which the sad sights of the world, and every suggestion of death, or age, sorrow, or pain, or sickness are studiously shut out. Three times, however, at his desire, the young prince is suffered to pass the boundary, and is roused from his epicurean existence by three incidents, viz., the sight of an old man tottering under the weight of years, of a young man tossing in the raging heat of fever, and of a corpse lying exposed by the roadside. When he learns that old age and suffering and dissolution are the sure lot of all, his sadness is alloyed with no selfish desire of

escape from such miseries, but seems to rise only from
intense sympathy with the sorrows of others. Henceforward the comforting of mankind and the deliverance
of the world from the pangs and mockeries and despairs
of transitory life become his dominant aims :

> Siddârtha turned
> Eyes gleaming with divine tears to the sky,
> Eyes lit with heavenly pity to the earth ;
> From sky to earth he looked, from earth to sky,
> As if his spirit sought in lonely flight
> Some far off vision, linking this and that,
> Lost—past—but searchable, but seen, but known.
> Then cried he, while his lifted countenance
> Glowed with the burning passion of a love
> Unspeakable, the ardor of a hope
> Boundless, insatiate : "Oh ! suffering world,
> Oh ! known and unknown of my common flesh,
> Caught in this common net of death and woe,
> And life which binds to both ! I see, I feel
> The vastness of the agony of earth,
> The vainness of its joys, the mockery
> Of all its best, the anguish of its worst.
> *   *   *   *   *   *   *
> The veil is rent
> Which blinded me ! I am as all these men
> Who cry upon their gods and are not heard
> Or are not heeded—yet there must be aid !
> For them and me and all there must be help !
> Perchance the gods have need of help themselves,
> Being so feeble that when sad lips cry
> They cannot save ! I would not let one cry
> Whom I could save ! "

Very striking is the account of the temptations which environ the young prince, and tend to shake his purpose to forego the delights which make his present home a paradise, and fare forth into the waste, seeking wisdom, after the manner of holy men, in hunger and nakedness and pain. Especially touching is the scene where he takes leave of Yasôdhara, who is about to become a mother. She has wept herself to sleep, and, stirring in her slumbers as if at the passing of some dream, her lips half framed the words : "The time—the time is come !" Whereat Siddârtha turned :

"I will depart," he spake ; "the hour is come !
Thy tender lips, dear sleeper, summon me
To that which saves the earth, but sunders us ;
And in the silence of yon sky I read
My fated message flashing. Unto this
Came I, and unto this all nights and days
Have led me ; for I will not have that crown
Which may be mine ; I lay aside those realms
Which wait the gleaming of my naked sword ;
My chariot shall not roll with bloody wheels
From victory to victory, till earth
Wears the red record of my name. I choose
To tread its path with patient, stainless feet,
Making its dust my bed, its loneliest wastes
My dwelling, and its meanest things my mates.
Clad in no prouder garb than outcasts wear,
Fed with no meats save what the charitable
Give of their will, sheltered by no more pomp
Than the dim cave lends or the jungle bush.
This will I do, because the woful cry

Of life and all flesh living cometh up
Into my ears, and all the soul is full
Of pity for the sickness of this world ;
Which I will heal, if healing may be found
By uttermost renouncing and strong strife.

   *   *   *   *   *   *   *

This will I do, who have a realm to lose,
Because I love my realm, because my heart
Beats with each throb of all the hearts that ache,
Known and unknown, these that are mine and those
Which shall be mine, a thousand million more
Saved by this sacrifice I offer now.
Oh, summoning stars ! I come ! Oh, mournful earth !
For thee and thine I lay aside my youth,
My throne, my joys, my golden days and nights,
My happy palace—and thine arms, sweet queen !
Harder to put aside than all the rest !
Yet thee, too, I shall save, saving this earth ;
And that which stirs within thy tender womb,
My child, the hidden blossom of our loves,
Whom if I wait to bless my mind will fail.
Wife! child! father! and people! ye must share
A little while the anguish of this hour,
That light may break and all flesh learn the law.
Now am I fixed, and now I will depart,
Never to come again till what I seek
Be found—if fervent search and strife avail."

Then passing through the barred gates of his pleasure-
place, and riding far enough from the city to baffle pursuit, he dismounts, strips himself of his princely robe,
and putting on a mendicant's dress takes an alms-bowl

wherewith to beg his daily bread, and determines henceforth to be known by no other name than Sakya-Muni, the Recluse of the Sakyas. To attain the enlightenment for which he had renounced the pride and joys of life, he first studies under the Brahmins, but gets no help from books. He next joins a group of ascetics, but after six years' patient endurance he finds that the road to wisdom does not lie through extreme austerities. Accordingly he forsakes them, and announces moderation in all things, or a medium course of discipline, as the fundamental principle of his system, declaring that "the man who would discourse sweet music must tune the strings of his instrument to the medium point of tension." Meanwhile his reputation as a sage and holy man had waxed so high that a neighboring monarch offered him a share in his kingdom, and he was constantly approached by poor and rich for counsel and consolation. It is to be noted, however, as a characteristic feature of his ministry, that neither at this time, nor at any period of his life, did he exercise or claim the power of interfering with the normal course of nature. Miracles, indeed, were imputed to Buddha by the legends that grew up in later ages among corrupt and degenerate votaries, but there is no trace of them in the early authentic record. It is a distinctive mark of Buddha's mission that he neither assumes to be invested with supernatural gifts, nor to speak from inspiration. What he achieves he achieves simply as man, and affirms that as much can be done by any of his fellows

14

who will as utterly throw off the thraldom of the senses and reach the same unselfish heights. When some enthusiast sought a sign from him to convince the people, he answered : " The miracle my disciples should show is to hide their good deeds and confess their short-comings."

We have pointed out that Buddha's gospel differs from all other faiths, in that its errand of love and pity is not to man alone, but to all sentient things. It is one of his cardinal tenets not only that it is infamous by the sacrifice of animals to seek favor for ourselves at the cost of another's suffering, but that it is a brutal abuse of force, and a slur on the bounty of earth's granaries to slay animals for food. The logical consequence of animal sacrifice was depicted in these words : " If a man, in worshipping the gods, kills a sheep of price, and so does well, why should he not kill his child, his parent, or his dearest friend by way of offering, and so do better ? " Buddha's teaching on this head is finely paraphrased by Mr. Arnold in a passage of his fifth book, where the Recluse of the Sakyas enters the palace hall of Bimbasara at the hour of sacrifice, and sees the priest's knife drawn to strike the victim. Then Buddha softly said :

"Let him not strike, great king !" and therewith loosed
The victim's bonds, none staying him, so great
His presence was. Then, craving leave, he spake
Of life, which all can take but none can give,
Life, which all creatures love and strive to keep,
Wonderful, dear and pleasant unto each,
Even to the meanest ; yea, a boon to all

Where pity is, for pity makes the world
Soft to the weak and noble for the strong.
Unto the dumb lips of his flock he lent
Sad pleading words, showing how man, who prays
For mercy to the gods, is merciless,
Being as god to those ; albeit all life
Is linked and kin, and what we slay have given
Meek tribute of the milk, and wool, and set
Fast trust upon the hands which murder them.
Thus spake he, breathing words so piteous
With such high lordliness of ruth and right,
The priests drew back their garments o'er the hands
Crimsoned with slaughter, and the king came near,
Standing with clasped palms reverencing Buddh ;
While still our Lord went on, teaching how fair
This earth were if all living things be linked
In friendliness and common use of foods,
Bloodless and pure ; the golden grain, bright fruits,
Sweet herbs which grow for all, the waters wan,
Sufficient drinks and meats.   Which when these heard,
The might of gentleness so conquered them,
The priests themselves scattered their altar flames
And flung away the steel of sacrifice ;
And through the land next day passed a decree
Proclaimed by criers, and in this wise graved
On rock and column : " Thus the king's will is :—
There hath been slaughter for the sacrifice
And slaying for the meat, but henceforth none
Shall spill the blood of life nor taste of flesh,
Seeing that knowledge grows, and life is one,
And mercy cometh to the merciful."

It is a mistake to suppose that the exceptional benignity of Buddha's creed in this particular was an inevitable corollary from his doctrine of transmigration. He did not invent, but merely ratified that belief in metempsychosis which in his day was universally held in India, but where, nevertheless, the slaughter of the lower animals, for one purpose or another, seldom provoked rebuke.

At length, after years of travail, when his eyes are dimmed and his strength spent, the truth is revealed to Gautama. We are told that the day of enlightenment came as he was seated one evening, under a banian tree which for centuries afterward was an object of pilgrimage, and of which a branch, transplanted to Ceylon 245 B.C., took root and grew and is still extant, being unquestionably the oldest historical tree in the world. The supreme moment was preceded by a touching temptation —a peasant woman leading her little child by the hand to offer food to the holy man, and thus carrying back his thoughts to the home he had left. But with the drawing on of night comes the supernatural side of the struggle, which is described with all the wealth of Oriental imagery. Mâra, the demon of love (who corresponds to Milton's Belial, in " Paradise Regained "), with his daughters and angels environ and caress him. The Buddhist account of this conflict between The Saviour of the world, and the Prince of Evil, is treated with such singular vigor by Mr. Arnold that we propose to collate it with a passage in " Paradise Regained," in which the reader will remark a certain correspondence. In the

poet's narrative Buddha has already repelled some of the
subtlest spirits of evil—the Sin of Self, the Sin of Doubt,
and Superstition disguised as Faith, when there draws
nigh a braver tempter, " The King of Passions who hath
sway over the Gods themselves : "

> And round him came into that lonely place
> Bands of bright shapes with heavenly eyes and lips
> Singing in lovely words the praise of love.
>
> *   *   *   *   *   *   *
>
> These hymned to Buddh
> Of lost delights, and how immortal man
> Findeth naught dearer in the three wide worlds
> Than are the yielded, loving, fragrant breasts
> Of Beauty, and the rosy breast blossoms
> Love's rubies ; nay, and toucheth naught more high
> Than is that dulcet harmony of form
> Seen in the lines and charms of loveliness
> Unspeakable, yet speaking, soul to soul,
> Owned by the bounding blood, worshipped by will
> Which leaps to seize it, knowing this is best.
> This the true heaven where mortals are like gods,
> Makers and masters, this the gift of gifts
> Ever renewed and worth a thousand woes.
> For who hath grieved when soft arms shut him safe,
> And all life melted to a happy sigh,
> And all the world was given in one warm kiss?
> So sang they with soft float of beckoning hands,
> Eyes lighted with love flames, alluring smiles;
> In dainty dance their supple sides and limbs
> Revealing and concealing like burst buds
> Which tell their color, but hide yet their hearts.

Beside this let us place the famous lines in the second book of the "Paradise Regained," where, in the council of fallen angels, Belial devises means whereby the Saviour of Mankind may be seduced from his high mission. It is curious to note how relatively lacking in pictorial power is the Miltonic sketch, the emphasis being laid for the most part on subjective effects :

> Set women in his eye, and in his walk,
> Among daughters of men the fairest found;
> Many are in each region passing fair
> As the noon sky ; more like to goddesses
> Than mortal creatures, graceful and discreet,
> Expert in amorous arts, enchanting tongues
> Persuasive, virgin majesty with mild
> And sweet allayed, yet terrible to approach,
> Skilled to retire, and in retiring draw
> Hearts after them, tangled in amorous nets.
> Such object hath the power to soften and tame
> Severest temper, smooth the ruggedest brow,
> Enerve and with voluptuous hope dissolve.
> Draw out with credulous desire, and lead
> At will the manliest, resolutest breast,
> As the magnetic hardest iron draws.

With the dawn the conflict ended, and Buddha's mind, unmoved from its fixed purpose, at length beheld the way of enlightenment and salvation for mankind. What was this "way" by which men should escape the griefs of age, disease and death ? It lay, we are told, in these four "Noble Truths," viz., that sorrow exists ; that sorrow waxes and accumulates through desires and cravings after objects of sense; that sorrow may be extinguished by entering on the "Four Paths," and that these paths of safety are perfect doctrine, perfect will, perfect speech, and perfect deed. These truths, absorbed and developed to their consummate flower in practice, conduct to the repose and the beatitude of Nivrâna. Before looking at the noble and winning forms which these conceptions take in Mr. Arnold's poem, let us glance at a few of the points brought out by Dr. Beal in his analysis of Buddha's system. The right doctrine contemplated is not to be acquired from books or evolved from metaphysical speculation, but to be gained through the purification of the mind from all unholy desires and passions. In Buddha's view, the perfection of wisdom is indistinguishable from the perfection of goodness. Flawless goodness once attained, the soul has no longer any need to be born again, and passes into that rest which is the perfection of being. In other words, Buddhism is a religion of ethical self-perfecting, based upon the corner-stones of self-conquest and self-sacrifice. Self-conquest is to be compassed by the observance of the five commandments, which we will cite presently in Mr. Arnold's paraphrase. Self-sacrifice is to be demonstrated by a limitless charity, a devotion to the good of others which rises to an enthusiasm for humanity, and an unwavering kindness to all sentient things. The motives to the practice of this religion are addressed partly to the egoistic hope of individual melioration, and partly to the altruistic sentiment of sympathy. Not only does each

man, by a life of beneficence and self-control assure himself a more thoroughly purged spirit in the next stage of
existence, but the sum of human weakness and human
misery will thus have been diminished.   Each new birth
is conditioned by the Karma—the aggregation of the
merit and the demerit of previous births in the same
family.   Moreover, we are collectively that which the
last generation has made us, and the next generation
will be that which we now make.   What is this but a
recognition of the two factors, heredity and environment,
for one of which we are wholly unaccountable, whereas
modern scientists agree with Buddha that we can, to an
appreciable extent, adjust and modify the other.   Comte's
Religion of Humanity contemplates nothing else than
such a strenuous and concurrent improvement of our
material and social and ethical conditions as shall inure
to the steady elevation of the race.   That sympathy plays
a far more active rôle than egoism in the Buddhist system is attested by the fact that its founder did not
preach or sanction the doctrine of conscious transmigration ; it is only in Nirvâna, or rather in that penultimate
state of absolute perfection preceding absorption, that
the good man's vision is quickened to perceive the steps
of his painful progress.   But the dominance of the altruistic side in Buddhism is best shown by its failure to
long commend itself to that stubborn individualism
which is the distinctive trait of the Aryan *Volkgeist* or
race spirit.   In its Indian birthplace scarce a trace of it
survives, and though its millions of devotees spread

from Ceylon to Java, from the Straits of Malacca to the
Kara Sea, and from Japan to Swedish Lapland, they do
not include a single people of Aryan origin. By a curious parallel in the history of the great rival faith, Christianity was rejected by the Semitic nation which gave it
birth, and it has failed to maintain a firm and fruitful
life among those more or less Semitized communities of
western Asia and north Africa, where it was first planted.
We may add that the only Aryan religion which has held
its ground in the land of its nativity is the Braminic
system, which in its caste institutions exhibits the most
stupendous embodiment of human selfishness.

The first seven books of the poem, as we have said,
are mainly narrative, and with them "The Light of
Asia," regarded as an epic, is rounded to a close. The
eighth book is devoted for the most part to an exposition of the Buddhistic philosophy and ethics, and here
the reader's power of comprehension and assimilation is
signally assisted by the author's intuitive grasp and illustrative imagery. It may be that all students will not
concur with Mr. Arnold's conception of Nirvâna, or
with his estimate of the Buddhist system as a means to
the regeneration of human life, but it will be frankly
conceded that he has approached his theme in that appreciative attitude and that reverential spirit which, in
the presence of vast facts, supply the torch of insight
and the key of veritable knowledge. Let us yet find
space for some citations from that large discourse delivered on his late home-coming by the holy man of India

14*

in presence of his father's court, his child between his knees, and his beloved Yasôdhara at his feet. Here, for example, are the five rules fashioned to guide aright amid the entanglement and stress of daily life, "the first true footfalls in the Fourfold Path : "

> Kill not, for Pity's sake, and lest ye slay
> The meanest thing upon its upward way.
>
> Give freely and receive, but take from none
> By greed, or force, or fraud, what is his own.
>
> Bear not false witness, slander not, nor lie ;
> Truth is the speech of inward purity.
>
> Shun drugs and drinks which work the wit's abuse;
> Clear minds, clean bodies, need no Soma juice.
>
> Touch not thy neighbor's wife, neither commit
> Sins of the flesh unlawful and unfit.

The following lines interpret Buddha's recognition of household and social duties, and of the modest paths in which the mass of mankind must walk :

> Manifold tracks lead to yon sister-peaks,
> Around whose snows the gilded clouds are curled ;
> By steep or gentle slopes the climber comes
> Where breaks that other world.
>
> Strong limbs may dare the rugged road which storms,
> Soaring and perilous, the mountain's breast ;
> The weak must wind from slower ledge to ledge,
> With many a place of rest.

*   *   *   *   *   *   *

Dear is the love, I know, of wife and child ;
   Pleasant the friends and pastimes of your years ;
Fruitful of good life's gentle charities ;
    False, though firm-set its fears.

Live—ye who must—such lives as live in these ;
   Make golden stairways of your weakness ; rise
By daily sojourn with these phantasies
    To lovelier verities.

So shall ye pass to clearer heights and find
   Easier ascents and lighter loads of sin,
And larger will to burst the bonds of sense,
    Entering the Path.

And here, finally, is Mr. Arnold's account of the philosophy of the Karma, or law of retribution, which teaches that no deed or speech or thought is sterile, but must figure somewhere on the debit or the credit side of humanity's account :

The books say well, my brothers. Each man's life
   The outcome of his former living is ;
The bygone wrongs bring forth sorrows and woes,
    The bygone right breeds bliss.

If he who liveth, learning whence woe springs,
   Endureth patiently, striving to pay
His utmost debt for ancient evils done
    In Love and Truth alway.

If making none to lack, he thoroughly purge
   The lie and lust of self forth from his blood ;
Suffering all meekly, rendering for offence
    Nothing but grace and good ;

If he shall day by day dwell merciful,
   Holy and just and kind and true ; and rend
Desire from where it clings with bleeding roots,
   Till love of life have end ;

He—dying—leaveth as the sum of him
   A life-count closed, whose ills are dead and quit,
Whose good is quick and mighty, far and near,
   So that fruits follow it.

No need hath such to live as ye name life ;
   That which began in him when he began
Is finished : he hath wrought the purpose through
   Of what did make him Man.

Never shall yearnings torture him, nor sins
   Stain him, nor ache of earthly joys and woes
Invade his safe eternal peace; nor deaths
   And lives recur.   He goes

Unto Nirvâna.   He is one with Life
   Yet lives not.   He is blest, ceasing to be.
Om, mani padme, om! the Dewdrop slips
   Into the shining sea.

The last stanza enbodies Mr. Arnold's conception of that ultimate state held up by Buddha as the goal and prize of perfect living. We need not say that Buddha's meaning has been variously expounded at different epochs and by different schools of commentators. The sublime but nebulous and elastic thought of absorption and repose lends itself to many definitions, and should doubtless be credited with much of the marvellous assimilative power displayed by Buddhism. Mr. Arnold's interpretation, he tells us, is not only the fruit of considerable study, but of a firm conviction that a third of mankind could never have been brought to believe in blank abstractions, or in nothingness as the issue and crown of being. His own view is further emphasised in the following six lines, with which our quotations from this remarkable book must end :

> If any teach Nirvâna is to cease,
>   Say unto such they lie.
> If any teach Nirvâna is to live,
>   Say unto such they err; not knowing this,
> Nor what light shines beyond their broken lamps,
>   Nor lifeless, timeless bliss.

We must now take leave of a poem which we venture to affirm will be held precious by more than one generation of Englishmen. Seldom in our day have so large poetic gifts been turned to such high and admirable account as in "The Light of Asia." Alike by its scheme and its execution, by the charm of its technical felicity and the capacious purport of its theme, this poem challenges no minor rank in the list of English epics. It is a work of thought and learning, and it is a work of art. There seems to be an exquisite propriety in such a tribute from an English hand to the greatest name of India. It constitutes a fitting monument to one of the most gracious, beneficent, and majestic lives which have dignified humanity and helped to purify the world.

The man must have a dull eye and a cold heart who can have followed the performances of Charles Reade during the past thirty years without cordial sympathy and sincere admiration. He has worked as hard in his vocation of man of letters as ever Southey worked, yet he shows no sign of exhaustion ; he has produced almost as much as that versatile, voluminous, and well-nigh forgotten writer, but, unlike him, has not inflicted one prosy sentence on the reader. Mr. Reade seems to have begun with a modest, under-estimate of his own abilities, and a just estimate of the scope and requisites of his art, and few things are more interesting or instructive than to mark the gradual unfolding of his talents and the patient improvement of his workmanship, under the pressure of a resolute will and the beacon light of clear and well-placed aims.

Those who choose to judge an author by the hasty letters which he occasionally indites for the newspapers in a burst of not unreasonable wrath, rather than by the elaborate works of art which embody his deliberate and conscientious effort, may not be prepared to see humility cited as a characteristic trait of Mr. Reade. As a matter of fact, however, a diffident self-appraisement is the key to his earlier vagaries in matters of type and punctuation, and it has been the main-spring of his growing success. We may perhaps find in it, too, an index of the quality and limitations of his talent. What distinguished this man from other novices in his beginning was the distinctness, we might say the piercing and discouraging distinctness, with which he perceived the essential, incurable defects of the written word as an instrument of transmission or portraiture. Anybody can see how far most weavers of English prose fall short in their power of expression of Bacon, or Swift, or Ruskin; but few discern how far these very models fell short of the writers' own conceptions. No student of style, if it be not Lessing, has descried more keenly the inseparable shortcomings of written language than the author of "Never Too Late to Mend." Now it is obvious that one who could lay his finger so unerringly on the flaws of the literary medium, could hardly fail to grade aright the skill of those who had found means to manipulate it, and therefore could not share the blind assurance of most tyros, or conceive himself competent at the start, if ever, to vie with the great masters of pictorial diction. In a word, Mr. Reade's short-lived attempt to compass the end of literary art by a flank movement, by the adventitious aids of mixed type, novel punctuation, broken sentences or any other device which should hit the reader's sense, and shoot the meaning into his brain, really attested an auspicious sincerity of purpose and a profound lack of confidence in the writer's powers of efficient work in the normal way—not the eccentricity and charlatanry which silly people saw in it. But whatever might be said for such mechanical helps to the projection of ideas, if they had long been naturalized on the printed page, it soon became evident to the innovator himself that their present application frustrated his main purpose, their strange and grotesque aspect diverting the reader's mind from the thought to the mere vehicle of utterance.

Accordingly Mr. Reade soon set himself to toil in the old ruts and to extort from the verbal apparatus handed down to us what potency of expression lay in it. He does not seem to have been born an artist in language; perhaps no man is, and yet we cannot but think Sterne and Thackeray must have owed quite as much of their nimble unwavering felicity to nature as to study; indeed, the aroma of their humor often seems too subtle and evanescent to consent to any but an intuitive embodiment. It is safer, however, to minimize the share of intuition and to magnify the share of industry in every artistic achievement, and if we are led to dwell with special emphasis on the painstaking habits of this particular author, it is because in his initial ventures the workman did not always hide his tools—his ideas and images moved somewhat stiffly in their dress of words, although the latter was uniformly trim and fresh, never second-hand or slovenly. But looking at his later books —for example, this new comer, " Woman-Hater "—we find his command of the English tongue almost unique among contemporary writers. His management of its structure and idiom is as deft and supple as Matthew Arnold's, and his vocabulary will be found, upon comparison, to have a wider range than George Eliot's, if hers in some directions seems to be more richly stored. If we except certain dainty, ethereal kinds of irony and humor, and also the loftier and least selfish strivings of human nature (about whose absence in the work of this author we may wish to say a word), there is scarcely any theme conceivable, short of abstract science, or technical art, to which Mr. Reade's style does not happily lend itself in the present volume. We come now and then (though not frequently) on bits of scenery to match whose cleanness and vividness of touch we should have to go to Ruskin and Walter Scott ; both of those famous landscape painters would have used more strokes of the brush. There are dialogues, too, whose dash and sparkle and exquisite economy of words might be paralleled, perhaps, in Congreve, but scarcely in any later English dramatist or novelist ; and, finally, there are embodied characters, human beings, which, on the somewhat homely plane of thought and purpose where they dwell, are as sharply outlined, as sinewy and as instinct with life, as are the figures of "Currer Bell." Such firm and large control over the resources of our language may have been gained, as the author more than once frankly tells us, by intense, methodical and unremitting labor, but it is not the less a splendid proof of genius.

This mastery of diction is well exemplified in the volume before us ; open it at random and on almost every

page you encounter some snatches of dialogue or fragment of description which will bear quoting. Thackeray, Dickens, and George Eliot can bear this simple but
conclusive test of finish and felicity, but let the reader
apply it to Scott, Fielding or Bulwer, and mark how
hard it is to hold the precise phraseology in the memory.
If we except some discourses of Parson Adams, and the
account of Partridge at the play, we doubt if even Lord
Macaulay could have cited a long paragraph from the
author of "Tom Jones." The burnished and incisive
style of Mr. Reade, his sedulous and sustained literary
workmanship, ought to commend him strongly to French
readers, who have been taught to exact a like merit from
their own novelists. Another characteristic trait would
be better appreciated on the other side of the Channel
than at home, and that is the dramatic quality of his
narratives. Many of them have been, and all might be,
adapted for the stage. We, however, have become so
accustomed to the biographical novel, that it rarely
occurs to us to dissect one of Dickens's or Thackeray's
stories and observe on what a meagre and incomplete
skeleton of plot their creations have been built. Thackeray himself often lamented the poverty of his invention
in this particular, and ranked the power of dramatic
construction and evolution high among the qualities
which, in his judgment, made Fielding unapproachable.
This latest work of Mr. Reade's, "The Woman Hater,"
is not only fertile in exciting situations, some of which
are new to fiction, but they are graduated with much

nicety to a climax, and seem to emerge one from another by a species of organic growth. Here and there the reader will note an incident which has no bearing on the movement of the tale, but we have found none which did not serve the turn of accenting the temper or motives of some one of the actors.

Owing to the fact that the two greatest humorists of the century chose to address it in the novel form, the English reading public accepts the most clumsily and loosely fashioned narratives, provided they introduce some striking or engaging types of character. There is, it seems to us, a tendency to underrate Mr. Reade's skill in characterization. It is true that none of his conceptions have niched themselves in our remembrance in the sense that Little Nell, Dick Swiveller, Colonel Newcome and Major Pendennis are household denizens; yet we venture to predict that Christie Johnstone and Peg Woffington, Triplet and David Dodd will be found to have a firm hold upon the next, as well as the present generation. We do not recall one book of Mr. Reade's whose chief actors are not individualized, and whose features, physical and mental, are not deeply printed on the mind, being almost always self-betrayed in action or dialogue, and very seldom catalogued by the author.

As regards, for instance, the two foremost characters brought on the stage in " A Woman Hater," we must recognize dramatic art both in the drawing of the figures and in the juxtaposition. The contrast between a profound, calm, loyal, and noble feminine nature,

and a shallow, graceless, but captivating scamp,—the
twain, moreover, being linked by marriage and the
still stronger tie of indestructible affection on the
woman's part—this contact and conjunction of irreconcilable elements is the *motif* of the tale. No doubt,
it suggests the groundwork of " Romola ;" but Ina
Klosking is more self-centred, less emotional, and less
etherealized, or in other words, of coarser clay, than
George Eliot's heroine, while Edward Severne is a Pito
duly Anglicized, that is, divested of physical timidity,
and transplanted into the nineteenth century and actual
social conditions. It is not easy to exaggerate the
adroitness with which the author portrays the tortuous,
insinuating, glittering, destructive course of this unique
impostor, who is an adept in every kind of roguery,
who forges bills of exchange to satisfy a whim, who
half kills one woman by an act of brutal violence, and
who hangs through the greater part of the book on the
verge of bigamy with another, yet who is handsome as a
picture, graceful, supple, and many-sided as a Greek,
irresistible to men as well as women, and a consummate
master of arts and hearts. In the hands of a second-rate
novelist such a figure would have been quite unman-
ageable ; we should have been proof against his alleged
seductions, and marvelled that the people about him
could be so egregiously taken in. But in this case we
yield to the fascination of the winsome, incorrigible
rascal ; he disarms us as well as his enemies ; indeed, he
proves in the end, like Frankenstein, too much for his

creator, and lest he should recapture the wife whom he had cruelly outraged, and so throw the story out of joint, the author is obliged to kill him.

Not only is the dialogue uniformly crisp and racy and not seldom studded with wit and epigram, but a piquant humor has been infused into several of the characters here presented. The writer contrives to make extremely diverting the figure of the woman-hater himself, who of course like most professed mysogynists is at heart a devout worshipper of the vilipended sex. Much of the comedy of this book is supplied by the brisk encounters between this disenchanted and philosophical young man, and a sprightly, unconventional specimen of the flirt species on the one hand, and a singularly astute and acrid maiden lady, who fills with relish the office of duenna, on the other. So, too, the advent of a female doctor among the hinds of an old-fashioned rural village is made to form a mirthful episode, in which the mode of life, ideas, and language of the English agricultural laborer are reproduced with an admirable realism.

Mr. Reade, in fact, is always a realist, as much so as was Mr. Trollope, although his realism is of an artistic, not a mechanical sort. For the most part the latter gave us only pale photographs reflecting with prosaic exactitude such commonplace scenes and persons as in the West End of London or the society of a cathedral town we should see every day but might not care to look at twice. The former, on the other hand, shows a painter's skill in culling and grouping, in heightening the colors of nature just enough to compensate for the imperfect medium in which he works, in devising situations calculated to quicken somewhat the pulse of normal human nature ; yet is he studious always to adjust the drawing, the tints, the movement of his picture to the proportions and the atmosphere of actual, or easily conceivable experience.   The result is that, while we readily admit that Mr. Trollope's characters may have lived in the flesh, a languid doubt too often arises whether such existence was worth describing ; we do not hunger for, although we could tolerate, their acquaintance ; we look with a listless eye on their insipid joys and small ambitions, and find it hard to care a straw whether the distressingly correct or mildly naughty youths who make shift to fill the rôle of heroes fare well or ill in their tame wooings.   But give a young woman one of Mr. Reade's books, and, ten to one, she will cry out with Miranda, "Oh, brave, new world, that hath such creatures in't !"   Certainly, there is no young man worth his salt who would not fall head over ears in love with any one of fifty damsels who gleam upon him from these volumes.

In this, as in other features which recall the great founder of the English novel, we can see that the author has been a faithful student of Henry Fielding.   But as in "Tom Jones," "Amelia," and "Joseph Andrews," so in all of Mr. Reade's novels (if we leave out one remarkable character brought forth in the present book, and at which we will presently glance), peopled as they are with virile and amiable beings, warm of color and quick with life, it must be said that the plane of thought and feeling is near the earth. The horizon of his actors is circumscribed to those sexual and domestic affections in which a personal, indeed a selfish, element is never absent—to that sphere of practical endeavor whose end is worldly comfort and content. To sow and to reap, to love and to wed, to be healthful and happy under the sun, is the goal and sum of their hope and motive. They know no deeper promptings, no higher strivings, the atmosphere they breathe is the hale, but somewhat heavy English air unleavened with that fine ether of anxious self-probing and self-discipline, of impersonal, wide sympathy, of sublime aspiration, which bathes some parts of "Romola" and "Daniel Deronda," lighting up what were otherwise a reflex of common existence with the mirage of an ideal and nobler life. It is true that such figures as Dorothea in "Middlemarch" and Daniel Deronda are of too lofty stature and fashioned of too dainty clay to suit Fielding's canvas, yet these are not impossible denizens of earth. If, then, there is such a thing as high art in novels as well as poetry, those beings are fit subjects for the highest who embody most completely and luminously the sweetness and self-sacrifice, the worth and majesty of human nature.

Viewing the general level on which his persons think and live, as well as the technical merits of the writer, we might have to place in the category of those who follow Fielding too faithfully, and fly too near the ground, Mr.

Reade, had he not in his latest work made known to us one woman—Ina Klosking—who almost deserves to rank with George Eliot's "Romola," that is to say, among the few high and spiritual creations with which English fiction has enriched us. The author is himself aware that he is here essaying a much loftier flight than any to which he had accustomed his readers. He tells us he has long marked and regretted that many able writers are doing much to perpetuate the petty vices of a sex, which, under the existing social system, is only half educated, by devoting thick volumes to such women as biography, though a lower art than fiction, would not waste pages on. They say, "we write the average woman for the average woman to read," but they are not consistent, for the average woman is under five feet and ugly, whereas their paltry creatures are all Homerically beautiful and tall. Now fiction, he continues, has just as much right to pick out large female souls as painting has, and a perverse selection is as false and ignoble in art, as to marry a pretty, brainless face is silly in conduct. Besides, it gives the female reader a low model instead of a high one, and so does her a little harm, whereas a writer might do her a little good, or try, at all events. Having all this in his mind and remembering how many noble women have shone like stars in every age and land, and feeling sure that, as civilization advances, such women will become far more common, Mr. Reade has tried in his novel to look ahead and paint "la Klosking."

IT is not impossible that the familiar field of social life to which the novel properly confines itself may be abandoned by some impatient writers, dazzled by the temporary success of psuedo-scientific romance. Before, however, we are flooded with imitation of Mr. Jules Verne's prolusions it may be well to inquire whether his books do not disclose grounds for believing that the revulsion of public taste will be far more unequivocal than its present propitious drift. Where a long series of volumes purporting to convey useful information in captivating form is put forth under the warrant of reputable publishers, set off with the most sumptuous embellishment that printer and engraver can bestow, and pushed into circulation by all the levers known to the bookselling trade, it is not surprising that the easy-going reader should accept the author for a time at his own valuation, and regard with naïve respect his pretensions to universal knowledge. But when a young woman with the help of a cheap atlas, and the school-boy, armed with his "Play Book of Science," may go on exposing blunder after blunder, the question is pressed upon us whether books like Verne's possess any claim to serious attention, or whether the slips and botches of the sciolist

15

are not so ubiquitous in his works as to render them impertinent and even contemptible.

The motive which prompts some persons to buy " The Mysterious Island " and its companion-pieces is perhaps sufficiently intelligible. So much prestige attaches just now to scientific attainments, that even the young woman of fashion and the average college graduate (perhaps not the least torpid member of society) are not unwilling to secure the materials of pyrotechnic display, provided they are not called upon for more strenuous headwork than is demanded by the perusal of an ordinary novel. And doubtless if it were possible to infuse a modicum of scientific truth by a species of hypodermic injection, our normal conversation would be the brighter for it. But the authors may be reckoned on the fingers who, knowing themselves competent to teach, have condescended to say profound things amusingly, and even with them the instructor is so far merged in the artist that they constantly forget to edify, and may be said to demonstrate the difficulty of drawing pleasure and profit from one fountain. The didactic poem has been ridiculed as a contradiction in terms, and no one probably would deny that even Virgil's Georgics, if read for their poetry (and of course in the present state of agriculture they could be read for nothing else), are hardly relieved from dulness by elaborate ornament; while the poem of Lucretius is delightful precisely in the ratio of its failure to offer a coherent exposition of the epicurean philosophy. And so with the historical novel, which never yet in any eminent degree (with the possible exception of Victor Hugo's "Notre Dame") has united dramatic vitality and authentic photography. Scott's essays, for instance, in that field, are notoriously inaccurate as pictures of mediæval manners, while books like Becker's "Charicles," or Helps's attempt to portray human life under the conditions of the Lacustrine epoch, are ingenious mosaics of established fact and legitimate induction, but, wanting plot and characterization, prove insufferably tiresome.

On the whole, the most successful experiments in the direction of didactic fiction have been made by De Foe and Swift, and the short-comings of Verne appear glaring by contrast with the methods of those artists. Neither accuracy nor congruity is sinned against by those masters of illusion. The rudiments of many technic arts as practised in De Foe's day are described in his best known work, and it was precisely the author's minute familiarity with the processes of their several crafts, and his dexterous application of them to rude instruments and materials, which persuaded artisans, at all events, of the authenticity of Crusoe's narrative. Crusoe's travels in Siberia and Tartary produced a like impression of verisimilitude on the Russian merchants of London, and the achievement was the more remarkable because so little information respecting those countries was then accessible in print. In short, De Foe's work, though it should be shorn of the artful, homely touches which impregnate his characters with life, would remain a tolerable manual or guide-book, and this manifestly should be the decisive test of the historical or scientific romance. A similar punctilious exactitude in details invests the chronicles of Gulliver with an atmosphere of reality. As it has often been pointed out, we need but to postulate the existence of human beings dwarfed to a given size, and straightway the microscopic kingdom of Liliput becomes a marvel of proportion and concinnity. We at once discover that the dimensions of domestic animals, of trees, ships, houses, are adjusted with mathematical precision to the scale of the puny inhabitants, while even the moral and social consequences of a diminutive physique are developed in the laws and customs, the statecraft and diplomacy of the little commonwealth. Again, how much minute and trustworthy observation of equine character and habits underlies the humor of the Houhynhms! And so with all of Gulliver's experiences—your credulity is taxed but once, at the outset of the narrative. If you are able to swallow the premise, your discernment and artistic sense will be cunningly flattered and stimulated by the coherence and symmetry of the structure reared on it.

Now, suppose a man of parts—like Swift, or Edgar Poe, whose " A. Gordon Pym " was framed upon good models—had undertaken to recount an aerial voyage, say to the planet Mars, what would be his preparation and procedure ? In the first place, doubtless, he would saturate his memory with the accepted facts of physical science, especially of dynamics, chemistry, and astronomy. Next he would so imbue his mind with the right methods of research, and so scrutinize the drift of speculation as at length to descry and discriminate those concentric penumbræ of the probable and possible which circumfold the known. In a word, he would aim to compass not merely the acquisitions of the savant, but that disciplined circumspect imagination which contributes the vital spark to scientific discovery. He would be constrained probably to deal with the awkward preliminary problem of aerial navigation through regions of space beyond our atmosphere, by some untenable, though specious, hypothesis, and would meet the difficulty of supplying his aeronaut with oxygenated air by an ingenious if impracticable device. But here his resort to subterfuge and obvious sophism would end. Henceforward every step of the process would be planted on the firm ground of demonstrative truth or legitimate inference, and would command the serious attention of the learned as well as the wonder of the uninstructed reader. And if he chose to delineate the marvels of some august civilization for which the age of the planet Mars might afford a plausible basis, we may be sure that the details of his picture would reveal at all events the correlation and gradation of a conceivable world, and a wary adaptation of social phenomena to the modified conditions of human life. We need not say that a romance of this character would not be disfigured by

puerile mistakes and oversights, much less betray an
ignorance of simple dynamic laws and the fundamental
data of chemistry.

The value of such a work regarded as a stimulus to
rational curiosity, or even as suggesting a possible clue
to systematic investigation, it might be difficult to exaggerate. We could well afford to excuse some deficiencies in the direction of mere human interest, since
no doubt the processes of the artist and the teacher,
which didactic fiction seeks to confound, are essentially
incapable of fusion. It will hardly be said that we
would place our supposed author on too high a plane
of technical knowledge. Although such acquisitions as
have been outlined might exact considerable application,
we submit that without approximation to them scientific
romance is an impertinence.

It is not perhaps a matter of supreme importance to
the average reader whether he derives his impressions of
English history from Freeman, Stubbs and Lingard, or
from Scott's novels and Shakespeare's plays, but some
correct notions of geography are necessary for the comprehension of current events, and nothing but flounder-
ing and bungling in very simple concerns can result from
an absorption of fallacy and error in those applied
sciences whose threads are interwoven in countless ways
with the warp of every-day life. Moreover, historical
blunders are tolerably sure of correction. There is little
harm to be apprehended from a book like Abbott's
"Napoleon," because the antidote is at hand in veritable

histories much more attractive in form. But ordinary people find scientific treatises hard reading, and we should be justified, therefore, in abating as a nuisance such works as apply the same spurious embellishment to the truths of physical science, and assuming to offer a banquet of curious information puts us off with scraps and heeltaps.

It is true that error is of trifling consequence in books written for children whose education has scarcely begun. They have time to winnow wheat from chaff, and at the outset, perhaps, sagacious instruction aims rather to interest than to edify. We have known a relish for botany and natural history to be awakened in young people by an absurd rhapsody called the "Swiss Family Robinson." But nobody would recommend to grown-up people Balzac's "Recherche de l'Absolu," in the hope that his nebulous speculations would prompt them to serious research in the domain of chemical affinities. We cannot shut our eyes to the fact that ordinary men and women, once immersed in the stream of business, of society, read chiefly for amusement ; and therefore in the case of adult persons the mass of vulgar errors held in solution in ephemeral literature has little chance of being precipitated through the action of systematic study. A notable contribution to the crudities and figments afloat in current conversation may be traced to the writings of Jules Verne. Every young woman in society has read them, every vivacious young man can quote them, and impart to his discourse a scientific glimmer which resembles knowledge as the phosphorescence of decayed bones resembles a calcium light.

The astonishing vogue of these productions constitutes their chief claim to criticism, but they may also be said to challenge it by a special eminence in worthlessness. In most works of the kind extravagant blunders are only occasional, or at worst sporadic, relieved by intervals of tolerable accuracy ; but our French author's unveracity must be accounted chronic, since he can rarely complete a dozen pages without some perversion of fact.

At the first glance, indeed, it seems improbable that books absolutely valueless should obtain exceptional success in more than one language ; and we may be reminded that French reviewers, who received Mr. Verne with quite unanimous approval, are by no means conspicuous for lenity, and have a particularly keen eye for charlatans.   But a very trite observation, which has escaped nobody at all conversant with the French press, may account for their charity on this occasion.   French journalists and litterateurs are in one direction exceedingly ignorant men.   It would be superfluous to qualify this statement by a reference to the distinguished record of French scientists, who are often masters likewise of effective statement, and whose lucid, methodical discussions of recondite topics contrast so agreeably with the clumsy expositions of German savans.   Of course no veritable student of science would waste consideration on a writer like Verne, but would silently turn him over to his confrères of the literary guild.   Now the Parisian litterateur *pur et simple* is a model in respect of workmanship and style, has often a profound acquaintance with the resources of his language, and its standards of artistic excellence ; is sufficiently familiar with the history of France, and has commonly explored with curious attention some phases of urban life. To the geography and history however of foreign countries he betrays a ludicrous indifference, and his attempts to delineate alien types of character—for example the English or the American—rarely transcend the limits of burlesque. The progress of physical science he surveys with Olympian unconcern, and it is probably demonstrable that his fund of metaphor has received scarcely any accessions from that source since the epoch of Voltaire. In short, a national tendency to regard form as of more moment than matter—which, to say the least, is not discouraged by the French Academy—is emphasized in the case of the journalist by tradition and education. Naturally, therefore, finding in Jules Verne the merit of an agreeable style, at once nervous and correct, he commends him heartily, avows himself captivated by the playful treatment of a novel theme, and is willing to take on trust statements of fact which might cost him some pains to verify. Once happily launched in France, the books soon found their way to England and America, where publishers, scenting a lucrative speculation, embarked some capital in the venture, and took the usual means puff their wares.

Unquestionably, if the love and reverence of the

15*

young is rightly deemed a precious guerdon of labor,
Jules Verne has not missed his reward, for we are informed by readers of "Sandford and Merton" that the
reputation of the brilliant Mr. Barlow has been totally
eclipsed by the cyclopædic Frenchman. So, too, if
Athenian many-sidedness stamps the ideal of culture, it
would perhaps follow that M. Verne is a cultivated
man, for if he does not squarely face, he certainly contrives to squint in many directions. If we accept, as
we have said, the dictum of Paris journalism, we must
acknowledge him to be an honor to France ; but we are
able to match him with that British worthy whose broad
and varied acquisitions were catalogued by Samuel
Butler. The latter's learning, we are assured, like our
French author's, was capable of most amusing applica-
tions :

> For he by geometric scale
> Could take the size of pots of ale,
> Resolve by sines and tangents straight
> If bread and butter wanted weight,
> And wisely tell what hour o' the day
> The clock doth strike by algebra.

And yet the biographer of that eminent savant
ventures to insinuate a modest doubt—which is beginning to suggest itself to some readers of Jules Verne—
as to the value of his extensive erudition :

> For't has been held by many that
> As Montaigne, writing of his cat,
> Maintained she thought him out an ass,
> Much more she would Sir Hudibras.

I.

A NEW novel by Henry James, Jr., is certain to commend itself to those who appreciate artistic workmanship. The circle of such readers is not a very wide one, and admiration, in this case, falls a good deal short of enthusiasm. It might have been supposed, however, that one of his latest stories—" Washington Square "—was intended to enlist the sympathies of a larger audience, being, as it is, a study of American men and women, viewed under the conditions of New York society, undisturbed by the introduction of English or Continental types. If the author had any such design, it has apparently miscarried. There is nothing in " Washington Square " to extend the esoteric reputation acquired by the author of " The American " and " The Europeans," and there is much in it to indicate that he is, in some degree, disqualified for writing a vivid, forceful American novel. In a word, this book discloses, in a specially palpable and emphatic way, the capabilities and limitations of Mr. James's literary talent.

It is a testimony to the sterling qualities of Mr. James's work within a certain sphere that his readers are instinctively impelled to judge him by a high standard. They are continually reminded, in his book, of

Matthew Arnold's dictum, that "we mean by art, not merely an aim to please, but also and more, a law of pure and flawless workmanship." If any American now seeking to please through the medium of English prose has recognized this law and striven to embody it in his own compositions, it is indisputably Mr. James. He has studied with incomparable patience, and with a striking measure of success, all the technical processes that go to make up effective literary exposition, grouping and perspective, projection and suggestion, the interplay of light and shade, boldness deftly interchanged with delicacy of drawing, distribution, accentuation, and economy of color. Far more keenly alive than most of his fellow novelists seem to be to the fact that an artist's work begins with the choice of a pregnant theme, and the selection of a new and promising point of view, he is also far more painstaking in that mental evolution and manipulation of the central thought which must, of course, precede the effort toward verbal exhibition. When we come to scan the visible results of this careful preparation, and test the writer's power of pictorial interpretation, we find that he has the power of saying just what he means, but not of saying it with electric intensity. While he has the admirable reticence which forbids expression to exceed by a hair's breadth the scope and intention of the thought, he has not in a superlative, but only in a moderate degree, the illuminating and procreative gift of thinking in metaphor. Moreover, his diction, while correct and finished, lacks grace and spontaneity, is nervous but not sinewy, neat and lucid, but seldom beautiful. On the whole, no one would deny that Mr. James is a singularly expert and accomplished artist with the pen ; that he is conspicuously well equipped for the task of reproducing what he sees and telling what he thinks. Unluckily, he does not see enough and he thinks too analytically. Here we strike shortcomings which lie altogether without the compass of technical attainment, and which suggest a qualification of Matthew Arnold's definition. Mr. James is sedulous, as we have said, about the choice of theme, but it commonly proves to be a narrow one. In his treatment, too, he seldom swerves from a point of view once taken, but his point of view is always that of an inquisitive psychologist, critical of his fellow-men, and tolerably well satisfied with himself.

When we call a man, says Mr. Arnold, emphatically an artist, a great artist, we mean by art not merely an aim to please, but also and more, a law of pure and flawless workmanship. Given, however, an equal approach to technical perfection, it is clear that we measure degrees of merit in an artist by the relative beauty or sublimity of the thing portrayed. We do not place the Dutch school on the same level with the school of Leonardo and Raphael. The mind tires of dwelling on the patient scrutiny and elaborate fidelity with which a Dutch master pries into and reproduces every insignificant detail of a mean or homely scene ; it irks us to see so much technical ability lavished upon objects whose originals

would scarcely win from us a glance.   Now, it seems to us
that the persons Mr. James selects for portrayal are, as
a rule, essentially common-place, their aims circumscribed, their motives petty, and their lives incapable of
rousing anything like eager or poignant interest.   They
are all trying to get into society, or, having gained a
certain rung on the social ladder, are pondering how
they shall mount higher toward the consummate assimilation of English manners, ways of thought, and modes
of speech which Mr. James, not perhaps unjustly, conceives to be the goal of refined Americans.   The author
never wearies of intimating the huge difficulty, not to
say hopelessness, of the undertaking, and marks with
quiet subacid irony the faults of judgment and blunder
of execution on the part of his aspiring countrymen.
He loves, for instance, to depict some Bostonian who,
after twenty years of observation and self-discipline, has
contrived to leave on the hasty Gallic or Teutonic eye
the impression of a sick Englishman, and after bestow-
ing cautious commendation on the counterpart to place
it suddenly in sharp and disenchanting contrast with
the Simon-pure article, a genuine English aristocrat.
See, the author seems to say, O men of Boston, how vain
are all your efforts ; you cannot elude my glance, and
it is doubtful whether I myself, who have exposed your
shortcomings, could deceive a Briton.   Now it does not
strike us that such types, though amusing, doubtless,
and in their small way edifying, are deserving of prolonged or very minute study.   Yet it must be owned

that Mr. James, so far as he draws Americans at all, has usually regarded them, not as illustrating elemental traits of human nature, or as interpreting the pressure of a unique environment, but rather as grotesque contrasts, or awkward approximations to representatives of European society, viewed in its most artificial and superficial aspect.

While his themes lack breadth and dignity, his treatment of them is wanting in creative power and pictorial vivacity. He seems to be a man distinguished for the fineness rather than the keenness of his sensations; for the delicacy of his insight rather than the intensity of his sympathies. He gives you the notion of one devoid of passions, and a little puzzled, not to say annoyed, by the passions of other people. His point of view is always that of intellectual attention, never that of profound, self-effacing feeling. In his lighter moods, he has the air of a sprightly quidnunc, who watches life as if it were a puppet show, while in his graver moments he has the searching cold look of a surgeon who treats the world as a dissecting room. The result is that his characters, for the most part, are destitute of objective vitality; we do not care much for them, for we cannot bring ourselves to believe in them. We are not always willing to affirm that they never were animated beings, but we are ready to aver that they are alive no longer. They are not abstractions, neither are they the living subjects of a surgical operation, whose blood spurts and whose flesh twitches under the knife ; they are the pale, inert subjects of a deliberate autopsy.

In the story " Washington Square " the author has confined himself more rigorously than usual to his rôle of psychologist. Although the title of the book leads us to expect a good deal of local color, there is really very little in its pages. There is nothing in the motive, the situations or the main characters which need have hindered the writer casting the scene of the narrative in Dublin or in Edinburgh. The four persons who figure in the foreground of the tale are a shrewd father, a dull daughter, a silly aunt, and a sly young man who means to marry a fortune. The father is a physician, and is obligingly credited with uncommon aptitudes for diagnosis and dissection, but the remarkable thing about the book is that the other three personages are only a step or two behind him in the fervor and minuteness of their analytical studies. The father pierces the young man's designs and tracks the slow evolutions of his daughter's intellect ; the daughter ponders the equation of duty and inclination with the speechless absorption of a mathematician ; the aunt revels in exploring the romantic aspects of the affair, and the young man concentrates his mind on its fiscal elements. Each of them goes about, so to speak, with a microscope, and when the author intervenes in his own person it is to verify discoveries, or re-adjust a focus, or substitute, it may be, his private lens of ostensibly superior power. Long before we have finished the tale we have become so immersed in psychological speculation that we have ceased to care a button whether the young woman and young man break off the match or marry; and, strange to say, the author exhibits the same indifference. It is true that something perfunctory is said touching a broken heart; but inasmuch as the victim loses none of her physical activity, and positively gains weight under the operation, we know that neither she nor the author believes a word of it. On the whole, Mr. James seems to have taken relatively little interest in this performance, owing, it may be, to the fact that the characters are all labelled American, and that no chance is offered to disclose and emphasize their social shortcomings through the juxtaposition of an Englishman, or even a Continental European.

II.

The situation whose elements and results are depicted in one of Mr. James's more expanded and substantial novels is suggested by the title, "Confidence." A man of mature years, who has indulged at college in the species of hero worship which is such a common outcome of academical conditions, is represented as retaining one of these juvenile friendships in its original effusive intensity. For the classmate who still seems to him the incarnation of all that is admirable and wise he carries respect and deference to such extraordinary lengths as to submit to his inspection and deliberate judgment the lady whom he desires to marry. He sends for him to come all the way from Italy to Baden to take note of the young lady's looks, and words, and ways, and to test them in the crucible of a frigid cynical analysis. In order that the experiment may be conducted with due leisure and circumspection, the undetermined lover leaves the lady and his friend together and departs on a journey of uncertain duration. Inasmuch as he is himself a rather slow-witted, unattractive person, as the young lady is both beautiful and captivating, and as the friend intrusted with the delicate functions of critic and arbiter is not, by any means, unsensitive to feminine charms, the consequence of such curious hesitation and childlike faith may be easily foreseen. The young lady and the friend fall in love with one another, and the cautious, trustful man, who wishes to have the impulse of his heart sanctioned by another's cool approval, finds himself rejected on his return. Thus nakedly and crudely outlined, the motive of the story seems to have nothing novel or specially suggestive in it ; and it may be said in general that Mr. James's constructive faculty is weak. It is remarkable, however, how much the author has succeeded in making by dexterous manipulation out of these somewhat meagre and shop-worn materials. By artful strokes in the use of subordinate incidents he has contrived to give the situation an air of originality, and he has in this instance infused so much distinctness and animation into his principal characters that we are able to follow their action with serious, if not precisely ardent, interest. The young man who is regarded by his over-trustful comrade as a sort of Bostonian Crichton has, of

course, an odious rôle to fill, and the skill with which
the author manages to make him, on the whole, accept-
able to the reader, and therefore eligible as an object
of the young lady's regard, is certainly striking. The
heroine herself is one of the few tolerably strong and engaging figures that Mr. James has drawn. For the confiding lover we are made to entertain a mild disrelish,
which ripens at last into frank contempt when we learn
that he has never known his own mind.

All the persons of this novel belong to the class of
partially Europeanized Americans, who are the favorite
subjects of the author's study. They all try to frame
their colloquial idioms on the models supplied by London
society, of which, as a rule, there is no adequate evidence
forthcoming that they have any intimate knowledge.
Such opportunities, however, as are afforded by the
American colonies in foreign cities, or the chance acquaintances formed at tables d'hôte or in railway car-
riages, they have turned to shrewd account, and their
careful reproduction of English modes of speech might,
very possibly, impress a stay-at-home American. Even
the author's best people, however—like the hero of this
novel for instance, for whom by the way he seems to
entertain a high respect—make some odd slips now and
then ; a painful phenomenon, since they apparently live
for no larger purpose than to completely weed their
speech of Yankee solecisms. One of these slips we may
note in passing, and that is the employment of "won't"
for the future indicative of the auxiliary verb. We

venture to say that Mr. James has never heard this word used for "I will not" in London drawing-rooms and clubs. No one, of course, would point out such a trivial blemish, if the repudiation of Americanisms and a close approach to the idioms in vogue among well-bred Englishmen were not avowedly or by implication commended in this book and other writings of Mr. James as the flower and crown of American culture and achievement. For our own part, we consider that the aim thus extolled is, in the first place, petty, and in the second futile, but a discussion of this topic would carry us too far.

Here we would direct attention, however, to a matter suggested by the present story. Why is it that the great mass of English gentlemen and ladies, excluding, of course, those gifted with exceptional powers of insight and reflection, persists in regarding well-bred Americans as an improved species of cads? Few persons who know England well will dispute that this curious prejudice is still impregnably rooted in English society, although its outward expression has been checked since the extraordinary increase of our national prestige which followed the collapse of the rebellion. We may well call this feeling curious, because no other people, no matter how rude and primitive its social structure may be, encounters this secret antipathy and persistent misconception. It is a fact that Brazilians, Mexicans, Peruvians, the natives of West India Islands, and of petty Central American States, while they doubtless have reason to observe that dislike of foreigners in general which is characteristic of the Briton, yet awaken less instinctive aversion and quiet, supercilious disdain than do we whose social appliances, standards, and customs are certainly higher than can be found elsewhere on this continent. This apparent anomaly, so grievous to our national self-love, is perfectly intelligible, and a recent story of Mrs. Oliphant's, "Mrs. Arthur," suggests the explanation.

The denizens of Mayfair and Belgravia cannot gauge the birth, breeding and social surroundings of a Chilian or Costa Rican Ambassador by the common test of phrase and idiom, because he speaks a foreign tongue. They are constrained to judge of him by his dress, carriage, and demeanor ; in other words, by those elements of social equipment which are most easily acquired. Our countrymen, on the other hand, stand in this respect on precisely the same footing as unknown Englishmen who are encountered for the first time in London society. They are approved or condemned according as their speech conforms to the standard accepted by well-bred people. This is a test which for obvious reasons a native of the United States cannot sustain. No American gentleman, either in New York or Philadelphia, or even in painstaking Boston, can use with even tolerable correctness the idiom of Mayfair. Indeed, no sensible man, who means to pass his days in his own country, would seek to do so. Mr. Motley did but recognize an inexorable fact when he said, as he was fond of saying, that we have an American language with canons of its own. It would be strange if the broad dissemblance in natural and social conditions to which the two sections of the English-speaking race have been subjected for two centuries had not left its mark upon their idioms. Of course, every spoken language, like every other living organism, is in a state of constant growth and decay, of accession and rejection, of adjustment to the physical and spiritual environment. Here in America the English language has been exposed not only to a different kind, but to a different rate of change. Now, no social odium attaches anywhere to the coinage of new words— terms which portray novel ideas and recognize altered circumstances. That is a process which is going on all the time among the English settlers in Australia, in India, at the Cape of Good Hope, in New Zealand, indeed, under all the multifarious conditions of the British colonial empire. What is more to the purpose, it is going on at the focus of English culture and refinement— in Belgravian drawing-rooms. We may venture, therefore, to say that so far as the speech even of San Francisco is really new—the genuine product of an endeavor to conform to strange surroundings—it will amuse and not disgust our English kinfolk.

It is not our new words, but our old, which are nauseous to Mayfair. While in many directions, doubtless, transformation has been more rapid, yet in others the American language has been more conservative than the English. We have kept many terms and idioms which were correct and elegant enough in Milton's day, or even Addison's, but which in the older country have been discarded—discarded, that is by the higher and better educated classes, since language like a deciduous tree begins to slough off at the top. There is not a single peculiarity due to conservatism in our American speech which cannot be found somewhere in the British Islands, in one or another of the lower walks of life. The secret of the mischievous effect produced upon the average Englishman by our verbal idiosyncracies, the greater part of which fall within the above category, is not that they are exotic and fantastic, but that they are unpleasantly familiar. They are as familiar to him as the dirty hands, vulgar leer and shambling gait of the country clown, or the town lout. He has heard them a thousand times before, but always in the mouth of menials of low grade, of farm laborers, bargemen, stablemen, petty shopkeepers, and generally by the typical representative of that subterranean world which he holds to be inhabited by cads. When, therefore, the tricks of speech thus hopelessly discredited fall from American lips, how can an English lady or gentleman of ordinary mental calibre fail to regard them as the ineffaceable stamp of mean birth and breeding? He or she does but obey the irresistible law of association, the law which even the clearest intellects escape only in moments of dispassionate reflection, not in the practical conduct of life.

A thing explained is half condoned. We shall bear,

perhaps, with more resignation the disapproval of our English kin when we can trace it to a hasty and irrational but entirely natural deduction from insufficient premises. All those—and their name is legion—who would fain understand how hard it is for the ordinary well-bred Briton to view us with more indulgence should study this book of Mrs. Oliphant's, wherein we are introduced to a family fairly representing the lowest grade of the middle class. In this stratum of society we shall meet to our infinite annoyance with the precise solecisms and vulgarisms which are oftenest laid to our charge.

THE END.